Eva Hesse SCULPTURE

Eva Hesse SCULPTURE

CATALOGUE RAISONNÉ

BY BILL BARRETTE

TIMKEN PUBLISHERS, INC.

NEW YORK

Published by Timken Publishers, Inc.,
225 Lafayette Street, New York, NY 10012

First published in hardcover in 1989

First paperback edition published in 1992

LIBRARY OF CONGRESS CATALOGING-IN-PUBLICATION DATA

BARRETTE, BILL.
EVA HESSE SCULPTURE / BILL BARRETTE.
P. CM.
BIBLIOGRAPHY: P.
ISBN 0-943221-02-1
1. HESSE, EVA, 1936–1970—CATALOGUES RAISONNÉS. I. HESSE, EVA,
1936–1970. II. TITLE.
NB237.H42A4 1989 88-22440CIP
730'. 92'4—DC19

Printed in Hong Kong

Set in Trump Medieval by EyeType, New York
Production by Stevan Baron
Design by Jerry Kelly and Jane Timken
Copy editing by Anna Jardine and Jean Wagner
Color separations by South Seas International Press Ltd.
Printed and bound by Everbest Printing Co., Ltd.

Contents

Acknowledgments

A project of this complexity requires the cooperation of many individuals, and I am grateful for the support and encouragement I have received during the three years it took to complete the book.

I am indebted first of all to Helen Hesse Charash for allowing the reproduction of her sister's work, and for access to one of the early diaries still in her possession; to Barry Rosen, consultant to the Hesse estate since 1982, for helping me locate many of the sculptures, a crucial part of this project; and to Cindy Nemser for allowing me to quote from her taped interview with Hesse.

Many people generously shared information about Hesse. In addition to those mentioned in the preface, I am grateful to various staff members of the Allen Memorial Art Museum at Oberlin College, Oberlin, Ohio; Larry Fineberg, curator of the Hesse Archive, facilitated my research at Oberlin; Kathy Siegel and Peter Bergmann prepared a list of the contents of the archive for the appendix; and Kimberly Gumz, registrar, provided a list of Hesse drawings at Oberlin.

I also received help from Jill Weinberg of the Fourcade Gallery and Nathan Kernan of the Robert Miller Gallery. Linda Norden undertook correspondence and assembled catalogue information during the first two years of the project. Joan Simon shared primary material that she had collected for her film on Hesse.

Most appreciated was the support that came from the late Victor Ganz; from Sally Ganz; and, above all, from my publisher, Jane Timken.

Preface

This book intends to present and in some way preserve Eva Hesse's sculpture. Her work has never been photographed or published extensively in color, and even though much of her work is not colorful, it is difficult to perceive it fully without color photographs. Eva Hesse made some one hundred sculptures between 1965 and 1970 when she died. Of these, ninety are shown in color, seventy of which have been photographed for this book; the remaining are destroyed or lost and no color photograph is available.

The only other major publication on the artist's sculpture is the critical biography by Lucy Lippard published in 1976, a memorial to Hesse by her friends and an invaluable source book. The main focus of the present publication is the reproduction of the sculpture in color, along with a discussion of how the work was made, as well as of Hesse's attitudes toward materials, craftsmanship, fabrication, permanence, and display. Some revisions in the sequence of the sculpture have been made where I feel the evidence warrents a change or where the grouping of certain pieces gives a clearer sense of the development of Hesse's work.

My sources for this book are above all my own experience with the artist and her art. I worked as a studio assistant for Hesse during the last year of her life and was involved in the fabrication of the last five sculptures. After her death, I was the person often called upon to install and repair her pieces. I also installed and supervised the photography of most of the sculptures for the book. This prolonged physical contact with the sculpture has allowed, indeed forced, me to think a great deal about Hesse's work, both its grand possibilities and its problems. Above all, this book reflects that tangible experience.

In addition to working with Hesse and her sculpture I have consulted her diaries and notebooks in the Hesse archive at Oberlin College and listened to the tapes of the extensive interview made by Cindy Nemser shortly before Hesse's death. I have had numerous conversations with the people directly involved in the fabrication of her sculpture, notably Doug Johns, Tom Doyle, Ray Donarski, and Sol LeWitt; and have interviewed her psychiatrist, Dr. Samuel Dunkell, and many more of Hesse's friends—Mel Bochner, Grace Wapner, Ethelyn Honig, Rosalyn Goldman, Ellen Johnson, Gioia Timpanelli, Mr. and Mrs. F. Arnhard Scheidt, Naomi Spector, and Victor Ganz. This was not done in order to rehash the intimate details of her very short life, but to see if I could gain new insights about Hesse and her relationship to her work now almost twenty years later, long after her death, and from the perspective of a very different art world.

Already in 1985, when I began to think of this book, information about Hesse and her sculpture was disappearing. Donald Droll, Hesse's friend, dealer, and executor, died. He more than anyone else had been responsible for her career for nearly twenty years. During the 1970s the Hesse estate moved from the Fischbach Gallery, where Droll was director, to the Knoedler Gallery, to Fourcade Droll, to the Droll/Kolbert Gallery, and then to Metro Pictures, following Droll's own trajectory through the art world. In 1984 the estate moved back to the Fourcade Gallery, and then in 1986, following Xavier Fourcade's death, it moved to the Robert Miller Gallery. The principal result of this movement was that much documentation of Hesse's work was lost or left in a state of disarray. Droll's memory was often the only source for facts about Hesse's career and with his death a great deal of information is now irretrievable.

The other key person in any consideration of Hesse's career is Victor Ganz. An enthusiastic supporter, he had already purchased three sculptures while Hesse was still alive. Then, in July 1972 Ganz, with typical courage, bought nine of Hesse's major works through Droll, a purchase that would have an important effect on Hesse's posthumous career. The funds from that sale made it possible for the estate to publish Lippard's book. But perhaps more important, the presence of so many key pieces in such an important collection, alongside works of Picasso, Johns, Rauschenberg, and Stella, was a strong statement not overlooked by the numerous curators and art historians who frequented the Ganz apartment. It was a very sad moment when Victor Ganz died in October 1987. His death reinforced the necessity of writing this book now, before more important primary sources of information about Hesse and her work disappeared.

BILL BARRETTE

For Victor Ganz

Introduction

This introduction and the entries that follow focus on Eva Hesse's sculpture, rather than her biography. However, no discussion of her work can or should be severed from the personal details of her life and I do not attempt to do so here. As Hesse remarked in 1970: "Art and life are very connected and my whole life has been absurd. There isn't one thing in my life that hasn't been extreme."[1] Unfortunately, the extreme and tragic details of her life have obscured her achievement as a sculptor. This is particularly true of the work produced during the last year of her life, when Hesse was in declining health. I have tried to use Hesse's biography only where I felt it might help clarify the motives behind her artistic choices or where it helps explain the unusual physical characteristics of her sculpture.

To recapitulate her early biography, Hesse was born to Jewish parents in Hamburg in 1936. Two years later she was put on a children's train to Amsterdam with her sister to escape Nazi persecution. They were then joined by their parents, and the family went to New York City in 1939 and settled in Washington Heights. Most of Hesse's family did not survive the war. Her father, who had been a criminal lawyer in Germany, became an insurance broker. Her mother, already depressed by the events of the war and her subsequent divorce from her husband, took her own life when Hesse was ten. Hesse was often sick, both as a child and as an adult, and for most of her life she suffered from extreme anxiety that was alleviated only when she gained success as an artist. Hesse describes this insecurity: "I used to feel a fraud all my life. The world thought I was a cute, smart kid and I kidded them. But at home I was called a terror. I was miserable. I had trouble—tremendous fear, incredible fear. I had my father tuck my blankets in tight into my German bed which had bars on the bottom which I would hold at night and he would have to tell me that we wouldn't be poor, and we wouldn't be robbed, and he'd be there to take care of me in the morning. [For me] as a child it was a ritual every night. There wasn't one day of security and then it never really got any better. So that gave me whatever strength I have. I have been a giant in my strength and my work has been strong and my whole character has it inside."[2]

Hesse determined early that she would become an artist, first studying at the High School of Industrial Arts, then Pratt Institute for Industrial Design and Cooper Union, from which she graduated. Hesse then entered the Yale School of Art and Architecture, where she studied painting with Josef Albers, Rico Lebrun, and Bernard Chaet. She graduated from Yale in 1959 and moved to New York. In 1961 she met and married sculptor Tom Doyle. Doyle, who was eight years older than Hesse, was well established as a sculptor and was also a gifted craftsman. At this time she worked in the shadow of her more successful husband, continuing to struggle with her drawing and painting.

Hesse's development as a sculptor began in June 1964, when she and Doyle left for what became a fifteen-month stay in Kettwig-am-Ruhr, West Germany, as guests of textile manufacturer and collector F. Arnhard Scheidt. Scheidt brought the Doyles to Kettwig and housed them in an enormous floor in one of his textile factories as a way of acquiring a certain amount of sculpture that Doyle was expected to produce and leave behind. Scheidt not only provided space and any materials that were needed but also put at their disposal the welders, carpenters, electricians, and plasterers who were working on the other floors of the factory.

For the first six months of her stay in Germany Hesse made a great number of drawings and tried to get some of these onto canvas, but was dissatisfied with the results. This frustration as well as the prompting of her husband turned her to sculpture. She began by cutting up and isolating images from her drawings, reworking them into collages. Hesse's next step was to combine painted, collage, and projecting elements onto a panel.[3] These experiments eventually led to a series of fourteen wood-and-masonite reliefs which combine painted areas with relief built up with cord, plaster, and sometimes found machinery parts.[4] Hesse describes her first attempt at a sculpture: "In the abandoned factory where we worked there is lots of junk around. Tom has used much steel and odds and ends for his sculpture. I have all these months looked over at much of the junk. I finally took a screen, heavy mesh which is stretched on frame like so and taken cord which I cut into smaller pieces. I soak them in plaster and knot each piece through a hole and around wire. It is compulsive work which I enjoy. If it were really a new idea it would be terrific. But it is not. However I have plans with other structures and working more with plaster. It might work its way to something special."[5] This first sculpture did not survive, but it contains the essential elements of a great number of cord sculptures Hesse would do in 1967.

The period spent in Germany was problematic for Hesse on a number of levels. In the beginning she was reluctant or hesitant to make peace with the country she had been forced to leave as a child and whose language she spoke fluently. She records in her diary that she experienced pains in her legs as well as continuing fear and anxiety which she attributed to her ambivalence about Germany and her difficulty working. Her marriage with Doyle was not going at all well, and Scheidt recalls a great deal of tension between the two, a tension that is repeatedly noted by Hesse in her diaries. Scheidt also recalls that she was bothered about not having children; the prospect was becoming more remote with the dissolution of her marriage. The erotic nature of her drawings and her first reliefs, which an artist friend referred to as birth machines upon seeing them in Kettwig, underscores her state of mind about having children. However, despite Hesse's difficulty in getting started in her work and despite the disintegration of the marriage, the stay in Germany was very important in Hesse's development as an artist. Ironically, it was in the country that had rejected her as a child that Hesse found her identity as an artist.

In September 1965 Doyle and Hesse returned to New York City and moved into a loft on the Bowery. The floor above them became available and Hesse used it for her studio. Doyle's studio was across the street and after three months he moved into it altogether when he separated from Hesse. This separation threw Hesse into deep despair; three notebooks chronicle the extreme ups and downs of this pivotal and chaotic year. Her father, with whom she had always been extremely close, died in August 1966, redoubling the sense of abandonment she had experienced when Doyle left. It was only through her art that Hesse was able to retain her sanity, producing a series of dark, disturbing sculptures that functioned to externalize the extreme anger and hatred she felt. The precarious and emotionally expressive quality of these works would appear again only in the sculpture she made at the end of her life.

By the fall of 1966 Hesse gained some recognition as an artist when she was included in Lucy Lippard's show "Eccentric Abstraction" at the Fischbach Gallery. In March of the following year, Donald Droll, the director of Fischbach, offered her gallery representation.

This attention increased her growing sense of confidence as an artist, allowed her finally to accept her separation from Doyle, and enabled her to begin gaining control of her persistent feelings of anxiety and abandonment. In early 1967 she abruptly stopped writing in the diaries she had been keeping since she was a child.

Donald Droll offered Hesse a one-person exhibition in the spring of 1968; it was postponed until November to allow extra time for the fabrication of the group of fiberglass sculptures that formed the core of the show. The exhibition was a success and established Hesse's reputation as an important new artist. Her career now accelerated rapidly and she was included in a number of important shows. But the period during which she enjoyed her triumph was brief. She collapsed in April 1969 and was diagnosed as having a brain tumor. During the next twelve months Hesse was operated on three times, yet she continued to work and produced six major sculptures and an important group of wash drawings before she died in May 1970.

In reviewing Hesse's work and particularly her sculpture, it is important to keep in mind that Hesse was a third-generation abstract expressionist who was trained as a painter. She had an expressionist's sensibility, darkly romantic with a strong belief in the redemptive power of art; she was hopeful that her traumatic personal history would be justified ultimately through the perfection of her art. As a student her heroes were de Kooning, Gorky, and Pollock.[6] But even as early as 1959, she was prescient enough to realize that the style she inherited was nearly exhausted. Like a number of the artists of her generation beginning their careers in New York during the early sixties, she realized that sculpture offered a way around the impasse caused by the decline of abstract expressionism on one hand and the ascendancy of pop art and other styles to which she was not sympathetic on the other. And like many of these artists, her sculpture was of a particularly painterly kind. More often than not it is frontal, dependent on the wall, constructed in layers, and especially concerned with surface and luminosity. Hesse later developed processes that emphasized working without a plan and in a spontaneous manner, reminiscent of the studio practice of abstract expressionist painters. Her success at infusing the formalist vocabulary of the sixties with a personal emotional quality has been influential for a number of artists in the seventies and eighties, particularly those rejecting painting in favor of sculpture.

Like the expressionists Hesse was inclined toward testing boundaries in her art as well as in her life. In her work there was an ongoing drama of a will to expansiveness played against a need for limits. In a diary entry from 1960 Hesse states: "I will abandon restrictions and curbs imposed upon myself. Not physical ones, but those restrictive tabs on my inner being. . . . I will paint against every rule I or others have invisibly placed. Oh how they penetrate throughout and all over. . . . I should like to achieve free, spontaneous painting delineating a powerful strong structured image. One must be possible with the other." In a great deal of her work Hesse was able to achieve a balance between the contradictory forces of structure and freedom. She elaborated on this idea in the interview with Cindy Nemser ten years later: "I remember always working with contradictions and contradictory forms, which is my idea also in life, the whole absurdity of life, everything for me has always been opposites, nothing has ever been in the middle. My life never had anything normal or in the center and it was always extremes."

Hesse's interest in contradictory phenomena and structures is constantly reflected in her sculpture. On its most basic level the primary polarity is male and female. This is most apparent in the German reliefs of 1965, with their overtly sexual combinations of organic and mechanical forms. During Hesse's minimalist interlude of 1966–1967, the oppositions become more developed and diffused. These include ascending and descending, expanding and contracting, light and dark, rigid and limp, ordered and chaotic forms. In the work of the last two years of her life Hesse extended the play of opposites through the material she used by combining the ephemerality of latex with the permanence of reinforced fiberglass.

In much of her sculpture Hesse maintains a fine line between the beautiful and the repulsive. She did not seek to make her sculpture beautiful, certainly not in a conventional way, but preferred instead that its ugliness be accepted as beautiful. Occasionally when she had made a piece that she felt was too beautiful, as, for example, *Repetition Nineteen III* (73) or *Right After* (96), she would compensate with an "ugly" version, *Area* (80) or "Rope Piece" (101). Her forms, vulnerable, empty, or with chaotic interiors, seem unusually susceptible to the pull of gravity and suggest decay. Yet these effects were part of a cycle of decay and regeneration. For the darker side of her sensibility would be balanced by imposing systems of order and by using translucent materials that resist the forces of degeneration and emit a transcendent luminosity.[7]

Having briefly outlined Hesse's biography, career, and some of the themes expressed in her work, we now turn to a closer examination of her procedures and materials to see what they might reveal about her attitudes toward fabrication, permanence, and display. Hesse was ill at ease with tools and bored by matters of construction and would often rely on others to help her realize her ideas. When she first started experimenting with sculpture during her stay in Kettwig, she stayed fairly close to painting and collage techniques such as cord with glue, torn-paper collage surfaces, and paint. When she encountered technical problems she turned either to Scheidt's workers, who, for instance, fabricated the fourteen wood-and-masonite relief panels for her, or to Doyle, who showed her how to build up forms with plaster which she would then paint. Doyle continued to help Hesse build her sculptures until their separation early in 1966. While she relied on others to help with the engineering and construction of her pieces, she would obscure the forms and the evidence of their facture by binding with cords or cloth, covering with thick layers of papier-mâché, and carefully gradating the surfaces from light to dark. She in effect drew attention away from how the pieces were made by emphasizing the more painterly concerns with surface, color, and light.

When Hesse began to gain recognition and opportunities to exhibit her work, insecurity about the fabrication and permanence of her sculptures led her to seek professional assistance. Two notebook entries from 1966 indicate her thoughts about this subject. In August she writes, "I realize how hung up I am about always feeling that what I do is wrong, not good enough, [that] in art my work will always break, wear badly, not last, that technically I failed. It does parallel my life for sure." In September, she developed a strategy for coping with this problem. "I must learn to have my work sent out. Not for work theory, but for permanence."

By the time she wrote this Hesse was just becoming part of a group of artists that included Robert Morris, Donald Judd, Robert Smithson, Sol LeWitt, Carl Andre, Mel Bochner, and Dan Graham. Many of these artists had incorporated the idea of outside fabrication into the philosophy of their work. Their motives for having work fabricated were very different from

Hesse's and were part of the minimalist/conceptualist thinking about the artist's relationship to the studio. Theirs was a movement away from the studio, questioning the very activity of making unique handmade objects resonating with the artist's touch and personality. Rejecting the handmade, the artist would assume a role closer to that of an architect, developing an idea and leaving the execution and handwork to others. It was a kind of sculpture diametrically opposed to that of Tom Doyle and thus more attractive to Hesse as a way of moving away from her husband. However, Hesse's work, with its concern for irregular surfaces and eccentric touch, would not seem to have lent itself to outside fabrication. It is a testimony to her considerable will and inventiveness that she succeeded in making the process work for her.

Hesse's first attempt at outside fabrication was in 1967 with *Accession II* (58), an open cube made of perforated metal that was constructed at Arco Metals in Manhattan. When the box was finished, however, she proceeded to cut and insert by hand thousands of pieces of vinyl extrusion. Thus she was able to have a box that was large and structurally secure while at the same time serving as a foil for the "hands-on" obsessional process that was part of her thinking from the beginning of her career.

Hesse turned again to outside fabrication early in 1968 when she began to plan for her first one-person show, which was scheduled to open in November of that year. Encouraged by friends and her dealer (who had agreed to pick up the costs), Hesse went to Aegis Reinforced Plastics on Staten Island. Even though she was told by Doug Johns, one of the owners of Aegis, that work could not begin until June, she nonetheless planned to make five very large pieces from reinforced fiberglass on a scale and in a material she had never used before. This experience with outside fabrication would have a profound effect on the course of her sculpture.

The first sculpture made at Aegis was a distinct failure and had to be discarded.[8] In spite of this inauspicious beginning, work on subsequent sculptures went quickly during the summer and early fall of 1968, and these formed the core of Hesse's successful show at the Fischbach Gallery. The collaboration between Johns and Hesse became extended and complicated when it turned into a romantic involvement as well. Johns moved into Hesse's studio after closing his business in September and then devoted himself full-time to the production of Hesse's work. Johns, describing their working relationship, said that he was the hands and she was the mind. He recalls that Hesse was indifferent to technical matters and it was the idea and the process that interested her.

She was somewhat ambivalent about her dependence on Johns and kept their relationship a secret from many of her friends. However, their collaboration produced larger and technically more complex pieces than Hesse had been able to achieve earlier, and because they worked so closely together, Johns was able to retain in the fiberglass sculptures the eccentric touch that was so characteristic of her work. Having Johns's technical skills at her disposal freed Hesse from having to consider problems of construction and allowed her to work in a much more spontaneous way. As a result she let go of her concern for minimalist structure in favor of pieces that became progressively more expressive. This collaboration, already in place before she became ill, initially allowed her to speed up the production of sculpture to meet the increased demand for her work, and, after she became sick, to continue to create innovative work even when her direct participation was severely restricted.

While the primary motive behind having the work fabricated was permanence, by 1969 Hesse willfully chose to make some of her pieces ephemeral. This change in thinking can be explained partially by the influence of the "anti-form" and "process" movements with which Hesse was becoming associated.[9] These movements, along with conceptual art, seeking to separate material from enduring form, were part of a trend away from minimalist order and geometry. Artists such as Serra, Smithson, Morris, Nauman, Saret, and Zorio were creating installations consisting of random pilings, hangings, and informal accumulations of industrial materials. The ephemeral nature of these installations, in addition to being a criticism of minimalism, was also a political stand that questioned the conventions of display and commodity status associated with more traditional art. This attitude in the art world coincided with the social upheavals of 1968–1969, the most politically volatile period of the decade. The spirit of the time was stridently antiauthoritarian and obsessed with inventing a wholly new order free from all tradition. This is reflected in much sculpture of the late 1960s which eliminates the pedestal, rejects bronze, carved wood, and stone, and disregards the general question of permanence. Hesse was not indifferent to these influences and ideas, and the "anti-form" and "process" movements formed the matrix of acceptance for her sculpture. However, Hesse's sculpture remained fundamentally different in spirit. Her work at the center remained expressionist: based on strong feelings and doubts, the inner forces of creation and destruction become annealed in the formation of her art.

One cannot explain Hesse's interest in the shift to the ephemeral solely on the basis of the artistic and political context in which her sculptures were made. Close examination of the materials and the way in which she used them helps to understand her intentions and to clarify what separates her work from that of her contemporaries. Hesse made sculptures in a wide variety of media, but she is closely identified with the use of latex and reinforced fiberglass. She began experimenting with latex in August 1967 and was immediately attracted to this unstable material, particularly to its flexible quality, which produces further distortion in an effortless way. Most important was the fact that latex could be used like paint and was a direct way of extending her painter's sensibility into three dimensions. She proceeded to use latex for some sixteen full-scale works, sometimes in combination with fiberglass.[10] At first Hesse was more interested in the casting properties of latex, and some of the earliest pieces, such as *Schema* (66), *Sequel* (67), and *Sans I* (69), are made of small, simply cast elements. Following the manufacturer's instructions, Hesse heated these in her oven to ensure a proper cure. Soon she began experimenting by adding fillers and pigments to the latex for greater painterly effect, as in *Stratum* (68) and *Aught* (84). And she moved away from casting latex to using it as a coating material, as in *Area* (80), *Seam* (81), and *Augment* (83). In the Nemser interview, Hesse remarked, "I don't want to use them [latex and fiberglass] as casting materials. I want to use them directly, eliminating molds and casts. I am interested in the process in a very direct connection." But this way of using latex—omitting the steps of drawing off water and heating—increased the chance that the latex would not cure properly. Also, the thin layers she used would oxidize more rapidly, change color, and become brittle. Hesse was aware that latex as she was using it was a fugitive material, and Doug Johns recalls that when he tried to discourage her from using it she lectured him and said that she considered its instability an attribute. She wanted the pieces to deteriorate. By late 1968

Hesse felt free to incorporate the instability of latex into the ongoing dialogue of opposed qualities that had characterized her sculpture from the beginning. In earlier work the forms and techniques suggest decay. Latex was to make these qualities literal.[11]

Reinforced fiberglass, the second of Hesse's signature materials, is entirely permanent.[12] Doug Johns recalls that she was as concerned with its stability as she was indifferent to the permanence of latex. If latex was an important way for Hesse to reintroduce an organic quality into geometric structures, reinforced fiberglass was equally important as a way of allowing her to stabilize these forms and elaborate them on a much larger scale without employing complicated construction techniques or technology. Another important quality of the material was its translucence, for this allowed Hesse to bring light back into her work. She had previously tried to incorporate light into her work by using gradated surfaces but had abandoned the technique in 1966.[13] The luminescent quality of fiberglass was to give a transcendent aura to much of the late work, especially in sculptures where it is the primary material. When used in combination with latex, as in *Expanded Expansion* (92), *Contingent* (98), and "Wall Piece" (100), the material creates an experience of light and color that is very affecting and perhaps singular in the art produced during the sixties.

Hesse related to reinforced fiberglass in a very direct way. In order to understand this it is necessary to understand something about the structure of resin. Polyester resin is similar to latex in that both materials are polymers—latex a naturally occurring polymer, and polyester resin a synthetic polymer produced from acids and alcohol. Polymerization is a chemical reaction usually carried out with a catalyst in which a large number of relatively simple molecules (monomers) are combined to form a chainlike macromolecule. Hesse was clearly interested in the structural aspects of materials she was using, for she titled her Fischbach exhibition "Chain Polymers." Further, the organizing principle of many of her sculptures executed between 1967 and 1969—for instance, *Sans I, II, III* (69, 79, 89); *Accretion* (78); *Vinculum I* and *II* (91, 90); "Ice Piece" (94)—mimics the various ways that a large number of simple units are repeated and joined together to form chainlike structures during the process of polymerization. This is not the only instance in which Hesse identified with the deeper structure of the materials she was using. The way she used extrusion, forcing it through small holes to reflect the process of its manufacture, as in *Ishtar* (21), *Constant* (49), *Accession I–V* (57, 58, 74–76), is another example.

One of the most consistent formal features of Hesse's development is the way she repeated and elaborated a single form or motif to create a more complex whole. Absorbing the influences of LeWitt, Judd, and other minimalists concerning serial repetition, Hesse made many sculptures during 1965 and 1966 that employed a repeated grid and module arrangement, most of them wall reliefs.

Late in 1967, however, Hesse began to disengage the modular units from their supports and at the same time distort their shapes. And this new step led to an important preoccupation late in her career, the theme of randomness. This new autonomy of the forms from the wall forced the artist to consider the problem of disposing her forms in space, a problem faced by many minimalist sculptors who wished to redefine the relationship between the viewer and the artwork by undermining the conventions of display. One solution, first put forth by Barry Le Va and quickly taken up by many artists, favored a random dispersal of units. This solution, in theory unbiased and free of pattern, avoided making aesthetic choices and subverted hierarchical relationships implied in the traditional ways of displaying sculpture. However, as mathematicians and scientists know, randomness is exceedingly difficult to achieve. Subtle patterns tend to emerge in even the most chaotic dispersal of elements, as my own experience in installing Hesse's sculptures confirms. Any attempt to arrange the units of her pieces so that they appear randomly dispersed is subjective and often self-defeating. Deciding what constitutes randomness ultimately requires aesthetic choices—which the idea of random dispersal was meant to circumvent.

Hesse incorporated the idea of random dispersal in twelve pieces done between 1967 and 1970. It allowed her to expand the scale of her sculpture, but more important, the unfixed relationship among the units suited her predilection for ambiguity. The increased number of options inherent in this approach to display greatly appealed to her, and after her show at Fischbach she sought to explore the idea of flexible structures even further.

During the last year of her life Hesse changed the orientation of her work from wall and floor to ceiling. Six of her last eight works, beginning with *Connection* (93) in 1969, are suspended from the ceiling and recall several sculptures she had made in 1966, such as *Vertiginous Detour* (28). The late hanging pieces are more problematic to install because Hesse's intentions regarding their display were often obscure and not fully developed in her lifetime.

The issue of display is central to an appreciation of Hesse's later work. The majority of sculptures from between 1968 and 1970 are made up of unfixed elements that have to be brought together into some kind of temporary whole during the process of installation. Her sculptures relate to space both personally and aesthetically. The potential of the works to expand and contract to accommodate the amount of space available for their display reflects Hesse's own feelings of dislocation, disconnection, and being too small for her environment. On an aesthetic level the almost limitless options possible for installation can have a daunting effect on even the most confident curator. Pieces such as *Accretion* (78), *Expanded Expansion* (92), "Ice Piece" (94), and "Rope Piece" (101) all have potential for extreme expansion or contraction and subvert conventional notions of what constitutes the monumental in modern sculpture by implying that its forms are only momentarily stable. Other sculptures, such as *Repetition Nineteen I* (62) and *III* (73), *Connection* (93), *Tori* (95), and *Seven Poles* (103), require randomness in the disposition of their units. The questions posed by the installation of all these works are the same: What were the artist's intentions? What liberties are possible in installation? Are some arrangements unacceptable?

I have tried to provide here and in the entries that follow an approach toward resolving these questions. Unfortunately, there cannot be a definitive answer, as Hesse died before she had time to experience the implications of her ideas about random structures. If she had lived longer and been faced with the realities of installing her work in many different spaces, I am sure that she, like many of her contemporaries, would have developed guidelines. What she was able to do during the last year of her life—as it became more difficult to supervise the installation of her sculptures and as her own ability to function in space was increasingly limited—was to ensure that her work not be restricted in its capacity to grow, to change and adapt to space. Her intention at this time was to push her work as far as it would go to achieve "another kind of vision" and to get to "a total other reference point" in her art.[14]

Indeed, a number of the late works hint at a new synthesis of opposites, a merging of the contradictory nature of her structures into a more unified theory. She felt that opposites need not be thought of as mutually exclusive, rather that they might encompass one another as part of the same structure. In a statement concerning one of her last pieces, "Rope Piece," she said, "When it is completed its order could be chaos. Chaos can be structured as non-chaos. That we know from Jackson Pollock."[15] By realizing that chaos possesses a structure and that order is ephemeral, Hesse was free to bequeath the installation of her sculptures to others, confident that any system of order imposed on her works would be by its nature temporary. This in turn demands that her work be reinterpreted every time it is installed, and endows these pieces with a tenuous but undeniable vitality.

NOTES

1. Hesse gave a series of taped interviews to Cindy Nemser a few months before her death. Parts of the interviews were published in *Artforum*, vol. 8, no. 9 (May 1970), pp. 59–63, and *Feminist Art Journal*, vol. 2, no. 1 (Winter 1973), pp. 13–14. Other sources for Hesse's biography are the diaries, notebooks, sketches, correspondence, and other papers that comprise the Eva Hesse Archive at the Allen Memorial Art Museum at Oberlin College in Ohio, the contents of which are listed in Appendix C.

2. Nemser interview published in *Feminist Art Journal*, p. 13.

3. A work of this type dated 1964 is in the collection of Editha and Gilbert Carpenter, Greensboro, North Carolina. Two undated collage, gouache, and ink drawings on craft paper that relate to this relief are in the Eva Hesse estate (EHEC-202 and EHEC-203).

4. For a discussion of Hesse's transition from painting to sculpture see Ellen Johnson, *A Retrospective of the Drawings* (Oberlin, Ohio, 1982), pp. 13–21.

5. Letter to Rosalyn Goldman, quoted in Lucy Lippard, *Eva Hesse* (New York, 1976), p. 29.

6. While at Yale, Hesse impressively demonstrated her understanding of abstract expressionist theory in two papers she wrote—"Significant Form" and "Abstract and Concrete Consideration of Form in Painting"—now in the Eva Hesse Archive at Oberlin.

7. The feelings Hesse's sculpture evokes in the viewer can be complex and emotionally suggestive. However, they are always achieved through very simple means—circles, rectangles, grids, and lines. For example, the circle-and-tail motif, used in such pieces as *An Ear in a Pond* (3), *Ishtar* (21), *Ennead* (32), *Ditto* (50), *One More Than One* (51), *Repetition Nineteen II* (63, 64), seems visceral, sexual, poignant. Hesse herself denied the obvious sexual overtones in her work, wishing to keep an interpretation of her work on a formal level that must be understood within the context of the late-sixties dogma about abstraction, that it be nonassociative, formalistic, and coolly objective.

8. See entry for *Repetition Nineteen III* (73).

9. These movements corresponded to Arte Povera in Europe.

10. Natural latex is a milky white suspension of a hydrocarbon polymer that is an exudation of the rubber tree. The formulation that Hesse used, L-200 casting latex, is a commercial product used in the production of molds for casting. The Cementex catalogue lists the material as containing sixty-one percent solids. It can be used alone or mixed with filler, and it is normally poured in a plaster mold that draws off part of the water in the curing process.

11. One should note, however, that the issue of instability and fragility in Hesse's work has become distorted in the public's mind; the impression that all her work is unstable is vastly exaggerated. Hesse experimented with a wide variety of materials in the construction of her sculpture and none of these present the problems that are inherent in latex. Furthermore, all the latex pieces did not disintegrate and certainly not to the same degree, an effect the artist could not have foreseen. Of the sixteen sculptures in which latex was used, seven remain in remarkably good condition twenty years later, four are no longer exhibitable, and five are in a somewhat compromised condition.

12. Polyester had been used by artists since the 1940s but did not become popular until the mid-1960s, when it was taken up by many sculptors searching for alternative materials and techniques. Fiberglass reinforced with polyester resin is used industrially for fabricating boat hulls, surfboards, and signs. Polyester resin appealed to artists because it was cheap and easy to use and large forms could be made that would be both strong and light. These qualities are in sharp contrast to more traditional sculptural methods of welding, stone and wood carving, and casting in plaster and bronze. The drawbacks to using polyester resin are its tendency to discolor as it ages, its unpleasant odor, and most significantly its toxicity. In spite of an important article by sculptor Robert Mallary that appeared in 1963 (*ARTnews*, vol. 62, no. 6 [October 1963], pp. 34–37, 60, 61) warning of the hazards of working with resin, its dangers remained poorly understood by artists. It was not until the early 1970s that many began to avoid using it.

13. See entry for *Oomamaboomba* (5).

14. See entry for *Contingent* (98).

15. See entry for "Rope Piece" (101).

GERMANY 1965

1 **Ringaround Arosie**

March 1965

MATERIALS: Pencil, acetone, varnish, enamel, ink, and glued cloth-covered electrical wire on papier-mâché and masonite

SIZE: $26\frac{3}{8} \times 16\frac{1}{2} \times 4\frac{1}{2}$ in. ($67 \times 41.9 \times 11.4$ cm.)

COLLECTION: Martin Bernstein, Birmingham, Michigan

PROVENANCE: Purchased from Droll/Kolbert Gallery, New York

Ringaround Arosie was the first of Hesse's German reliefs and a touchstone for many pieces that followed. The watercolor shown here—executed two months before the relief—is helpful in understanding her transition from a graphic to a sculptural medium and shedding some light on the meaning of this first relief, named for her closest friend, Rosalyn Goldman. The watercolor, done just at the time Hesse learned of her friend's pregnancy, refers to themes of ovulation, intercourse, and gestation, themes that would appear in many of the German reliefs. Hesse's pleasure in Goldman's pregnancy must have been tempered by her concern that she herself might not have children. Hesse uses the central image of the watercolor, transforming it into relief. By naming the relief after her closest friend she both commemorated and identified with the event.

In a letter to Sol LeWitt, Hesse referred to this piece as looking like a "breast and a penis." The conjunction of male and female forms is one of the most consistent iconographic elements of her sculpture, and the great variety of ways Hesse was able to synthesize this idea indicates that it arose out of a psychic necessity. The relief establishes many of the techniques she would use in her sculpture of the next two years: building up surfaces with papier-mâché, binding forms with cords, activating the surface with pieces of torn paper.

2 **Two Handled Orangekeyed Utensil**

April 1965

MATERIALS: Enamel, tempera, black ink, plaster, and cord on particle board

SIZE: $16\frac{1}{2} \times 26\frac{3}{8} \times 3\frac{1}{2}$ in. ($41.9 \times 67 \times 8.9$ cm.)

COLLECTION: Private collection, New York

PROVENANCE: F. Arnhard Scheidt, Kettwig-am-Ruhr, West Germany (acquired from the artist). Sold at Christie's, New York, November 7, 1985, lot 202

This relief retains the tension between organic and mechanical forms that was characteristic of the "machine drawings" made in West Germany in the winter of 1964–1965. As in those drawings Hesse has isolated the machine image against a white ground. The emphasis in this relief is on the suggestive bulges and hidden organic forms built up from papier-mâché that lie just beneath the surface. The handles, key, and other protrusions refer to mechanical as well as sexual coupling. The drawings illustrated here and on page 26 are the only two that relate closely to the composition of the reliefs (see Ellen Johnson, *Eva Hesse: A Retrospective of the Drawings*, page 18).

3 An Ear in a Pond

Completed April 27, 1965

MATERIALS: Enamel, tempera, paper, plaster, and cord on masonite

SIZE: 26⅜ × 17¾ × 7¾ in. (67 × 45.1 × 19.7 cm.)

COLLECTION: Mr. Robert M. Kaye, Rumson, New Jersey

PROVENANCE: Estate of Eva Hesse. Purchased from Metro Pictures, New York, in 1983

CONDITION: Paper brittle and lifting away from masonite support; flaking in green tempera areas

INSCRIPTION: On verso, "turp., varnish, tempera, black is enamel, 'An Ear in a Pond' "

A number of themes appear here that Hesse was to develop more fully in later work; for example, the circle with a tail on the right and the phallic form on the left will occur in a number of sculptures of 1965 and 1966. Also, the male and female elements that were first combined in *Ringaround Arosie* (1) are seen here in a more dynamic context: a raised line extends from the bright green phallus, enters behind the pink ear, and emerges as a limp bound red cord. Hesse has moved further away from drawing in this relief by allowing gravity to play a role. The interplay between rigid and limp will be used to great effect in such works as *Laocoon* (31), *Vinculum I* (91), and *Expanded Expansion* (92).

4 **Legs of a Walking Ball**

May 1965

MATERIALS: Enamel and tempera on cord, papier-mâché and metal on masonite panel mounted on a wooden stretcher

SIZE: 17¾ × 26⅜ × 4¼ in. (45.1 × 67 × 10.8 cm.)

COLLECTION: Estate of Eva Hesse

CONDITION: Restored in blue area and at end of the ball

INSCRIPTION: On verso, "Eva Hesse 65, yellow and red enamel—rest is tempera with varnish, 'Legs of a Walking Ball' "

Legs of a Walking Ball was the first of Hesse's reliefs that incorporated movable elements: the red lever and the orange rod with the cord-bound terminal bulb can be moved to create various pictorial options. The ideas of kinetic sculpture were very much in the air at this time, and according to Doyle, Hesse visited and was influenced by both Jean Tinguely and Hans Haacke, sculptors who used playful moving parts in their work. She would develop the idea of unfixed and movable parts more fully in later sculptures in which she wished to incorporate the role of chance. The image is a female one; the inner bulge suggests a fetus in a womb. The title is very close to that of a sculpture by Ruth Vollmer from 1961 called *Walking Ball*; however, Doyle claims neither he nor Hesse knew Vollmer at this time.

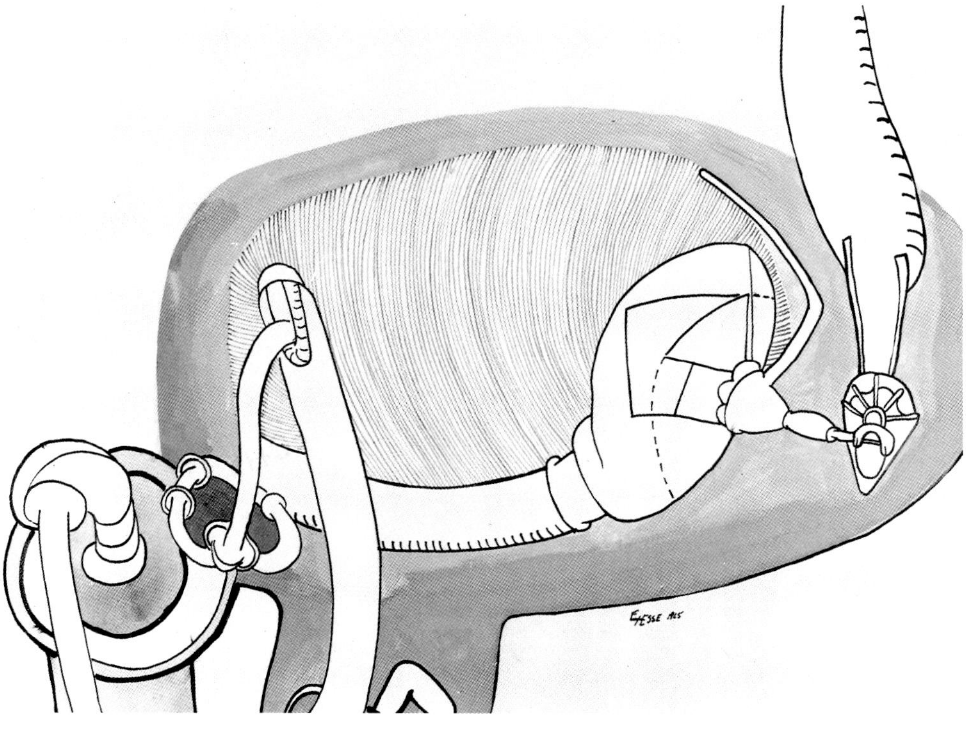

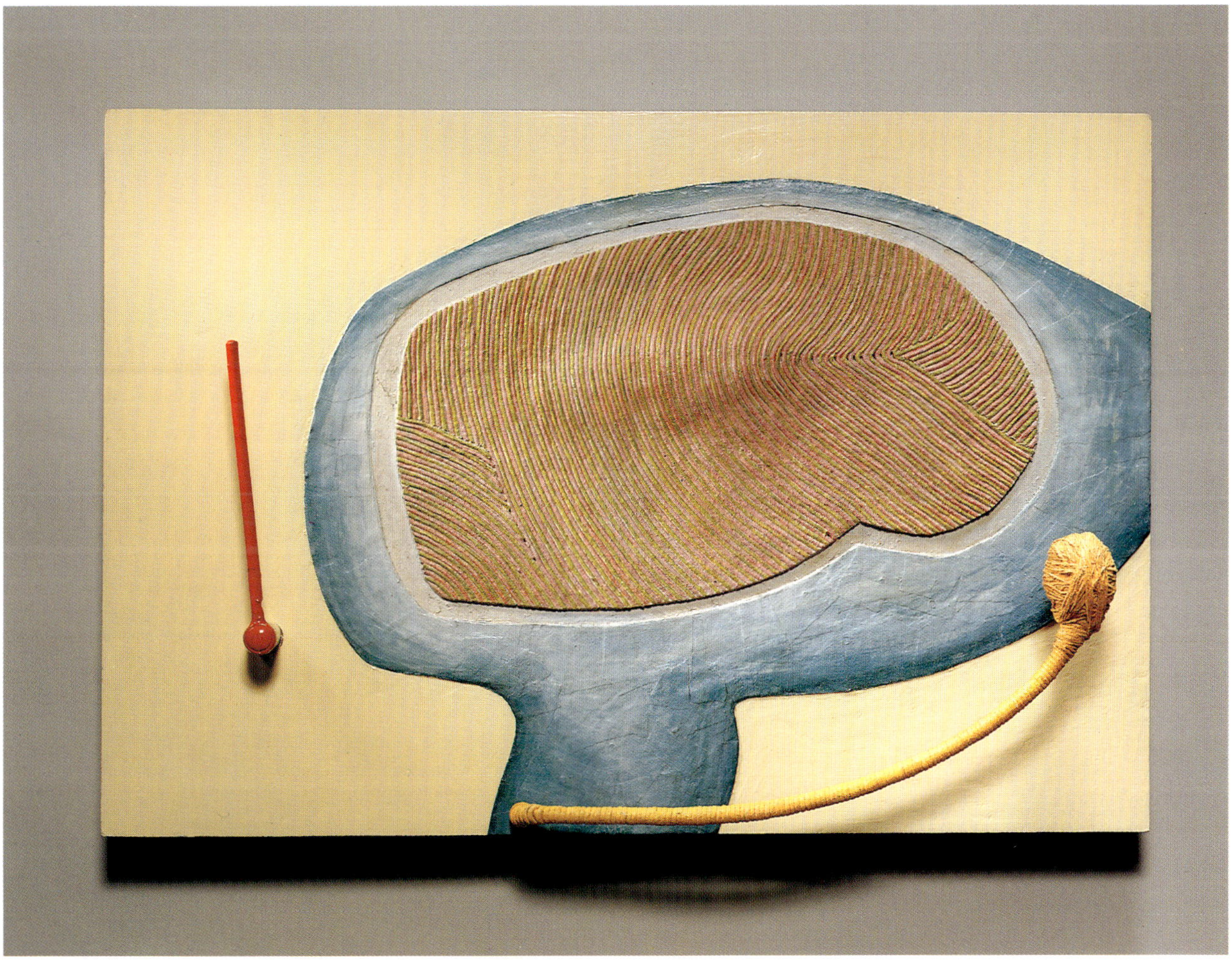

5 **Oomamaboomba**

May 1965

MATERIALS: Paint, cord-wrapped metal, and plaster on masonite

SIZE: 21¼ × 25⅝ in. (54 × 65.1 cm.)

COLLECTION: Stolen circa 1984

PROVENANCE: Estate of Eva Hesse

The zigzag line in *An Ear in a Pond* (3) is here set into space, forming a loop that joins two parts of the relief, a composition that was to appear in a much exaggerated fashion in *Hang Up* (22). This cord-bound loop is carefully gradated from pink to purple: Hesse used painted gradations in some seventeen sculptures of 1965 and 1966. The technique of gradation, which Hesse learned from Albers's color courses at Yale, is more appropriate to painting than sculpture. In painting it indicates the fall of light as well as advancing or receding space, phenomena which occur naturally in sculpture. As Hesse used gradation in her sculpture it had the effect of dematerializing the forms. Sometimes the gradation follows the logic of the sculpture so that the piece appears lighter at the top (6, 21, 22). Other times the gradation is darker at the top (19, 20, 32), giving the impression that gravity has been reversed.

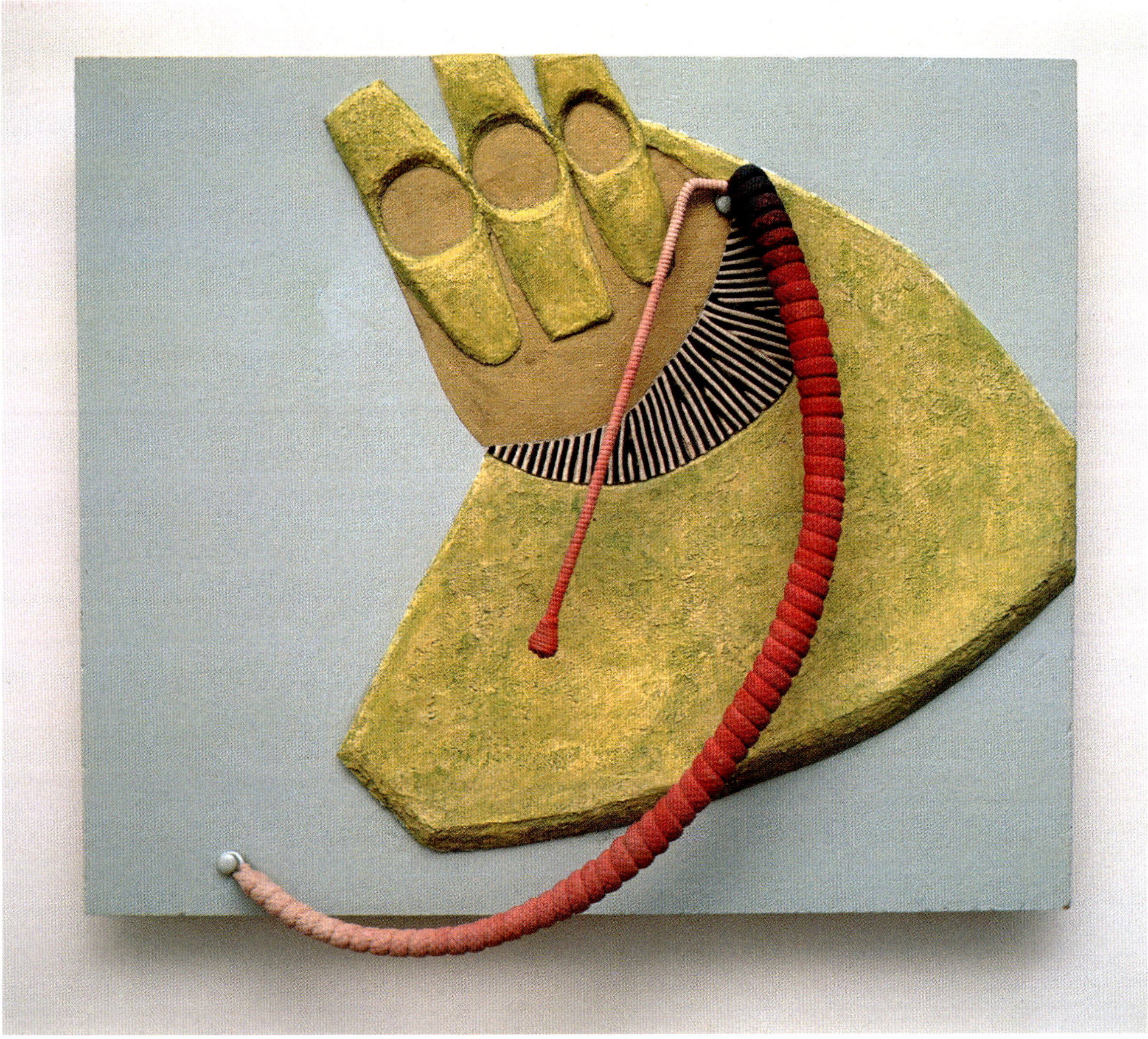

6 **Tomorrow's Apples (5 in White)**

June 1965

MATERIALS: Painted concretion, enamel, gouache, varnish, cord, and papier-mâché mounted on chipboard

SIZE: 25¾ × 21⅞ × 6¼ in. (65.4 × 55.6 × 15.9 cm.)

COLLECTION: Tate Gallery, London

PROVENANCE: Estate of Eva Hesse. Purchased from Donald Droll, acting for the Estate of Eva Hesse, through Whitechapel Art Gallery, London, in 1979 (grant-in-aid)

INSCRIPTION: On verso, "Eva Hesse, 1965, '5 in white,' white is Ducolux enamel 88-50, colors are gouache (Scminke), varnish alcohol"

Five differently colored bound cords, gradated from light to dark, connect two areas of low relief. Four of them tentatively touch the margin of the relief areas, and the red one plunges into the middle of the lower form, thereby enlivening the whole. This connection of two neutral areas by cords, incorporating the effect of shadow, anticipates the composition of the *Metronomic Irregularity* series (37, 38, 39). Binding had an important meaning for Hesse both as a compositional device and as an obsessional activity. She doubled the notion of binding by linking the two sections of the relief with bound cords.

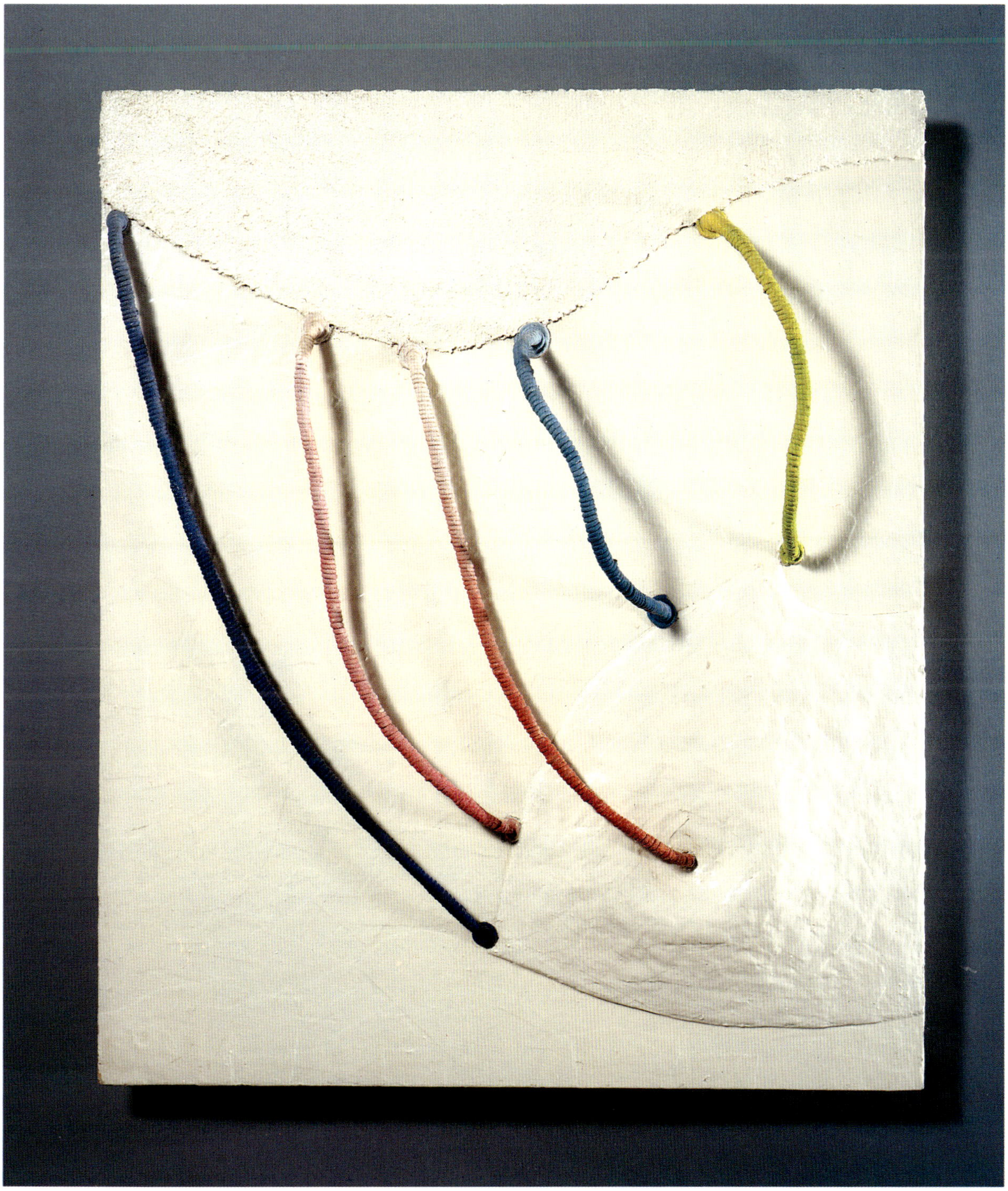

7 **2 in 1**

June 1965

MATERIALS: Enamel, tempera, purple ink, cord, and painted metal bolt on particle board

SIZE: 21¼ × 27⅛ × 9 in. (54 × 68.9 × 22.9 cm.)

COLLECTION: Private collection, New York

PROVENANCE: F. Arnhard Scheidt, Kettwig-am-Ruhr, West Germany (acquired from the artist). Sold at Christie's, New York, November 7, 1985, lot 200

2 in 1 takes the sexual forms of *Ringaround Arosie* and further animates them with the addition of a four-inch carriage bolt jutting out from the circular forms in an antic display of maleness. At the same time the frankly phallic form and the whirling breasts—appearing like large orbs or eyes—have an aggressive or ferocious quality that is apotropaic rather than sexy. The effect of the piece is one of power, not invitation. Hesse used painted bolts in later pieces—*Pink, C-Clamp Blues,* and *Top Spot* (10, 11, 14)—but the associations there are much less sexual.

8 **H + H**

June 1965

MATERIALS: Enamel, gouache, alcohol varnish, ink, papier-mâché, wood, cord, and metal conduit on particle board

SIZE: 27 × 27½ × 4⅞ in. (68.6 × 69.8 × 12.4 cm.)

COLLECTION: Private collection, New York

PROVENANCE: F. Arnhard Scheidt, Kettwig-am-Ruhr, West Germany (acquired from the artist). Sold at Christie's, New York, February 8, 1986, lot 97

CONDITION: Restored

INSCRIPTION: On verso, "1965, white is enamel paint, yellow-gouche [*sic*]—over is alcohol varnish—over that purple ink—over that is varnish, pink and orange gouche [*sic*] + green black—ink, 'H + H' "

Like *Oomamaboomba* and *Tomorrow's Apples, H + H* contains a loop projecting into space connecting two parts of the relief. The white phallic form at the top is joined to the painted ovoid shapes nestled in the interior by the loop, and the ovoids themselves are joined by a painted yellow line. The white wooden form at the top of the relief was a discarded piece from one of Doyle's sculptures, and the title refers to a brand of pipe tobacco that he used. According to Doyle, even though their domestic life was very strained at this time, he and Hesse continued to be involved with each other's work. Hesse advised him on matters of color, while he helped her with problems of construction, like a number of other artists throughout her career. The titles too at this period were something of a collaboration and were the type favored for abstract expressionist painting, with references to jazz, slang hipsterisms, free association, and mythology.

9 Cool Zone

July 1965

MATERIALS: Aluminum base for a stand and painted cloth-bound cord

SIZE: Diameter of stand: 15 in. (38.1 cm.); length of cord: 45 in. (114.3 cm.); depth: 10 in. (25.4 cm.)

COLLECTION: Estate of Eva Hesse

Cool Zone was made from a metal base, perhaps for a sculpture stand, that was found in the studio at Kettwig. In a reversal of its function it is here attached to the wall and threaded with a limp cord dangling pathetically and further negating the supporting function of the base. *Cool Zone* shows a drastic reduction to more linear forms and neutral color and anticipates a number of later pieces such as "Spoke Piece" (15) and "Moderna Museet" (20).

10 **Pink**

July 1965

MATERIALS: Silver paint, enamel, wood, plaster, painted cotton cord, and painted metal button on masonite

SIZE: 21⅝ × 25⅝ × 5¾ in. (54.9 × 65.1 × 14.6 cm.)

COLLECTION: Saatchi Collection, London

PROVENANCE: F. Arnhard Scheidt, Kettwig-am-Ruhr, West Germany (acquired from the artist). Sold at Christie's, New York, February 8, 1986, lot 96

Woven cords, graded from light to dark gray, animate and stitch together the three painted zones of this relief; the zones, also graded, give an illusion of depth. The raised wooden forms in the center—one similar to the orange shape in *Two Handled Orangekeyed Utensil* (2), the other to the white form in *H + H* (8)—are pinned down by a pink bolt that gives the relief its name and its only note of color. The move from strong colors to neutral grays anticipates Hesse's complete abandonment of color some months later.

11 C-Clamp Blues

July 1965

MATERIALS: Painted concretion, metal wire, painted bolt, painted hollow plastic ball with rattle on particle board

SIZE: 25⅝ × 21⅝ × 1½ in. (65.1 × 54.9 × 3.8 cm.)

COLLECTION: Saatchi Collection, London

PROVENANCE: F. Arnhard Scheidt, Kettwig-am-Ruhr, West Germany (acquired from the artist). Sold at Christie's, New York, February 8, 1986, lot 98

CONDITION: Cleaned in 1986

In technical terms *C-Clamp Blues* marks a turning point in the development of Hesse's relief sculpture. The artist is moving away from building up the surface with plaster and papier-mâché, and here used a flat neutral background as a foil for a projecting V-shaped wire and ball. The sexual tone of the motifs apparent in the earlier reliefs is here much more abstract, and consequently more enigmatic.

12 **Up the Down Road**

July 1965

MATERIALS: Aluminum paint, tempera, styrofoam, and cloth-bound cord on masonite

SIZE: 25¾ × 19¾ × 7½ in. (65.4 × 50.2 × 19 cm.)

COLLECTION: Saatchi Collection, London

PROVENANCE: F. Arnhard Scheidt, Kettwig-am-Ruhr, West Germany (acquired from the artist). Sold at Christie's, New York, November 7, 1985, lot 201

CONDITION: Fair; restored in 1987

Hesse used another neutral background here, styrofoam painted with aluminum paint against which a graded purple cord moves from one corner to another. The fact that the lighter gradation of purple is at the bottom gives a note of refined ambiguity to the piece. The title, with its suggestion of going against the current, aptly describes Hesse's own position in relation to her art as well as her life. In an interview with Cindy Nemser given five years after making the German reliefs, she said of them: "There was nobody doing anything like this. At the time, I mean, this was totally absurd to everybody. . . . That was the height of minimalism and pop. I mean, not that I care. I really don't ever work like that. . . . All I wanted was to find my own scene, my own world. Inner peace or inner turmoil, but I wanted it to be mine."

13 **Eighter from Decatur**

July 1965

MATERIALS: Enamel, tempera, cord, and metal weaving-machine part on particle board

SIZE: 27⅛ × 21¼ × 7½ in. (68.9 × 54 × 19 cm.)

COLLECTION: Estate of Eva Hesse

In *Eighter from Decatur,* Hesse incorporates a mechanical part used for winding cords in textile manufacture. She reuses the part in a way that exaggerates its spinning and binding capabilities, and turns the relief into a comment on her own attraction to compulsively repeated binding gestures. The pink graded breast shape used in the earliest reliefs, *Ringaround Arosie* and *2 in 1* (1, 7), is the center of the rotating spokes here. The illustration indicates Hesse's own arrangement of the movable spokes when the relief was first shown at the Kunstverein in Düsseldorf in August 1965.

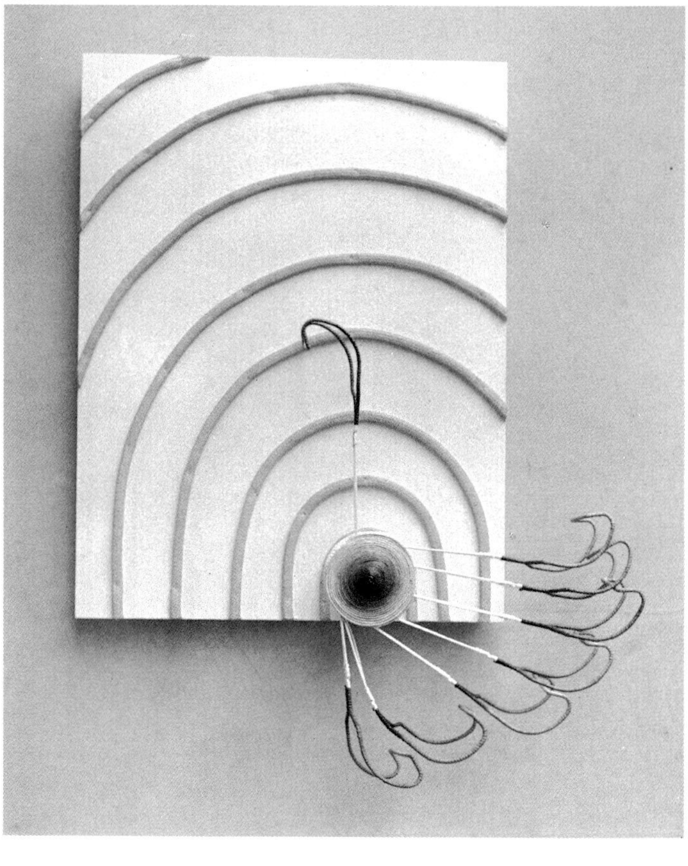

14 **Top Spot**

July 1965

MATERIALS: Enamel, tempera, found wooden fixtures, plastic pipe, metal conduit and bolt, clamps and screws, porcelain socket, and cloth-bound cord on particle board

SIZE: 27⅝ × 21¼ × 11 in. (70.2 × 54 × 27.9 cm.)

COLLECTION: Saatchi Collection, London

PROVENANCE: F. Arnhard Scheidt, Kettwig-am-Ruhr, West Germany (acquired from the artist). Sold at Christie's, New York, November 7, 1985, lot 199

INSCRIPTION: On verso, "Top Spot 1965"

There is a playful quality in *Top Spot*—missing from most of the other reliefs—which in fact is not generally characteristic of Hesse's work. A colorful confusion of painted cords and metal conduit plays on the surface of the relief. While there is a recapitulation of a number of motifs—for example, the cord dropping to the ground, a painted metal bolt, the use of graded cords—the sculpture lacks the psychological intensity of the earlier reliefs and suggests that Hesse had exhausted the possibilities of the relief form.

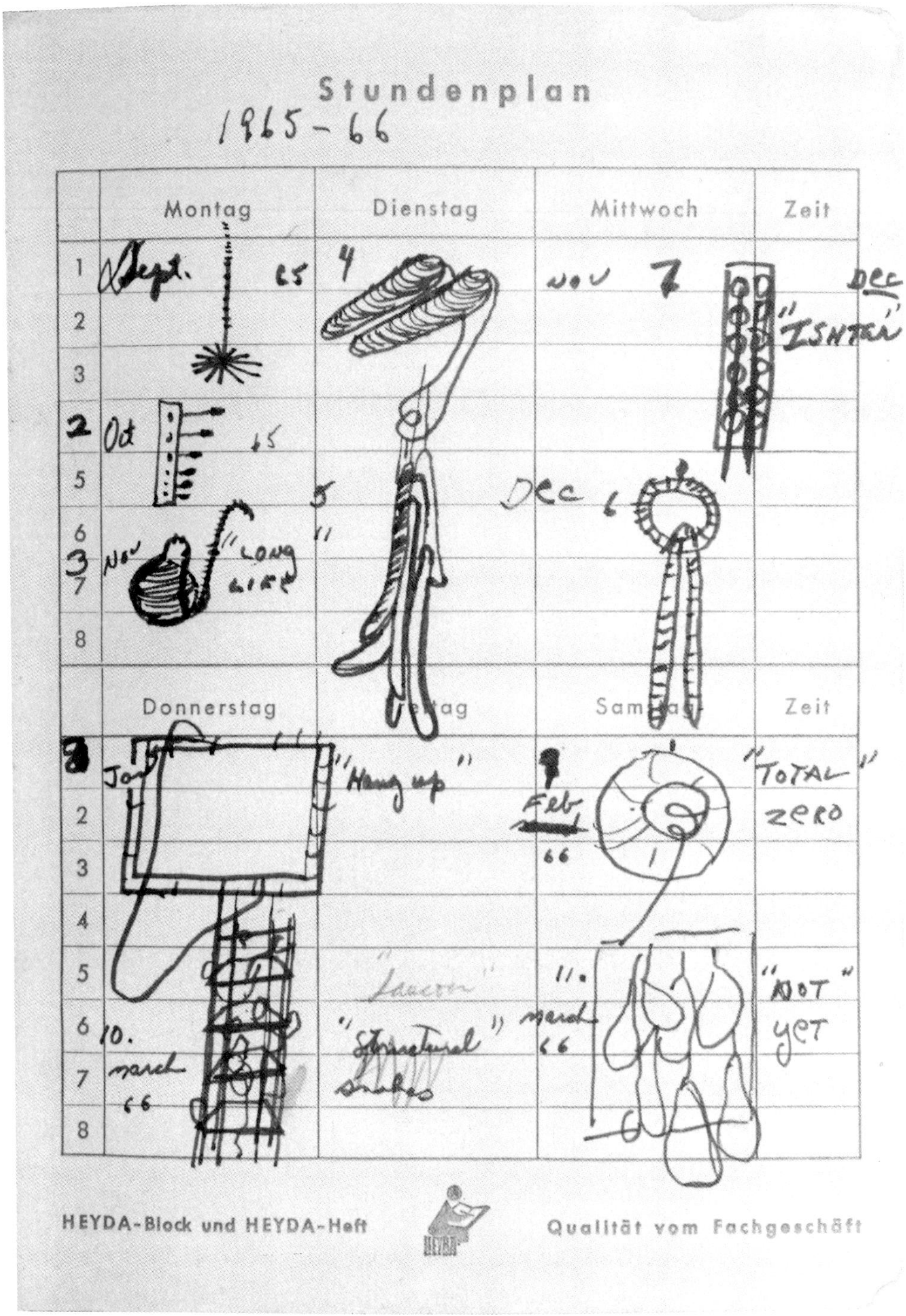
Stundenplan
1965-66
Montag
Dienstag
Mittwoch
Zeit
Sept. 65
Oct 65
Nov "LONG LIFE"
NOV 7
DEC "ISHTAR"
DEC 6
Donnerstag
Zeit
"Hang up"
Feb 66
"TOTAL ZERO"
10. march 66
"Structural snakes"
11. march 66
"NOT YET"
HEYDA-Block und HEYDA-Heft
Qualität vom Fachgeschäft

NEW YORK 1965

15 **Untitled ("Spoke Piece")**

September 1965

MATERIALS: Painted wood and iron bound with cord

SIZE: Height: ca. 126 in. (320 cm.); other dimensions unknown

COLLECTION: Destroyed at the request of the artist in 1970

When Hesse and Doyle returned from West Germany in September 1965, the floor above their Bowery apartment became available for her to use as a studio. She vigorously applied herself to making new work in her new environment and by the end of the month had already completed this sculpture. The construction was largely done by Doyle, to Hesse's specifications. The rim was removed from the wheel of a sanitation cart and the spokes were then mounted to a base from a bar stool by a very long, slender pole. Hesse bound the spokes and pole with cords and painted them so that the piece was graded from black at the bottom to light gray at the top. The pole thus seemed to disappear as it rose to the full height of her studio, testing the limits of the new space. The pole fits into a base so that it can spin around, a motion reinforced by the binding and recalling the spinning of *Eighter from Decatur* (13), an earlier piece in which she used found parts. The exaggerated display of verticality along with severe reductiveness was on the other hand to appear in two later sculptures, *Sans III* (89) and "Ice Piece" (94). "Spoke Piece" was her first freestanding sculpture and, in fact, is one of the very few freestanding pieces she made. At her request it was destroyed shortly before she died.

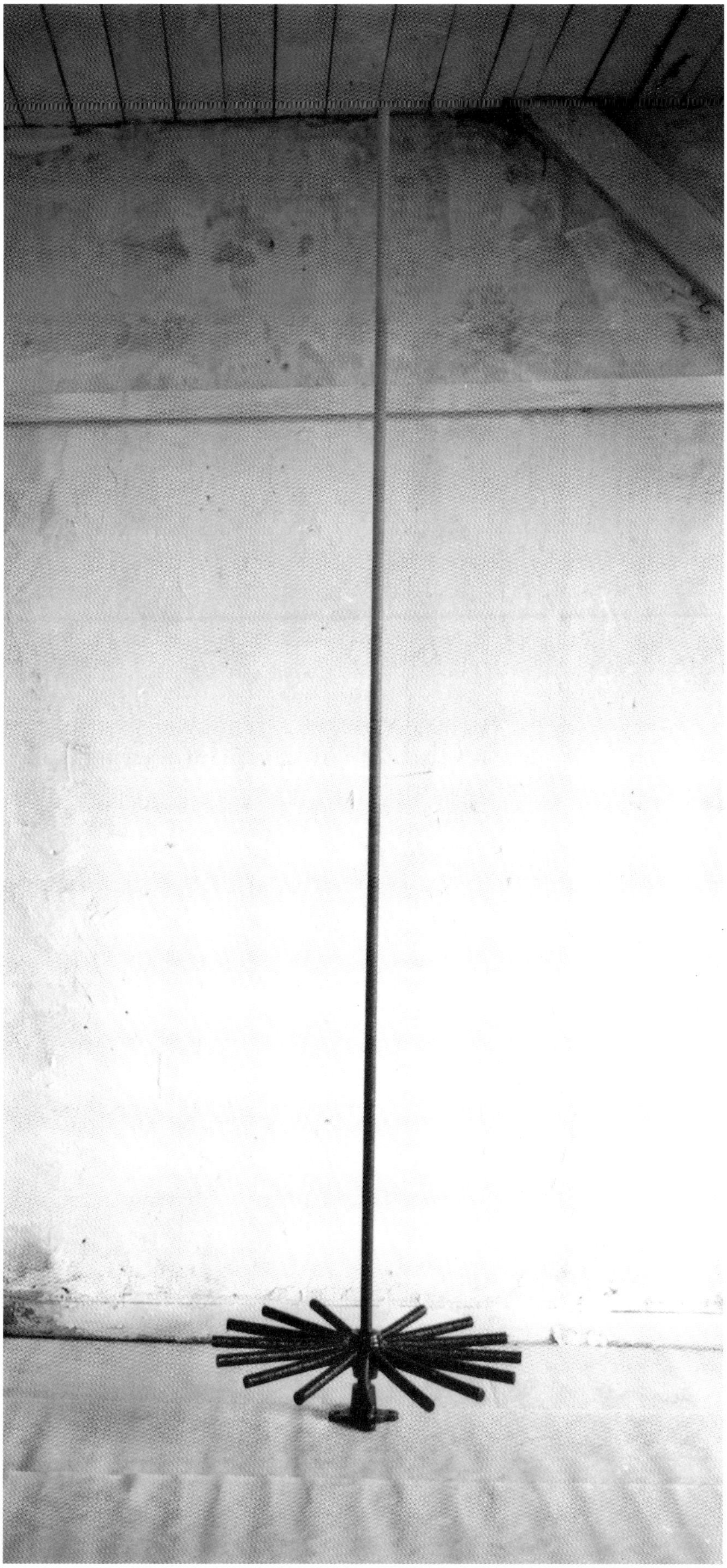

16 Untitled ("Purple Piece")

October 1965

MATERIALS: Acrylic paint on wood

SIZE: 45 × 8–21½ × 2½ in. (114.3 × 20.3–54.6 × 6.3 cm.)

COLLECTION: Estate of Eva Hesse

CONDITION: Some losses along the top edge

Like the previous sculpture, this one was constructed with Doyle's help. It was made of varying-sized handles from bar clamps that had been left in Hesse's studio by the previous occupant. The eight handles project out from the side of a vertical piece of wood. Holes were drilled on the face of the vertical piece corresponding in number and location to the handles. Hesse painted the piece the same finely graded purple she had used in *Up the Down Road* (12). Altogether this sculpture is rather reminiscent of the German reliefs in the use of color, the somewhat mechanical appearance, and the male and female sexual references. However, a sense of precision, a serial arrangement, and the repetition of forms are new in her work and recall some of Donald Judd's and Robert Smithson's work. A drawing from 1967 shows Hesse's continued interest in this type of structure, as does "Model for Unrealized Sculpture" (70). Hesse abruptly abandoned the use of color at this point and would not use it until late 1967, when she was to introduce color through the use of latex.

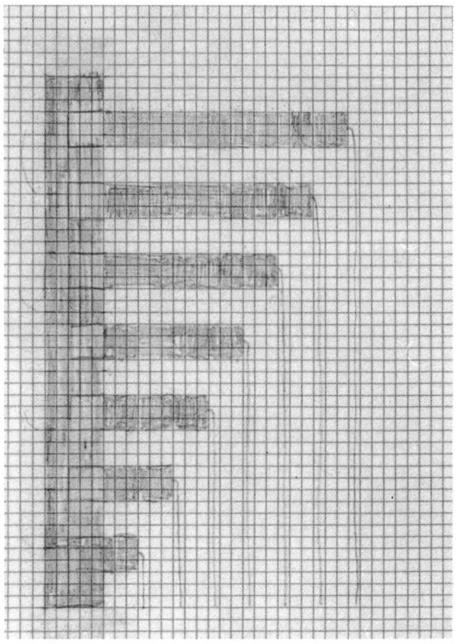

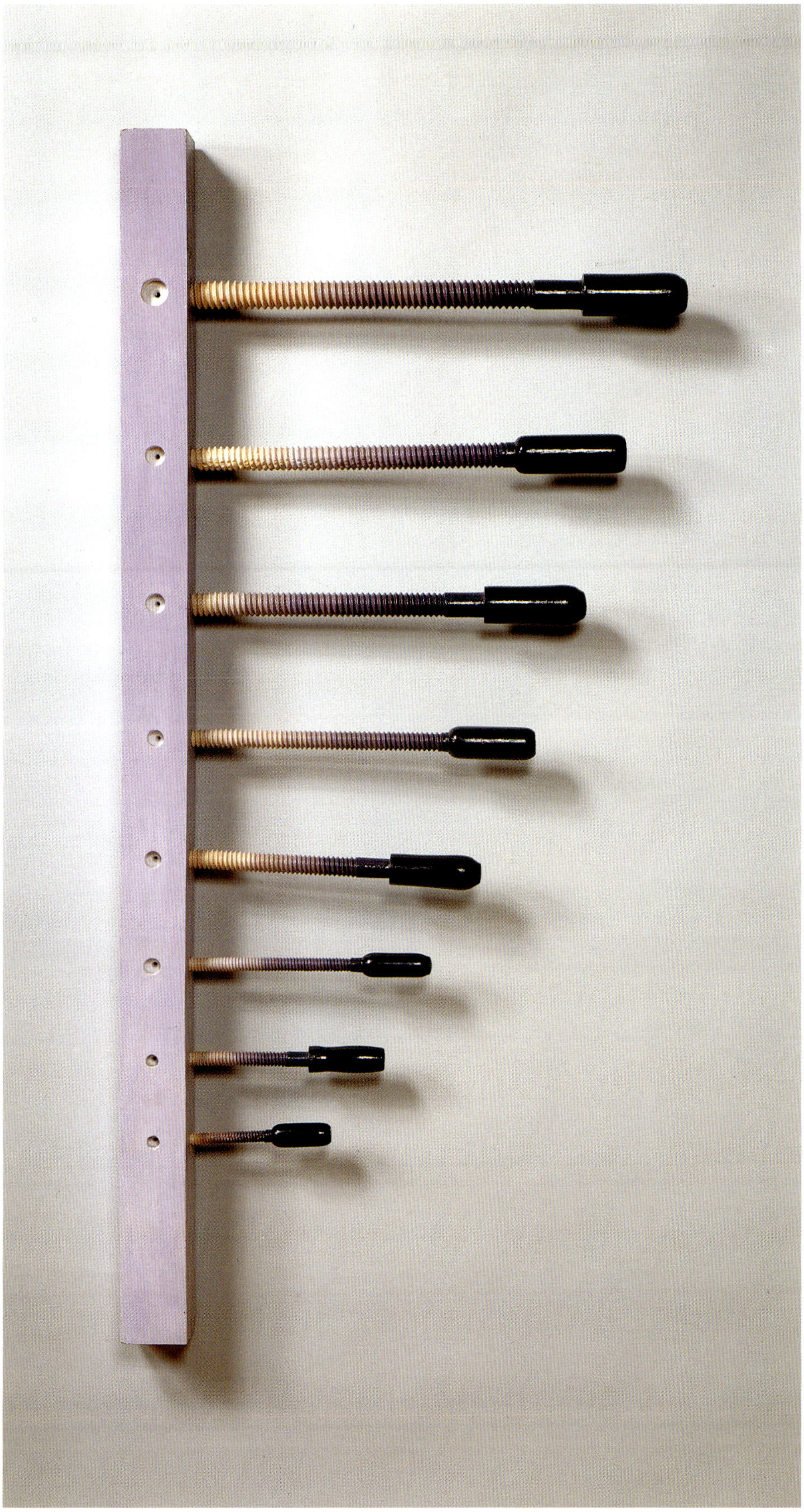

17 **Long Life**

November 1965

MATERIALS: Cord, papier-mâché, epoxy, and enamel over a beach ball and hose

SIZE: Length of hose: 84 in. (213.4 cm.); diameter of ball: 20 in. (50.8 cm.)

COLLECTION: Destroyed at the request of the artist in 1970

Hesse employed a technique for the construction of *Long Life* that she would use in at least ten sculptures of this period. She covered a hollow form, in this case a beach ball, with papier-mâché and then covered that with cord and glue. A tube, also cord-bound, and graded from dark to light gray, rose from the ball and was attached to the wall. According to Ray Donarski, an artist friend of Hesse's, a likely source for this technique was Henry Pearson's papier-mâché-and-yarn-wrapped beach balls. Pearson had begun making these spheres in 1963 and it is most likely that Hesse would have seen them in Donarski's studio. It is easy to understand her attraction to this construction technique, for it allowed her to make large three-dimensional forms without any particular knowledge of tools and therefore without anybody else's assistance. The fact that the resulting forms were hollow also suited Hesse's developing aesthetic. The image is a sexual one, suggesting a womb with an umbilical cord, as in *Ear in a Pond* (3). Its size and blackness give the sculpture a disturbing and powerful presence. The concept of connecting the form to the wall with a kind of tether is very close to a sculpture made by Robert Morris in 1964, now in the collection of Philip Johnson. Although Hesse liked *Long Life* enough to exhibit it in the spring of 1966, she asked that the piece be destroyed before she died.

18 **Ingeminate**

November 1965

MATERIALS: Surgical hose, papier-mâché, cord, and sprayed enamel over balloons

SIZE: Length of hose: 144 in. (365.8 cm.); each element: 22 × 4½ in. (55.9 × 11.4 cm.)

COLLECTION: Saatchi Collection, London

PROVENANCE: Purchased from Droll/Kolbert Gallery, New York

Here a pair of balloons were covered with papier-mâché and bound with cord. The balloons were painted with a glossy black enamel and connected by surgical tubing. The impression is oddly that of mummified phalluses joined by an umbilical cord. The title means "to emphasize through repetition," a concept that would become fundamental to Hesse's art. As she moved away from relief to more three-dimensional forms, she was faced with the problem of positioning them in space. In the photograph of her studio on page 64, *Ingeminate* is shown on a cloth-covered pedestal with the cord section looping to the ground; she hardly ever used this solution again, however, preferring instead to hang her sculptures from the ceiling or on the wall, or to place them directly on the ground.

19 **Several**

November 1965

MATERIALS: Acrylic paint, papier-mâché over balloon with rubber cords

SIZE: 84 × 11 × 7 in. (213.4 × 27.9 × 17.8 cm.)

COLLECTION: Saatchi Collection, London

PROVENANCE: Purchased from the artist by Donald Droll in 1966. Purchased from Droll/Kolbert Gallery, New York

CONDITION: End of one unit broken and repaired

Several is made of seven balloons covered with very thin shells of papier-mâché, painted graduated shades of dark to light gray. It lacks the wound cords and glue used in *Long Life* (17) and *Ingeminate* (18), and as a result appears light and fragile. At the same time the scale of the piece is surprisingly large, as the photograph of Hesse standing with the sculpture indicates. Like *Ingeminate*, *Several* is composed of paired phallic forms joined by cords. Significantly, one of the units lacks its partner; it is the first indication of a trend in Hesse's work away from joining and pairing forms. Here she begins to isolate forms and display them singly or, if she shows them in clusters, groups them into an odd number of units. This tendency is underscored by the title; *several* can mean "severed" and "separate" as well as "indefinite number more than two."

20 **Untitled ("Moderna Museet")**

November 1965

MATERIALS: Enamel-painted cord over wood or metal ring and over hose

SIZE: Length of hose: 148 in. (375.9 cm.); length of hose and ring (variable): ca. 106 in. (269.2 cm.); diameter of ring: 32 in. (81.3 cm.)

COLLECTION: Moderna Museet, Stockholm

PROVENANCE: Purchased from Droll/Kolbert Gallery, New York

This is a more compelling version of *Cool Zone* (9) and is the first sculpture that is hung from the ceiling. It reverses the structural principle of *Long Life* (17): rather than a cord-bound sphere on the floor from which issues a graded tube, an empty hoop is suspended in space and a graded tube hangs through it, growing lighter in color as it approaches the floor.

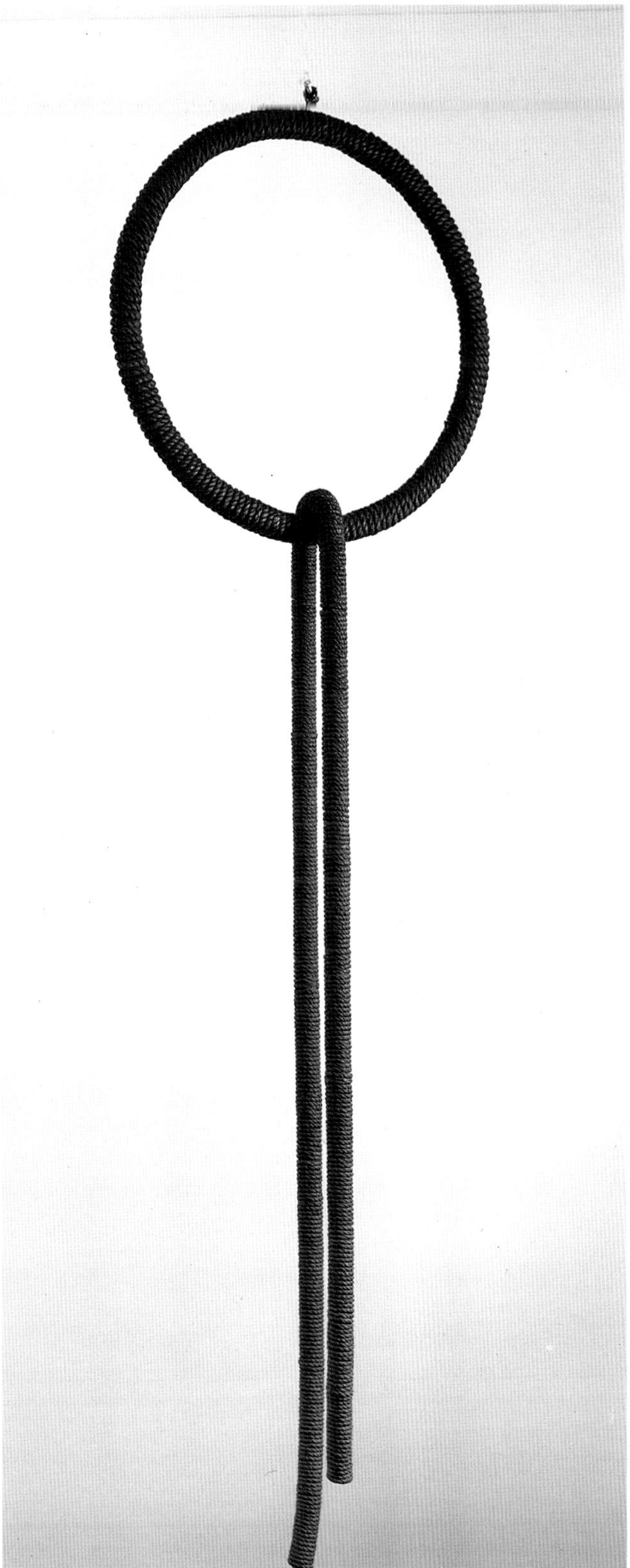

21 **Ishtar**

December 1965

MATERIALS: Twenty cord-bound and painted hemispheres (3 in. in diameter) with black plastic cords protruding from their centers, mounted on heavy paper stapled and nailed to wood; paper gessoed and painted with acrylic

SIZE: 36 × 7½ × 2½ in. (91.4 × 19 × 6.3 cm.); height with cords: 42½ in. (107.9 cm.)

COLLECTION: Florette and Ronald B. Lynn, New Jersey

PROVENANCE: Acquired from the artist in 1965

CONDITION: Darkened and somewhat dirty

INSCRIPTION: On verso, "Eva Hesse 1965"

Ishtar uses the breast-and-cord motif from the German relief *Ear in a Pond* (3) and repeats it. As Hesse absorbed the influence of minimalism, repetition would play an increasingly important role in her work. However, for Hesse repetition implied exaggeration and absurdity and—unlike the canonical work of the minimalists—did not indicate an interest in mathematical ordering. The repetition of the breast forms in *Ishtar* creates a powerful female presence and does indeed recall the many-breasted Diana of Ephesus, a Roman variant of the Semitic goddess of fertility and war from whose name the sculpture takes its title. The division of the sculpture into equal zones of dark and light, along with the contrast between the fullness of the breast forms and the thin, black pendulant cords, echoes the opposed aspects of birth and death associated with the ancient female divinities. Hesse would have seen the Ishtar Gate and a large collection of Near Eastern antiquities when she visited the Pergamon Museum in Berlin in 1964.

NEW YORK 1966

22 **Hang Up**

January 1966

MATERIALS: Acrylic on cloth, wood, and steel

SIZE: 72 × 84 × 78 in. (182.9 × 213.4 × 198.1 cm.)

COLLECTION: Art Institute of Chicago

PROVENANCE: Purchased from Fourcade Droll, New York, by Victor Ganz, July 10, 1972. Purchased from the Estate of Victor Ganz by the Art Institute of Chicago, April 1988

Hang Up, finished in January 1966, is one of Hesse's most arresting sculptures. Whenever it is installed, it invariably creates a surprising impression that is hard to explain and almost impossible to sense from a photograph. Perhaps it is the integrity of the numerous contradictions that are held in taut suspension that accounts for the powerful presence, a presence made all the more remarkable because the piece is made up of negative spaces.

The construction of the work was carried out by Doyle and LeWitt to Hesse's specifications. A stretcher was wrapped with bedsheets and a half-inch steel tube wrapped with cord was made to project from it—sweeping from the upper right corner of the frame out into the room and back into the lower right corner. Both frame and tubing were then painstakingly graded from light to dark gray, causing the structure to appear strangely insubstantial.

The looping out into space has its origin in several of the German reliefs, most notably *Oomamaboomba* (5), *H+H* (8), and *Up the Down Road* (12). In *Hang Up,* however, rather than combine the loop element with a variety of mechanical and organic shapes, Hesse distilled the components into the most basic constituents and thus created a dialogue between the properties of two- and three-dimensional space. *Hang Up* concerns the tension between seeming opposites—painting and sculpture, real and depicted space, darkness and light, expansiveness and limitation. The tautness of the wire and the way it forms a circuit with the wrapped frames makes *Hang Up* quite different from the sculptures that follow, in which lines hang limply to the ground like severed umbilical cords.

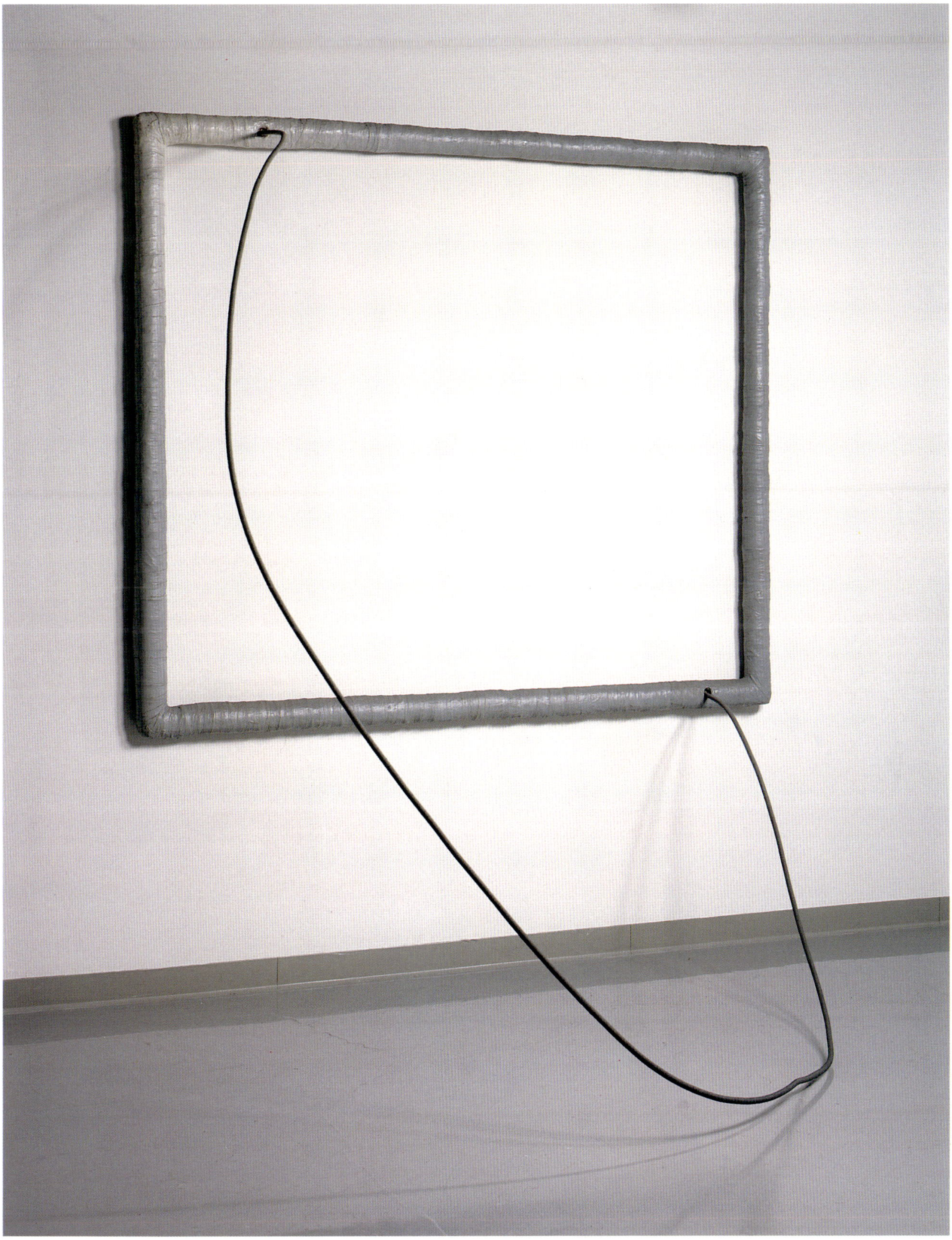

23 **Total Zero**

February 1966

MATERIALS: Rubber, plastic, epoxy, acrylic paint, polyurethane, metal, papier-mâché over inner tube

SIZE: 27 × 27 × 36 in. (68.6 × 68.6 × 91.4 cm.)

COLLECTION: Destroyed at the request of the artist in 1970

Continuing the technique used in *Several,* Hesse covered the inner tube with papier-mâché and painted it a shiny black enamel. The tube has a bulge on one side, and a hollow metal rod painted in graduated tones from black to pale gray projects from the nozzle. This rod is looped and then directed straight out, giving a strong impression of either deflation or inflation. Hesse had previously worked with this polarity in a pair of sculptures from 1965, *Long Life* (17) and "Moderna Museet" (20).

Total Zero is a very disturbing piece. The tension and wholeness achieved in *Hang Up* (22) are here abruptly punctured. The title of the piece refers to the woman who had replaced Hesse in her husband's affections. Hesse's diaries from this period offer ample evidence of the fury and anxiety she felt when she and Doyle separated. The title is equally a projection of her own feelings of inadequacy and fear of being left alone and empty. She felt uncomfortable about the piece and asked that it be destroyed shortly before her death. The combination of rage and loss informs the whole group of singular works at this time. Although she would not follow this path for long, the strong emotive charge that runs through her later work has its origin in this and the following dark pieces.

24 Untitled ("Estate Balloons")

1966

MATERIALS: Enamel paint over papier-mâché and rubber cord

SIZE: Original length unknown, but appears from the photograph to be ca. 30 in. (76.2 cm.); height of extant section: 16½ in. (41.9 cm.); diameter of long section: 2½ in. (6.3 cm.); length of gourd-shaped section: 9½ in. (24.1 cm.); diameter of gourd-shaped section: 4½ in. (11.4 cm.); length of connecting cord: 122 in. (309.9 cm.)

COLLECTION: Estate of Eva Hesse

CONDITION: Badly damaged, unexhibitable

This and the three balloon pieces that follow are technically and stylistically related to *Ingeminate* (18) and *Several* (19). Numbers 25, 26, and 27 recall *Ingeminate* in the way they are bound with black cord, strongly suggestive of mummification. "Estate Balloons" was fabricated in the same manner as *Several*, being a thin shell of papier-mâché over a balloon. The two sections are joined together as in *Ingeminate* and are presented as a balanced, albeit dead, pair of forms. The piece therefore probably precedes numbers 25–27, which stand as desiccated single units and are closer to *Total Zero* (23) in giving an impression of dejection. Hesse's work seems to be moving in the direction of isolated parts, sometimes grouped but not connected. The phallic aspect of these pieces contrasts markedly with the sexual content of earlier works such as *Ear in a Pond* (3), where the phallus is bright green and erect. A line emerges from it and zigzags before entering the female "ear," which seems to absorb and transform this aggressive energy into the red cord. In these balloon pieces, on the other hand, the phallus is presented alone in a blackened state of decay and in one example (27) is revealed to be hollow. There is an atmosphere of poignant isolation and death.

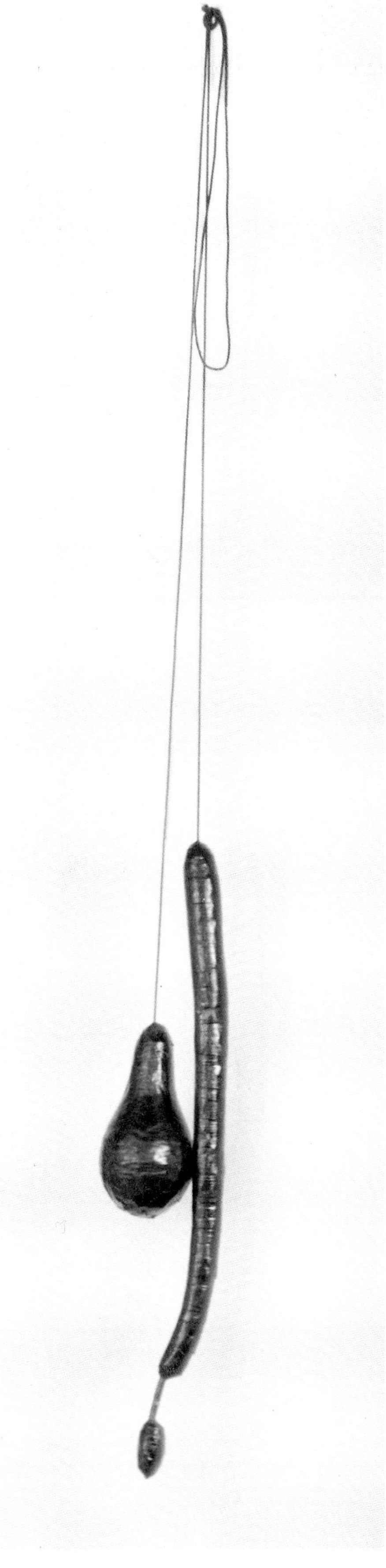

25 **Untitled ("Vollmer Balloon")**

1966

MATERIALS: Enamel paint and cord over papier-mâché and latex balloon with elastic cord

SIZE: Height of rigid element: 33½ in. (85 cm); variable diameter: 2–2½ in. (5.1–6.3 cm.); overall height varies with the installation

COLLECTION: Museum of Modern Art, New York

PROVENANCE: Bequest of Ruth Vollmer (gift of the artist)

See number 24. This piece appears positioned differently in a photograph of Hesse's studio (page 64) taken in August 1966.

26 **Untitled ("Lenk Balloon")**

1966

MATERIALS: Enamel paint and cord over papier-mâché and balloon

SIZE: 94½ × 9 1/16 × 2 in. (240 × 23 × 5.1 cm.)

COLLECTION: Thomas and Maria Lenk, Schloss Tierberg, West Germany

PROVENANCE: Acquired from the artist by exchange in 1967

See number 24.

27 **Untitled ("LeWitt Balloon")**

1966

MATERIALS: Enamel paint and cord over papier-mâché and latex balloon

SIZE: 47 × 11½ × 2½ in. (119.4 × 29.2 × 6.3 cm.)

COLLECTION: LeWitt Collection, on loan to the Wadsworth Atheneum, Hartford, Connecticut (temporary loan no. 146.327.1976)

PROVENANCE: Acquired from the artist by Sol LeWitt

See number 24.

28 **Vertiginous Detour**

March 1966

MATERIALS: Enamel, rope, net, plaster, and papier-mâché

SIZE: Length of net: 23 in. (58.4 cm.); circumference: 40 in. (101.6 cm.)

COLLECTION: Ganz Collection, New York

PROVENANCE: Purchased from Fourcade Droll, New York, July 10, 1972

Like *Long Life* (17), *Vertiginous Detour* was probably formed over a beach ball. The cords, instead of being wound tightly around the ball, come unraveled through a net and give the sculpture a variety of sexual associations. The title refers to balance temporarily threatened and through it the artist acknowledged the precarious emotional state in which she found herself. The sculpture hangs from the ceiling and is the last one to be so oriented until *Connection* (93) in 1969.

29 **Untitled ("Three Nets")**

March 1966

MATERIALS: Painted rope, net, papier-mâché, weights

SIZE: 42½ × 11½ × 6 in. (107.9 × 29.2 × 15.2 cm.)

COLLECTION: Peter Palumbo, London

PROVENANCE: John Coplans, New York. Mayor Gallery, London

This and the net piece that follows, executed around the same time as *Vertiginous Detour*, complement and continue the ideas of the black balloon sculptures. Both net pieces contain weighted elements; here the weights are wrapped with paper and twine and painted a glossy black; and in the next piece the weights are loosely wrapped in milky-white polyethylene and appear more sensuous. Weighted pendular sacks, they seem very much like testicles, which conceptually and physically accompany the phallic forms of *Several* (19) and the black balloon series (24–27). Like these pieces "Three Nets" and "Nine Nets" belong to a period of high anxiety and rage, expressed in her diaries as Hesse was separated from her husband.

30 **Untitled or Not Yet ("Nine Nets")**

March 1966

MATERIALS: Nine dyed bags with weights and clear polyethylene

SIZE: 72 × 24 × 14 in. (182.9 × 61 × 35.6 cm.)

COLLECTION: Ganz Collection, New York

PROVENANCE: Purchased from Fourcade Droll, New York, July 10, 1972

See number 29.

31 Laocoon

March 1966

MATERIALS: Acrylic paint, cloth-covered cord, wire, and papier-mâché over plastic plumber's pipe

SIZE: 120 × 24 × 24 in. (304.8 × 61 × 61 cm.)

COLLECTION: Allen Memorial Art Museum, Oberlin College, Ohio

PROVENANCE: Fund for Contemporary Art and gift of the artist and Fischbach Gallery to the Allen Memorial Art Museum (accession no. 70.32)

Laocoon ranks with *Hang Up* (22) and *Metronomic Irregularity II* (38) as Hesse's most important sculptural achievements of 1966. Begun in 1965, *Laocoon* passed through an intermediate version shown in a photograph (page 87) taken before the work was completed in March 1966. Hesse turned to Ray Donarski for technical assistance with the construction of the plumber's-pipe armature of the piece. According to Donarski, the plastic pipe appealed to Hesse because it could easily be cut with a hacksaw and glued together with epoxy, work she could do by herself. Hesse covered the rigid pipes with papier-mâché and painted them a light gray. The "snakes," as she calls them in her diary, were made by wrapping wire with cloth and covering the forms with papier-mâché and thinner wire, and were then painted a light gray. Despite the technical advantages of this technique and the ease of execution, Hesse never used plastic pipe again.

Laocoon is one of her very few freestanding sculptures. More frequently her structures depend on the wall or ceiling for support or fall limply to the floor. The problem of support was a central theme in her sculpture and was intertwined with her recurrent dependence on other artists for technical assistance.

In *Laocoon* Hesse achieved a tension that expresses a synthesis of her most basic artistic and personal concerns. A diary entry soon after the completion of the piece demonstrates how she conceived the oppositions within herself. "Underlying theme: two conflicting forces inside Eva. 1) Mother force, unstable, creative, sexual, threatening my stability, sadistic-aggressive. 2) Father/stepmother force, good little girl, obedient, neat, clean, organized, masochistic." In her life these contradictory forces would remain in conflict, but in her art she came to resolve them in many surprising ways.

In formal terms *Laocoon* contains a number of elements that were to appear in Hesse's later work. For example, the ladderlike ascending structure counterpoised with earthbound descending cords would be used again in *Vinculum I* and *II* (91, 90); and the balancing of structured and chaotic elements is the main theme of such disparate works as *Ennead* (32), *Metronomic Irregularity I–III* (37, 38, 39), *Inside I* (53), and *Accession I–V* (57, 58, 74, 75, 76).

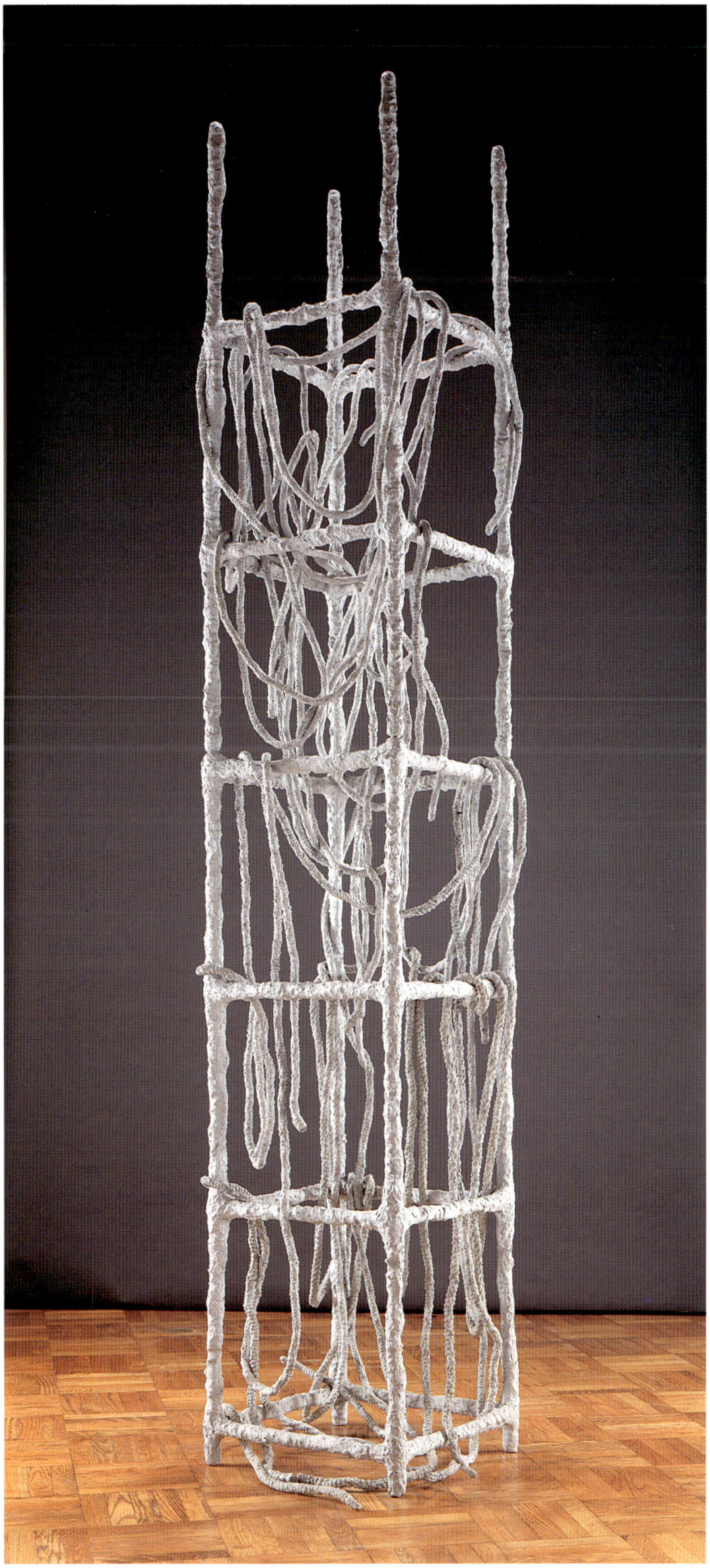

The title is a reference to the Hellenistic sculpture in the Vatican Museum in Rome that depicts the punishment of a priest, Laocoön, and his two sons for violating the temple of Athena. In retribution Athena caused two snakes to emerge from the sea and strangle the father and his sons. Hesse visited the museum in the fall of 1965 and would have known the sculpture also from her art courses at Yale.

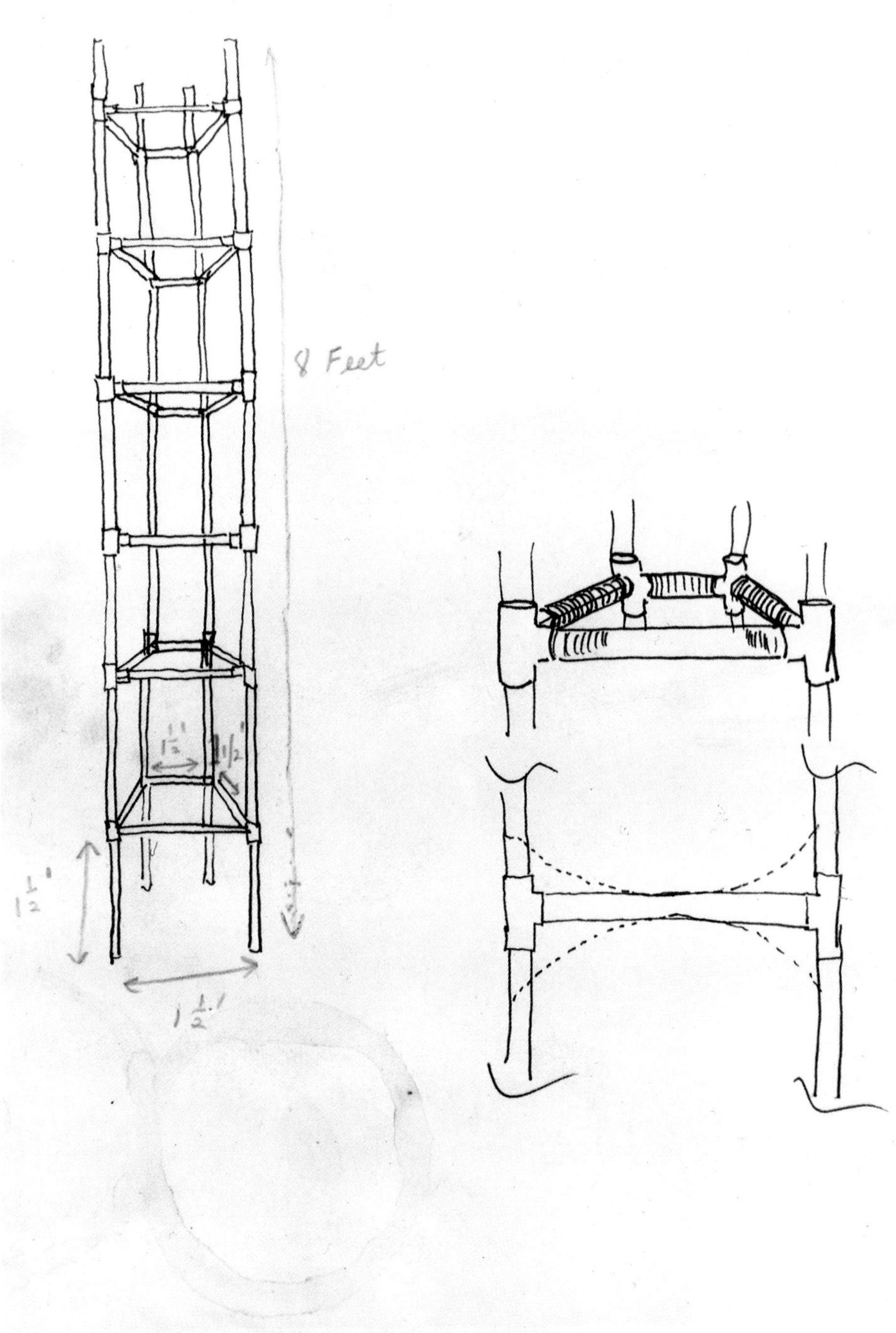

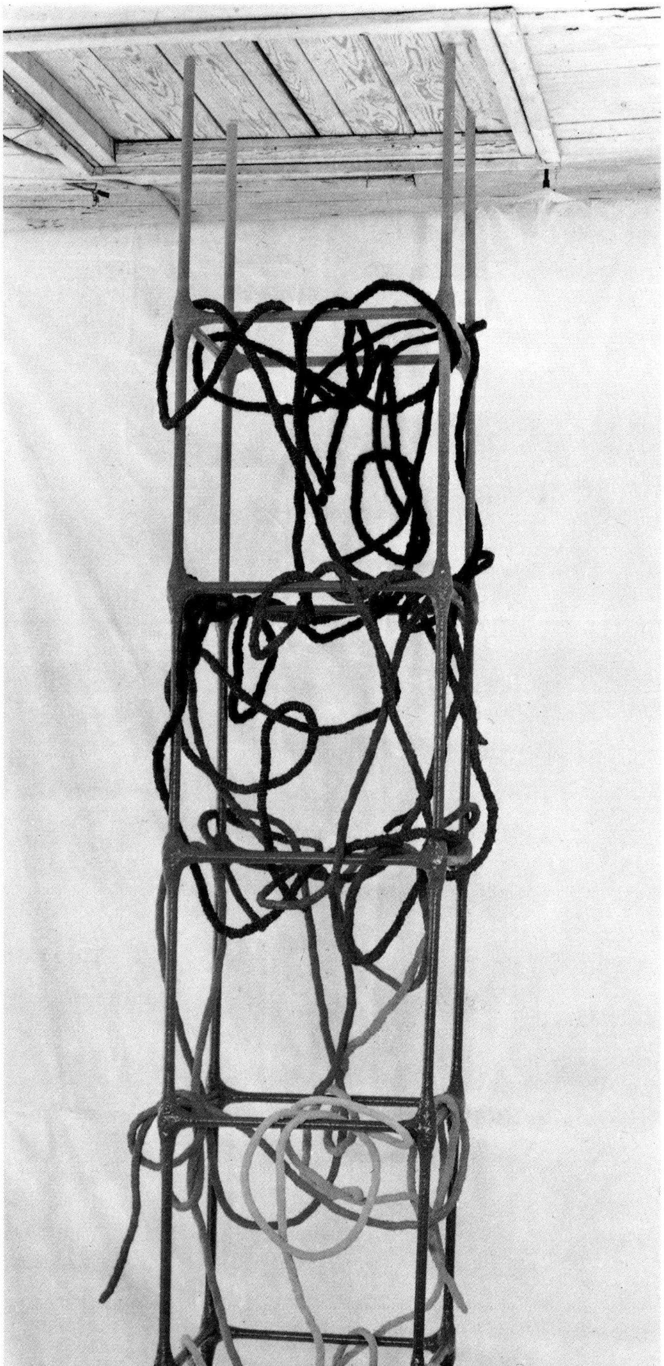

32 **Ennead**

1966

MATERIALS: Dyed string and painted papier-mâché

SIZE: 36 × 22 × 1½ in. (91.4 × 55.9 × 3.8 cm.)

COLLECTION: Ganz Collection, New York

PROVENANCE: Purchased from Fourcade Droll, New York, July 28, 1972

Ennead is actually a development from *Ishtar* (21). A close examination of the piece shows a grid of small hemispheres, much smaller than those of *Ishtar*, and each one, like those in that work, contains a string; here they are thickened and lengthened until they become a thick, tangled mass of hair. The shrinking of the hemispheres, the proliferation of their number, and the lengthening of the string are good examples of Hesse's reuse of the vocabulary of *Ishtar* to create an entirely different effect. The way the strings-as-hair hang down in disarray in front of the panel to which they are attached suggests mourning and implies a sense of resignation as well. The title, which, as the artist notes, means "a set of nine," suggests the imposition of a system, an idea that will be more clearly expressed in the works of 1967. But *Ennead* also refers to a grouping of nine gods associated with the mythology of ancient Egypt and is reminiscent of the mythic titles *Laocoon* and *Ishtar*. It was about this time that Mel Bochner gave Hesse a thesaurus, which she began to use for obtaining the more esoteric titles of her works. *Ennead* was the last sculpture in which she used gradation, both on the board and on the strings. She transferred the technique as well as the proliferation of circles to a group of drawings done in the summer of 1966.

33 **Compart**

1966

MATERIALS: Acrylic paint and cord over papier-mâché and masonite

SIZE: Height when installed: 48 in. (121.9 cm.); width of panels: 9–12 in. (22.9–30.5 cm.); depth: 1–2½ in. (2.5–6.3 cm.)

COLLECTION: Mr. and Mrs. Melvin Kolbert, Bloomfield Hills, Michigan

PROVENANCE: Mr. and Mrs. Y. S. Tang, New York. Sold to Droll/Kolbert Gallery, New York, circa 1979

INSCRIPTION: Signed on verso of panel 4, lower left corner

With *Compart* and the next piece Hesse began to impose a sense of order on the more chaotic elements of her work. It is useful to remember that 1966 was the year of the "Primary Structures" exhibit at the Jewish Museum and "Systemic Painting" at the Guggenheim. Certainly the art world was abuzz with talk about series, set theory, Fibonacci numbers, and many of the artists in Hesse's circle of friends figured prominently in both exhibitions. Although Hesse was not by temperament disposed to these ideas, they would influence her work for about a year. And by submerging the emotional content of her work, she was able to pass as a minimalist long enough to gain a foothold in the art world. This diversion also enabled her to reformulate her ideas about sculpture. *Compart* and the related pieces (34, 35, 36) reuse the formal elements of *Ringaround Arosie* (1), namely circular motifs and wound cord. In *Compart* Hesse cut the circles and thus activated the voids between the sections; and in the series *Metronomic Irregularity* (37, 38, 39) she developed segmentation further. The notebook page reproduced with "Small Compart" (34) indicates that Hesse envisioned *Compart* both horizontally and vertically. The circle as a motif was particularly important at this time, as these pieces and the concentric-circle drawings suggest.

34 Untitled ("Small Compart")

1966

MATERIALS: Acrylic paint, cord, and papier-mâché over masonite

SIZE: Height when installed: 38 in. (96.5 cm.); top section: 10 × 10 × $1\frac{1}{2}$ in. (25.4 × 25.4 × 3.8 cm.); middle section: 11 × 11 × $1\frac{1}{2}$ in. (27.9 × 27.9 × 3.8 cm.); bottom section: 12 × 12 × $2\frac{1}{4}$ in. (30.5 × 30. × 5.7 cm.)

COLLECTION: Private collection, Chicago

PROVENANCE: Estate of Eva Hesse. Purchased from Rhona Hoffman Gallery, Chicago, May 1988

See number 33.

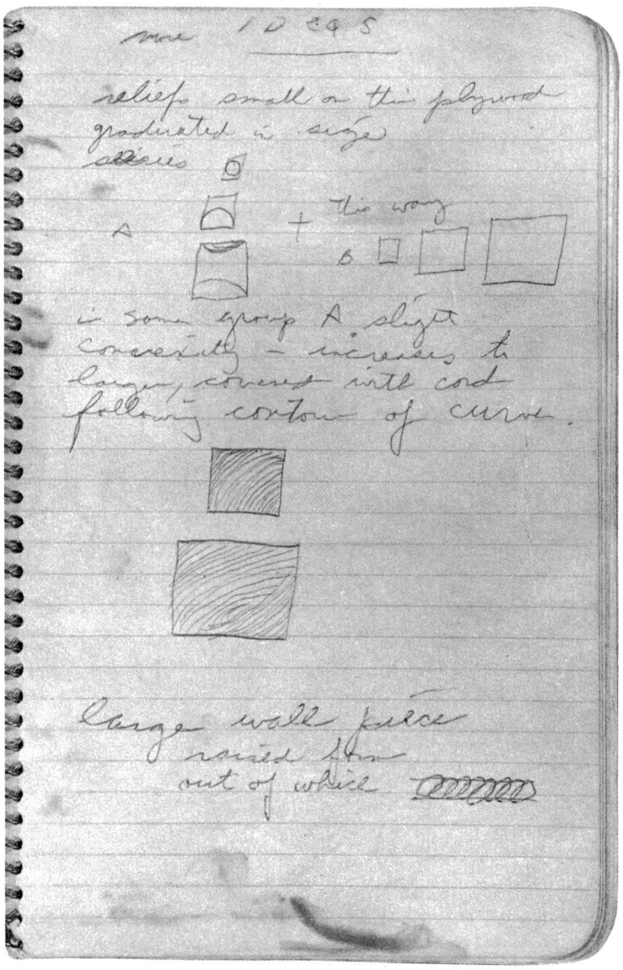

35 **Untitled ("Bochner Compart")**

December 1966

MATERIALS: Acrylic paint and cord over papier-mâché and masonite

SIZE: 9 × 9 × 2 in. (22.9 × 22.9 × 5.1 cm.)

COLLECTION: Mel Bochner, New York

PROVENANCE: Acquired from the artist

INSCRIPTION: On verso in gray paint, "M.B. E. Hesse, 66"

This and the next sculpture, related to numbers 33 and 34, were given to Sol LeWitt and Mel Bochner, respectively, at a Christmas party given by Ruth Vollmer in 1966. Probably they were originally planned to be part of a larger piece.

36 Untitled ("LeWitt Compart")

1966

MATERIALS: Gray acrylic paint, cord, papier-mâché on wood

SIZE: 7½ × 7½ × 4 in. (19 × 19 × 10.2 cm.)

COLLECTION: LeWitt Collection, on loan to the Wadsworth Atheneum, Hartford, Connecticut (temporary loan no. 146.317.1976)

PROVENANCE: Acquired from the artist by Sol Lewitt

CONDITION: Good; some yellowing

INSCRIPTION: On back center, "for Sol"; signed in ink, "Eva Hesse, 1966"

See number 35.

37 **Metronomic Irregularity I**

1966

MATERIALS: Painted wood, Sculp-Metal, and cotton-covered wire

SIZE: 12 × 18 × 2 in. with cords (30.5 × 45.7 × 5.1 cm.)

COLLECTION: Estate of Robert Smithson, Nancy Holt, New York

PROVENANCE: Acquired from the artist in 1966

Metronomic Irregularity I and *III*—models for the large sculpture *Metronomic Irregularity II*—were made for Lucy Lippard's show "Eccentric Abstraction" at the Fischbach Gallery in September 1966. In all three versions identical gray panels were divided into a grid and a small hole was drilled at the intersection of each line. From many of the holes cloth-covered wires protrude to connect the panels. The negative space between the panels is identical to the size of the panels and is activated and pulled into the composition because of the shadows cast by the tangled wires. Hesse had used connecting wires earlier in *Tomorrow's Apples* (6) and the concept of negative space in *Hang Up* (22).

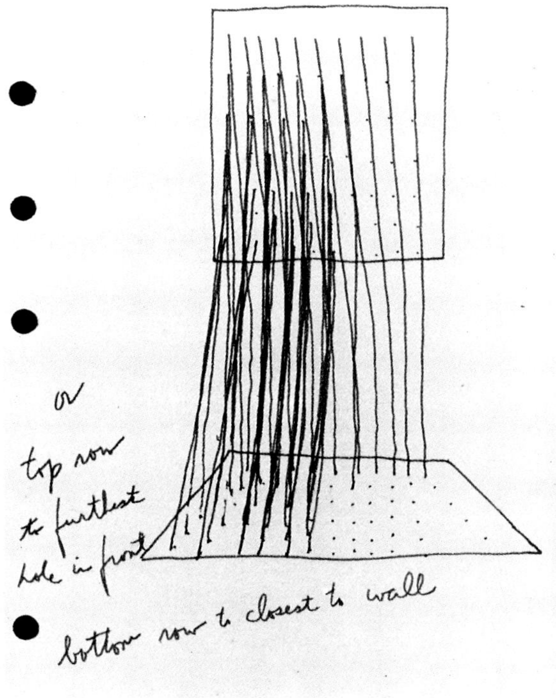

38 **Metronomic Irregularity II**

1966

MATERIALS: Painted wood, Sculp-Metal, and cotton-covered wire

SIZE: 48 × 240 in. installed (121.9 × 609.6 cm.); width of each panel: 48 in. (121.9 cm.)

COLLECTION: Present location unknown

PROVENANCE: Panels at Fourcade Droll, New York, in 1976

Spanning 20 feet, *Metronomic Irregularity II* marks a big change in terms of scale and orientation. Hesse's sculptures up to this time were almost always vertical, the tallest being around 10 feet. Here she expanded horizontally, an orientation that would be taken to extremes in *Addendum* (52), *Accretion* (78), *Sans II* (79), and *Expanded Expansion* (92). This development seems to mark Hesse's emergence from a long and difficult period of self-absorption and confinement. In contrast to the feeling of weight and gravity in such earlier pieces as *Ennead* (32) or the net pieces (29, 30), *Metronomic Irregularity I, II,* and *III* as well as *Compart* demonstrate a taut balance of tension between units and give a very strong sense of Hesse's growing confidence.

The work was dismantled after the 1966 Fischbach show and was not reassembled again in the artist's lifetime. The panels and wires were in her studio at the time of her death but their present location is unknown.

39 **Metronomic Irregularity III**

1966

MATERIALS: Painted wood, Sculp-Metal, and cotton-covered wire

SIZE: 10 × 50 × 2½ in. (25.4 × 127 × 6.3 cm.)

COLLECTION: Ganz Collection, New York

PROVENANCE: Purchased from Fourcade Droll, New York, July 20, 1972

See number 37.

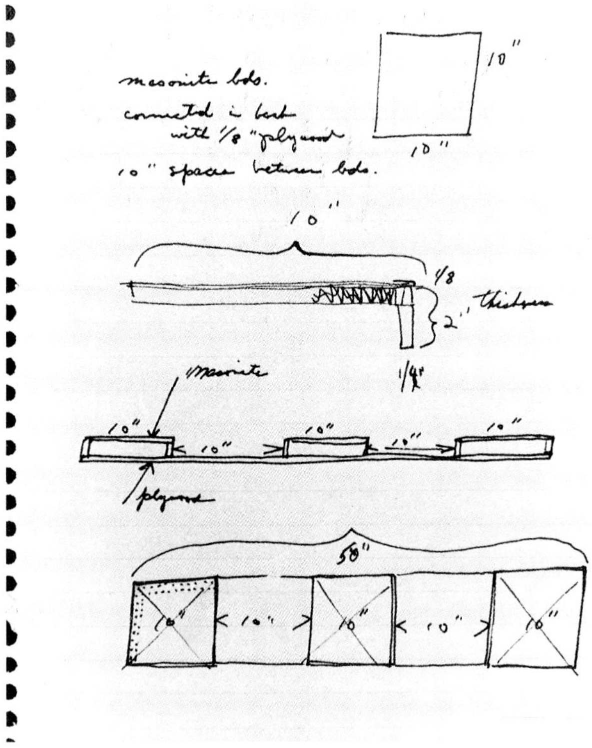

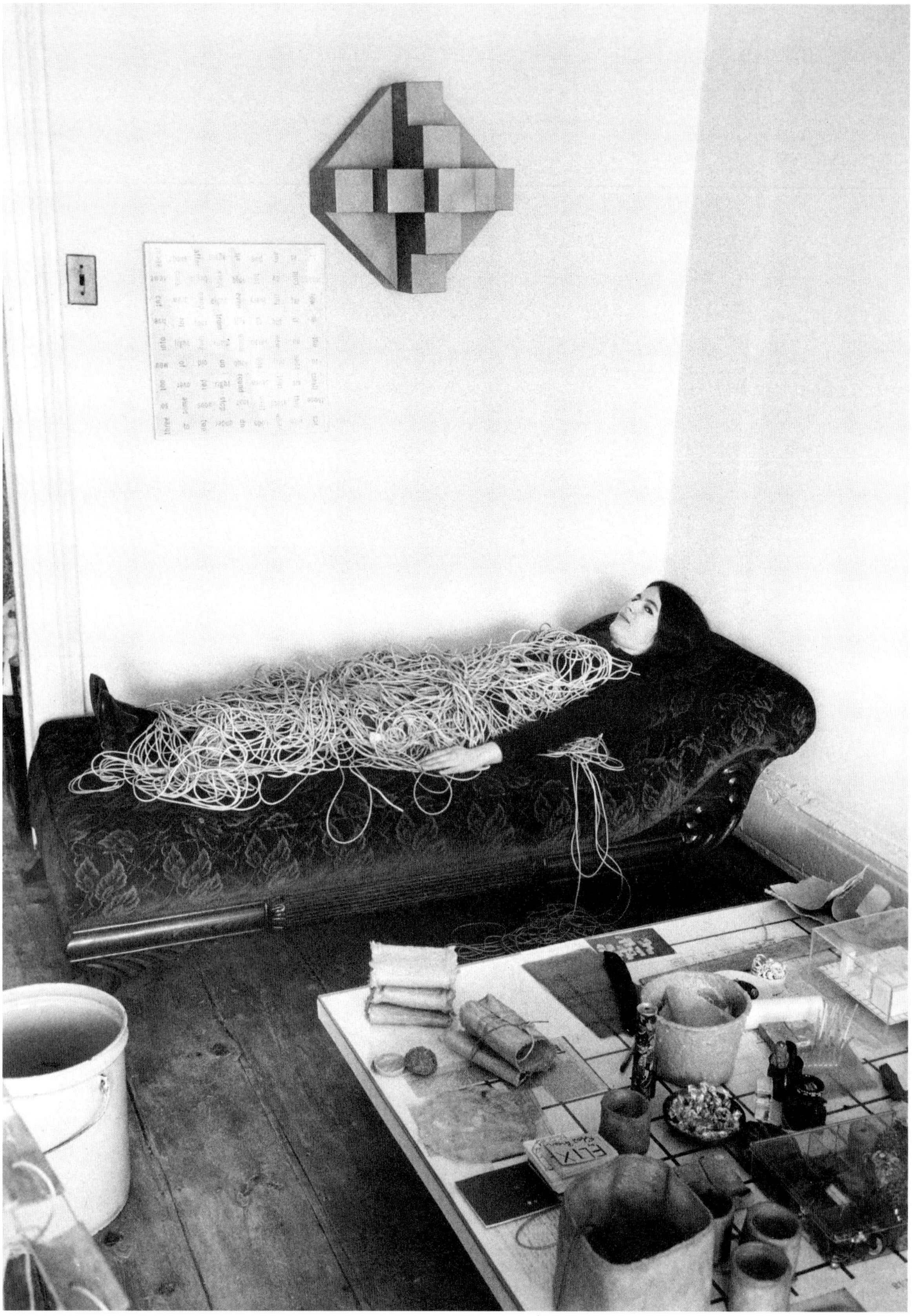

NEW YORK 1967

40 Compass

1967

MATERIALS: Steel washers and Sculp-Metal on wood

SIZE: 10×10×1 in. (25.4×25.4×2.5 cm.)

COLLECTION: Marilyn Cole Fischbach, New York

PROVENANCE: Acquired from the artist in 1967

In August 1966 Hesse began making a series of concentric-circle drawings. The circles are generally organized into rows and placed within a grid framework. The framework is sometimes obscured, other times left visible. Delicate washes of gray to black ink give the drawings a luminous evanescent quality, similar to the gradation of color on many of her sculptures in this period. Referring to the trauma from the death of her father in August 1966, and her separation from her husband a few months earlier, she remarked in a notebook entry, "I go in circles, maybe therefore my drawings." She continued this obsession with circles by making them three-dimensional and substituting real circular elements (washers and grommets) for drawn circles. In order to bind the washers and grommets together she used Sculp-Metal,* a material she used for nine other sculptures, most of them in 1967. Hesse was able to build up the surface in thin layers and retain the feeling of the layered washers of the drawings. The medium is a very direct one and required no intermediate steps such as casting or curing. These qualities would have appealed to Hesse, who was searching at the time for ways to make her work more substantial while using techniques that were familiar to her from painting and collage. A number of artists, among them Jasper Johns and Robert Morris, had used Sculp-Metal to similar effect in their work; the dull gray metallic surface had a density that was well suited to the developing minimalist esthetic of the early 1960s.

*Sculp-Metal is the trade name for a modeling compound made of atomized aluminum, a solvent (methyl ethyl ketone), and a vinyl binder. It has the consistency of clay and is usually applied with a palette knife in thin layers. The material dries to a very hard surface that can then be sanded and polished.

41 **Range**

1967

MATERIALS: Aluminum grommets and Sculp-Metal on cardboard

SIZE: 12 × 12 × 1/4 in. (30.5 × 30.5 × 0.6 cm.)

COLLECTION: Marilyn Cole Fischbach, New York

PROVENANCE: Acquired from the artist in 1967

INSCRIPTION: Signed on verso, lower right, "Eva Hesse, 1967"

See number 40.

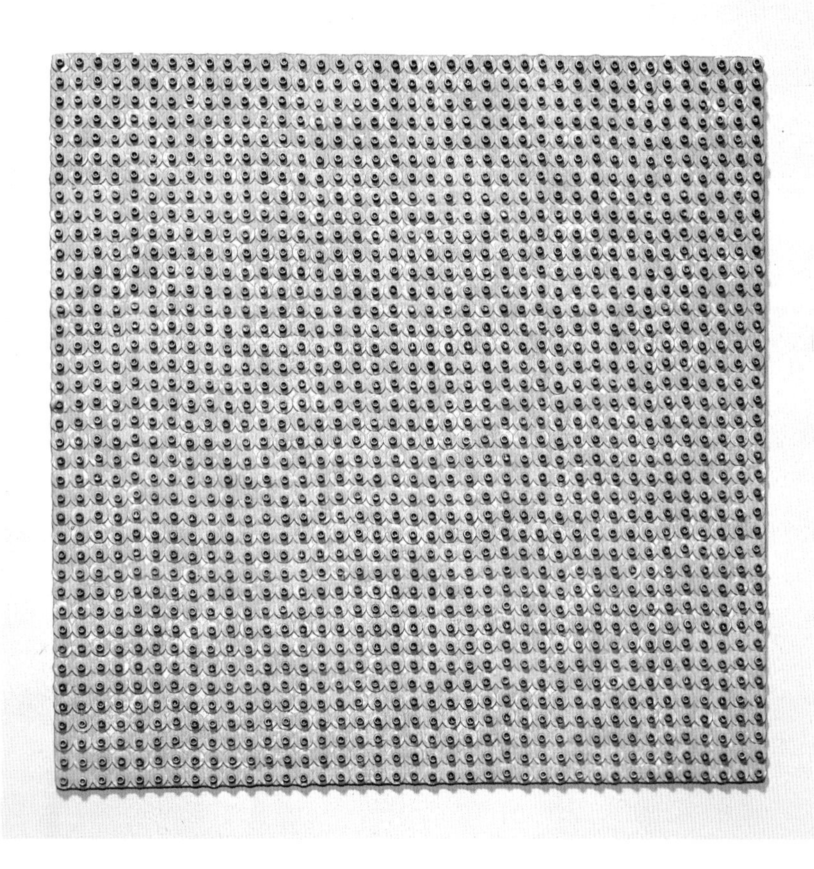

42 Cincture

1967

MATERIALS: Sculp-Metal over steel washers and plastic extrusion on masonite

SIZE: 10 × 10 × 2 in. (25.4 × 25.4 × 5.1 cm.)

COLLECTION: Marilyn Cole Fischbach, New York

PROVENANCE: Acquired from the artist by Fischbach Gallery, New York

CONDITION: Damaged lower left corner; restored

The title of this piece refers to the U-shaped plastic extrusions that are here pushed through adjacent holes from the back. A washer is placed over each end on the front surface. *Cincture* is perhaps the most notable of the washer pieces. Hesse was to exaggerate this process in *Iterate* (46) and *Constant* (49) and then take it even further with the *Accession* boxes (57, 58, 74, 75, 76) later that year. The title here refers to an encircling enclosure. This piece is related to *Compass* (40).

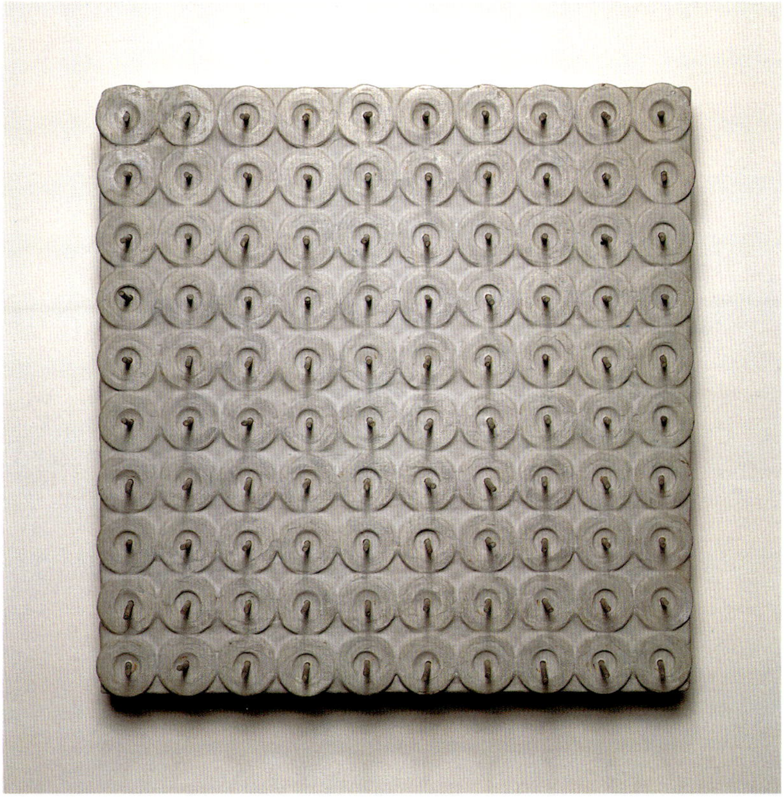

43 Untitled ("Washer Piece")

1967

MATERIALS: Sculp-Metal over steel washers on wood

SIZE: 36 × 36 × 1 in. (91.4 × 91.4 × 2.5 cm.)

COLLECTION: Philadelphia Museum of Art (lent anonymously)

PROVENANCE: Probably acquired from Droll/Kolbert Gallery, New York

CONDITION: Some rusting of washers in areas not covered by Sculp-Metal

See number 40.

44 **Washer Table**

1967

MATERIALS: Rubber washers on wood and metal

SIZE: 8¼ × 49½ × 49½ in. (21 × 125.7 × 125.7 cm.)

COLLECTION: LeWitt Collection, on loan to the Wadsworth Atheneum, Hartford, Connecticut (temporary loan no. 146.326.1976)

PROVENANCE: Acquired from the artist by Sol LeWitt

The base of *Washer Table* was built by Sol LeWitt and given to Hesse. See number 40.

45 **Magnet Boards**

1967

MATERIALS: Sculp-Metal on wood and magnets

SIZE: Each unit: 12 × 12 × 2 in. (30.5 × 30.5 × 5.1 cm.)

COLLECTION: Louise R. Noun, Des Moines, Iowa

PROVENANCE: Fischbach Gallery, New York. Mr. and Mrs. Henry Feiwel, New York. Sold at Sotheby's, New York, May 5, 1986, lot 40

CONDITION: Good, with some losses of Sculp-Metal

INSCRIPTION: Signed and dated on verso

Magnet Boards is the most beautiful and mysterious of Hesse's Sculp-Metal pieces. It is also unique within her oeuvre as the only work in which she used magnets. A notebook drawing (see illustration) shows that Hesse originally planned to have the magnets connected by wires, creating a movable version of the *Metronomic Irregularity* series (37, 38, 39). The use of unfixed elements that could be moved within a certain set of limits was also to appear in later pieces, *Sequel* (67) and *Vinculum II* (90). *Magnet Boards* is closely related to the graph-paper drawings of 1967. It was possibly inspired by Alfred Jensen's checkerboard paintings of the early 1960s. Jensen was a friend of Hesse's and did influence her ideas about grids and numbers.

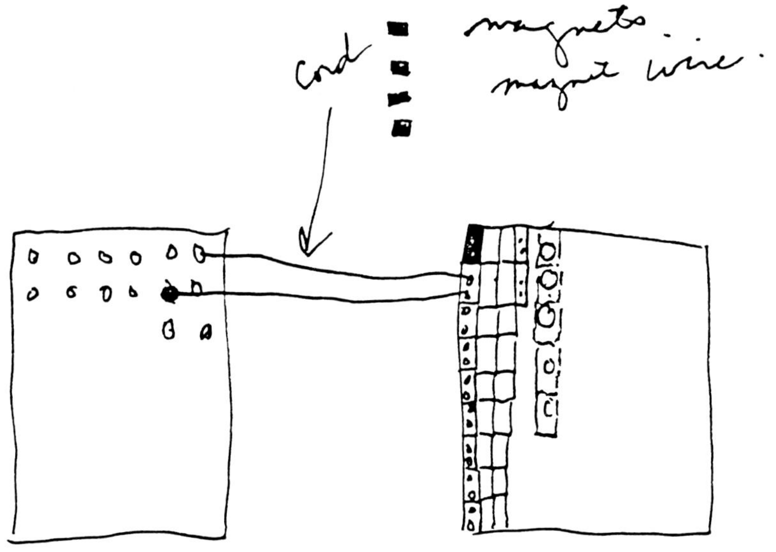

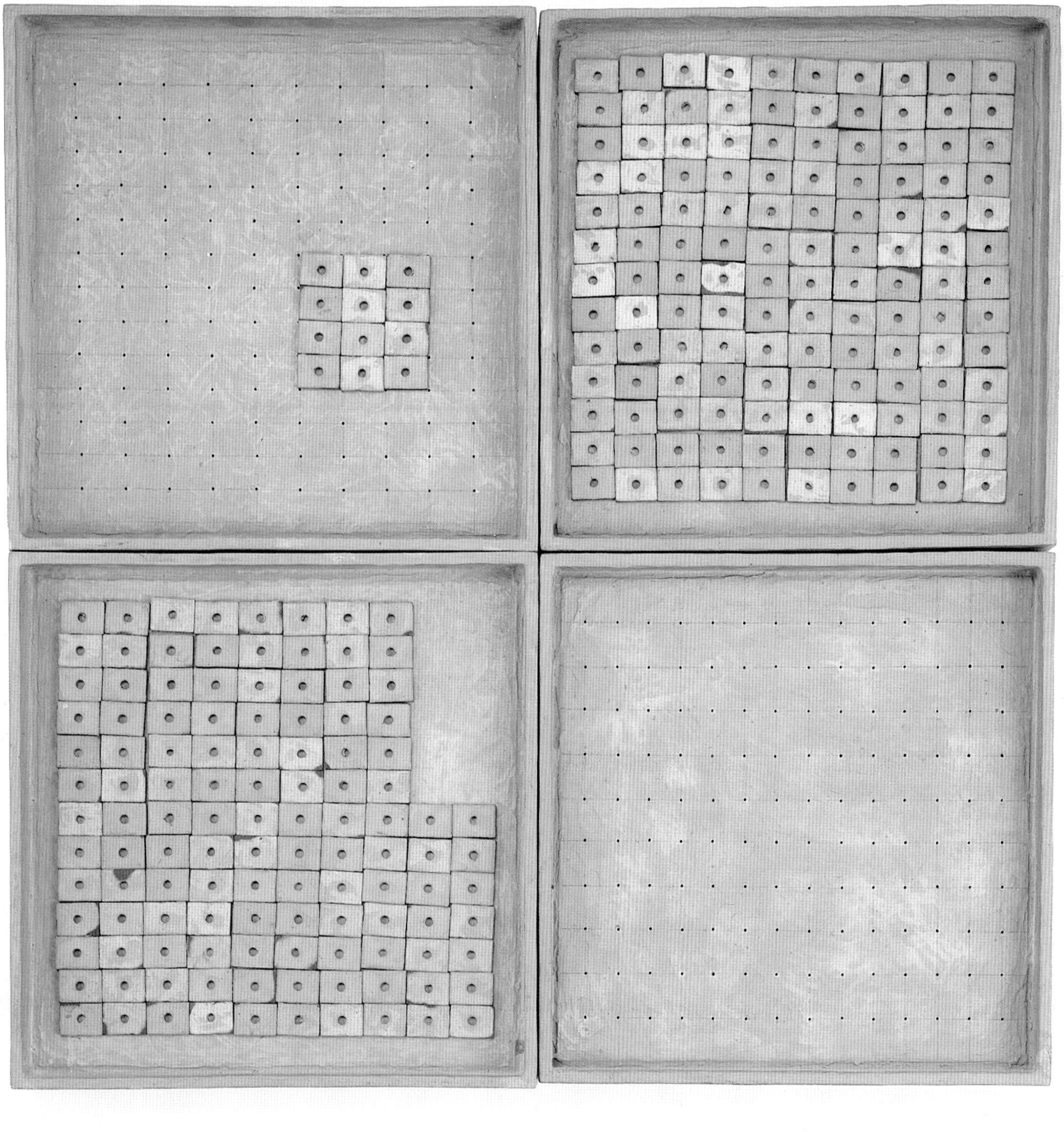

46 **Iterate**

1966–1967

MATERIALS: Wood shavings and glue, cord and acrylic paint on perforated masonite

SIZE: 20⅛ × 20¼ × 1 in. (51.1 × 51.4 × 2.5 cm.); height with cords: 22 in. (55.9 cm.)

COLLECTION: Dr. Robert Pincus-Witten, New York

PROVENANCE: Estate of Eva Hesse

CONDITION: Cracking at three corners and general yellowing of surface material (glue or varnish)

INSCRIPTION: Signed twice on verso: in gray paint, "Hesse 66," and in black ink along the top edge, "Eva Hesse 67"

With *Ishtar* (21) and *Ennead* (32), Hesse had begun to establish a preferred set of motifs—repeated circles, grids, lines—that she would use for the rest of her career. She used these simple motifs alone or in combination with remarkable and far-ranging variety, achieving quite different effects with this restricted vocabulary. It was her ability to assign emotional and psychological intensity to these simple formalist devices that makes her work still so compelling and differentiates it from the cooler art of her minimalist contemporaries.

This relief and the next four sculptures take the grid as their basis. In each case the grid is obscured under a thickly textured crust of material from which short knotted cords protrude through holes drilled at the intersection of the horizontal and vertical grid lines. The effect is reminiscent of the process used for the *Metronomic Irregularity* pieces (37, 38, 39), except that here the cords are cut and knotted and the backgrounds are more richly textured. The surfaces of *Iterate* and the study for a sculpture (47) are divided into a nine-by-nine grid, while that of *Constant* (49) is nineteen by nineteen. Odd numbers had special associations with femininity for Hesse and recur in many of her pieces; the odd numbers also work to introduce an element of irrationality into the cool, rigid logic of the grid. Nine is used in "Nine Nets" (30), *Ennead* (32), *Ditto* (50), the study for *Schema* (65), and *Tori* (95), and in the original plan for *Contingent* (98). Nineteen occurs in *Metronomic Irregularity III* (39), *Repetition Nineteen I* and *III* (62, 73), and the model for *Accretion* (77).

47 **Study for Sculpture ("Woman's Museum")**

1967

MATERIALS: Sculp-Metal, cord, Elmer's glue, acrylic paint, and varnish on masonite

SIZE: 10 × 10 × 1 in. (25.4 × 25.4 × 2.5 cm.)

COLLECTION: National Museum of Women in the Arts, Washington, D.C., gift of Wallace and Wilhemina Holladay

PROVENANCE: Fourcade Droll, New York. Metro Pictures, New York. Purchased from Sidney Janis, 1984

CONDITION: Some losses from cords, due to wear

See number 46.

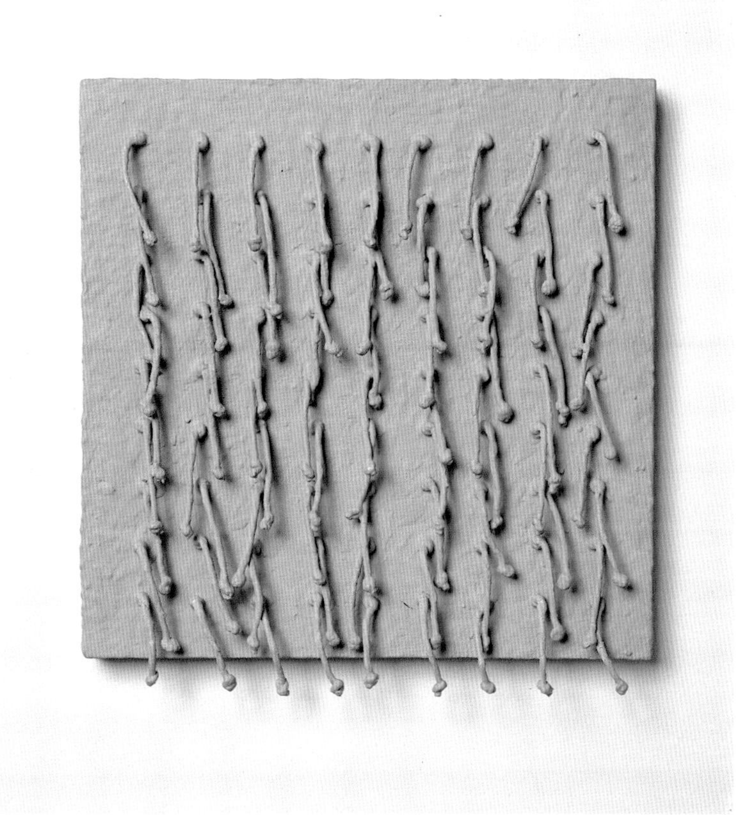

48 Untitled ("Composition for Sylvia")

1967

MATERIALS: Acrylic paint, wood shavings, and glue on masonite, rubber tubing

SIZE: 12 (with cords) × 10 × 2½ in. (30.5 × 25.4 × 6.3 cm.)

COLLECTION: Sylvia Mangold, New York

PROVENANCE: Acquired from the artist

CONDITION: Rubber tubes replaced

This piece is identical in construction and materials with *Constant*, number 49.

49 **Constant**

1967

MATERIALS: Acrylic paint, wood shavings, and glue on masonite, rubber tubing

SIZE: 60 × 60 × 5¾ in. (152.4 × 152.4 × 14.6 cm.)

COLLECTION: Ganz Collection, New York

PROVENANCE: Purchased from Fourcade Droll, New York, July 10, 1972

CONDITION: Surface lifting away from wood on lower right side; rubber tubing replaced in 1972

In *Constant* and number 48 Hesse pushed black rubber extrusions through a dense black square whose surface was made of a thick concretion of wood shavings, glue, and acrylic paint. The black field is energized by the imprint of the artist's fingers obsessively tracking over the surface, and by numerous knotted extrusions. Extrusion is a plastic or rubber tubing that has been formed by being forced through a small opening after a previous heating of the material. By pushing the rubber extrusion through the holes in *Constant,* Hesse refers to the process of making extrusion, and at the same time viscerally evokes that artistic process so central to her work, extruding, or drawing out of herself. This subtle conflation of image, process, and material occurs earlier, as in *Eighter from Decatur* (13), and later, for example, in the *Sans* series (69, 79, 89).

50 **Ditto**

1967

MATERIALS: Sculp-Metal on plexiglass and wire-bound electrical cord

SIZE: 15 × 14½ × ⅛ in. (38.1 × 36.8 × 0.3 cm.); height with cords: 70 in. (177.8 cm.)

COLLECTION: Private collection, New York

PROVENANCE: Mr. and Mrs. John Lloyd Taylor, Milwaukee, Wisconsin. Purchased from Paula Cooper Gallery, New York, in 1987

CONDITION: Small loss in lower right-hand corner, painted in lighter gray color; plexiglass bowing concavely

INSCRIPTION: Signed on lower right verso, "Eva Hesse 1967"; inscribed, "Droll/Kolbert Gallery no. DKS117"

Ditto is similar to the washer pieces (40–44) and the concentric-circle drawings. The slight sculptural presence it possesses is achieved by the protrusion of steel wires falling from the center of individual circles, activating the wall space below the relief. Hesse applied a scumbled layer of Sculp-Metal over a thin sheet of plexiglass. The nine circles were then built up from the background by an additional layer of Sculp-Metal and appear like collapsed hemispheres. The shielded hookup wire falling from the Sculp-Metal circles has an awkward relation to them and is not as evocative as the softer cords and tubing used in the other reliefs of this type (51, 52, and Appendix A, 3).

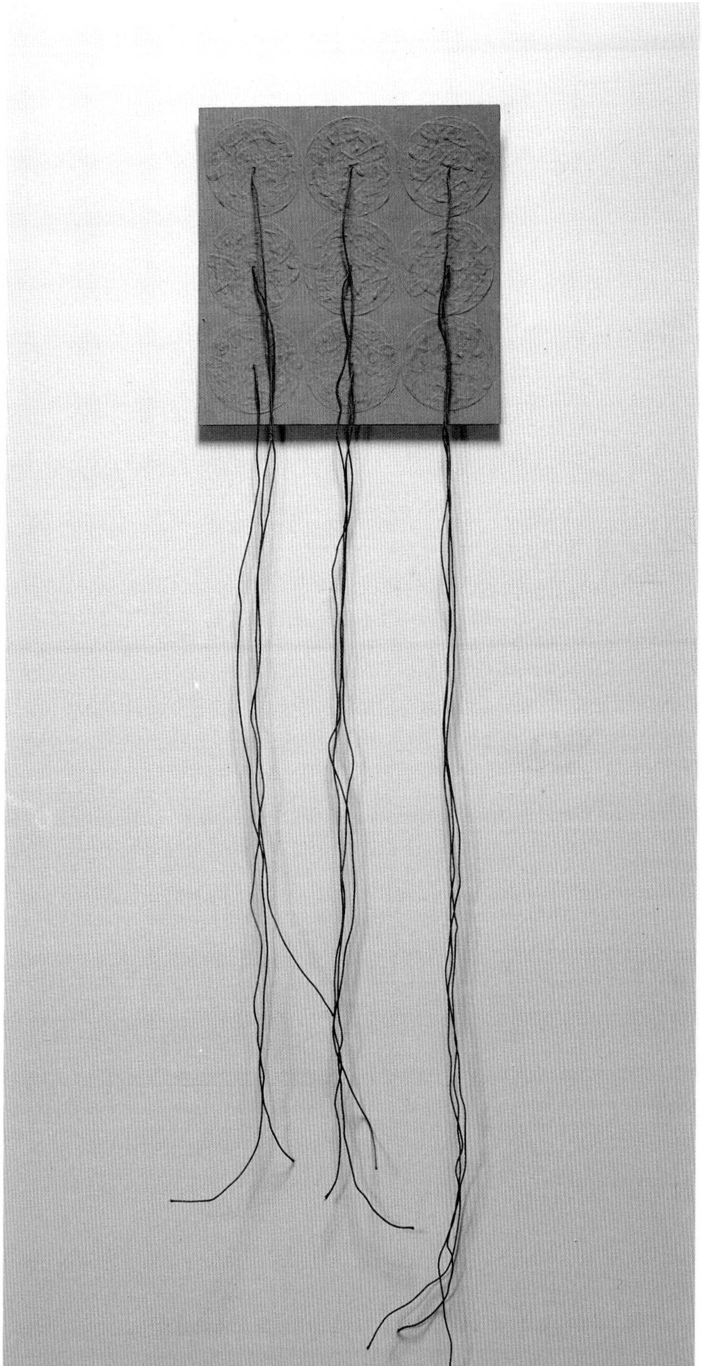

51 **One More Than One**

1967

MATERIALS: Acrylic paint on papier-mâché over wood and plastic hemispheres, painted cord

SIZE: 8½ × 15 × 5½ in. (21.6 × 38.1 × 14 cm.)

COLLECTION: Stephen Antonakos and Naomi Spector, New York

PROVENANCE: Acquired from the artist by exchange

CONDITION: Yellowish discoloration on cords, darkening of varnish or glue

Hesse used the same technique as in *Constant* (49), building up a highly textured surface over a wooden form (both forms were made by Donarski). Here the breast shape ubiquitous in Hesse's work has collapsed totally and turned inward. The tendency in the work of 1967 was toward desexualizing the forms of the previous year by diffusing them through repetition or systematization. *One More Than One* still retains some of the emotive sexuality of the earlier pieces, but it is negatively expressed. The thickness of the hanging cords and their involvement of a considerable amount of floor and wall space create an impression of rather large scale, despite the small dimensions of this piece. The title and the hemispheres recall *2 in 1* (7).

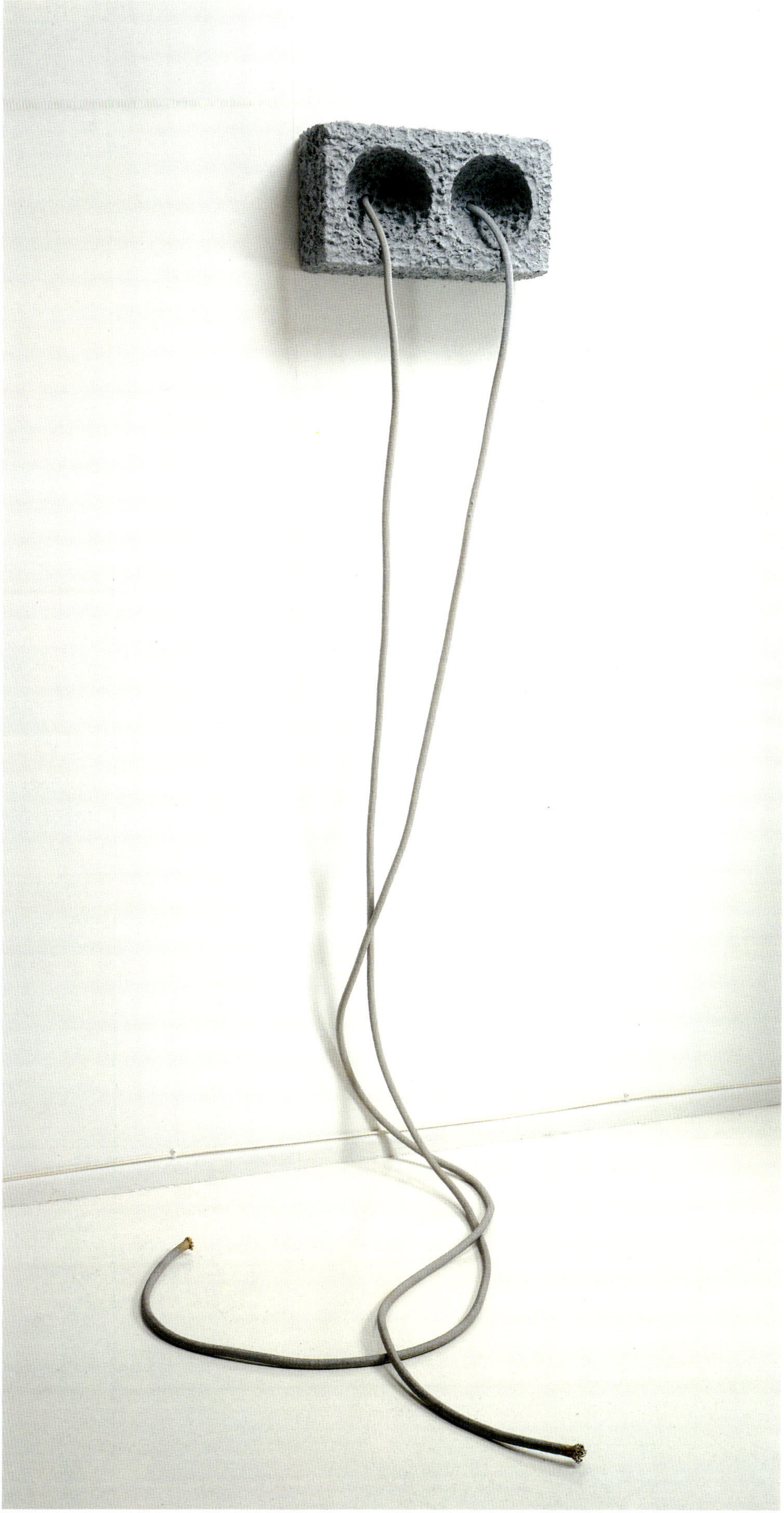

52 **Addendum**

1967

MATERIALS: Painted papier-mâché, wood, and cord

SIZE: 4⅞ × 119¼ × 5⅞–8⅛ in. (12.4 × 302.9 × 14.9–20.6 cm.); length of cords: ca. 118⅛ in. (300 cm.)

COLLECTION: Tate Gallery, London (accession no. T.2394)

PROVENANCE: Victor Ganz (purchased from Fourcade Droll, New York, in 1972). Purchased from Ganz by the Tate in 1979 (grant-in-aid)

Addendum was included in the exhibition "Serial Art" at Finch College in November 1967. It is the last version of hemispheres, cords, and textured support, and in its eccentric display of systematic abstraction it is very far indeed from the sexually biased combination of the same elements in *Ishtar* (21). Hesse prepared a statement about this piece (printed in full in Lippard, *Eva Hesse,* page 96) which demonstrates how quickly she had absorbed the minimalist ideas of abstraction and incorporated them into her ongoing and more deeply felt ideas of contradiction and absurdity. After describing the title, the measurements of the work, and the careful sequencing of its components, she writes: "The chosen nine foot eleven inch structure, the five inch diameter semi-spheres—and the long thin rope are as different in shape as possible. The choice of extremely different forms must reconcile themselves. To further jolt the equilibrium the top of the piece is hung seven feet high. The cord is flexible. It is ten feet long, hanging loosely but in parallel lines. The cord opposes the regularity. When it reaches the floor it curls and sits irregularly. The juxtaposition and actual connecting cord realizes the contradiction of the rational series of semi-spheres and irrational flow of lines on the floor. Series, serial, serial art, is another way of repeating absurdity."

There is a full-scale drawing for this piece (18 × 122 inches) in the LeWitt Collection at the Wadsworth Atheneum in Hartford, Connecticut (accession no. 146.328.1976).

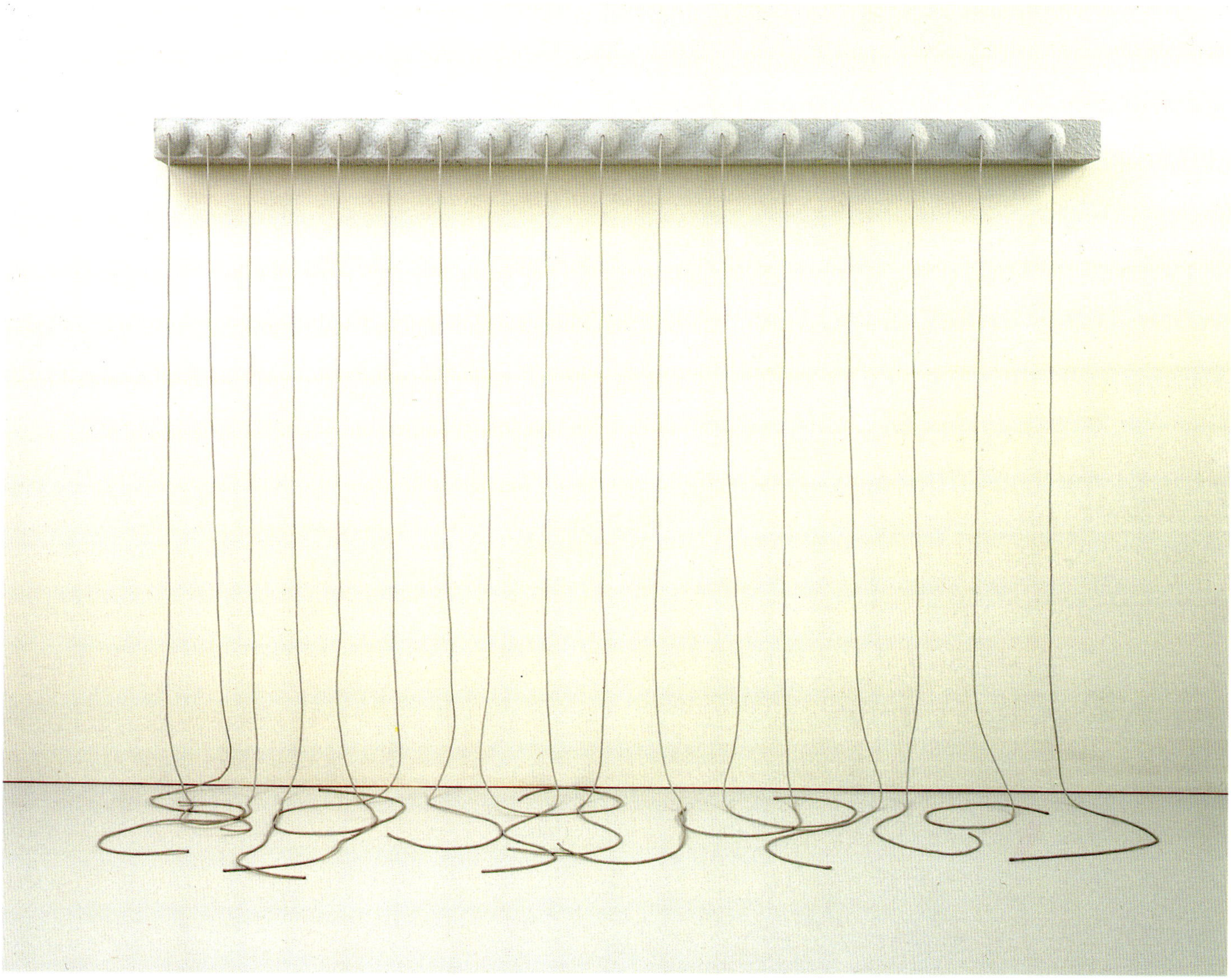

53 **Inside I**

1967

MATERIALS: Acrylic paint over papier-mâché, twine, and wire over wood

SIZE: 11¾ × 11¾ × 12 in. (29.8 × 29.8 × 30.5 cm.)

COLLECTION: Raymond J. Learsy, New York

PROVENANCE: Estate of Eva Hesse until 1986. Purchased from Arnold Herstand Gallery, New York

INSCRIPTION: Signed and dated on the bottom, "Eva Hesse 1967"

In the early summer of 1967 Hesse moved away from wall reliefs in favor of enclosing forms in boxes. At the same time, as Lippard notes *(Eva Hesse,* page 105), Hesse left her large upstairs studio and restricted her working space to the two small rooms of her apartment. This sense of containment is certainly echoed in the work of the next few months. *Inside I* is an open wooden box covered with painted papier-mâché; deep in the bottom of the box sits a snarly tangle of painted cord and wire. The snakelike tangle recalls *Laocoon* (31) and anticipates "Rope Piece" (101). In two small related pieces (54) the tangle appears to be bursting over the sides of the shallow container, reversing the relationship of tangle to box seen in *Inside I.*

54 **Small Pieces Related to *Inside I* and *Inside II***

1966

MATERIALS: *Inside I:* Gray enamel paint over cord, wire, and metal cans; *Inside II:* Weight wrapped with paper and cord, gray acrylic paint

SIZE: Height of units: *Inside I:* 2¼ in., 1½ in. (5.7 cm., 3.8 cm.); diameter of units: 2½ in., 3 in. (6.3 cm., 7.6 cm.); *Inside II:* height: 2 in. (5.1 cm.); diameter: 3 in. (7.6 cm.)

COLLECTION: *Inside I:* Helen Hesse Charash, Cliffside, New Jersey
Inside II: Gioia Timpanelli, New York

PROVENANCE: Estate of Eva Hesse

See number 53.

55 **Inside II**

1967

MATERIALS: Acrylic paint mixed with sawdust over wood, papier-mâché, cord, weights, and acrylic

SIZE: 5¼ × 7 × 7 in. (13.3 × 17.8 × 17.8 cm.)

COLLECTION: Estate of Eva Hesse

CONDITION: Minor losses on one of the weighted units

Inside II, another thick-walled box, contains two weights wrapped in paper, bound with cord, and painted a light gray. A third wrapped weight exists (54). Binding forms with cord, such a common process in Hesse's earlier work, was not to occur after *Inside II.* Wrapped cord-bound weights appear in an earlier sculpture, "Three Nets" (29).

56 **For Joseph**

1967

MATERIALS: Painted papier-mâché over wood and lock of hair sewn in plastic with nylon thread

SIZE: 2½ × 3½ × 2¾ in. (6.3 × 8.9 × 7 cm.)

COLLECTION: Joseph Goldman, New York

PROVENANCE: Given by the artist to Joseph Goldman

For Joseph was made as a present for the son of Hesse's closest friend, Rosalyn Goldman, on the occasion of the boy's second birthday (June 21, 1967). A shallow wooden box covered with roughly textured papier-mâché contains a lock of the boy's hair and commemorates his first haircut. It is not surprising that Hesse signals this event, for she had recently cut her own very long hair. For Hesse, cutting her hair must have been an important event, the sign of change and a new beginning.

57 **Accession I**

1967

MATERIALS: Aluminum and rubber tubing

SIZE: $9\frac{1}{8} \times 14\frac{1}{4} \times 14\frac{1}{4}$ in. ($23.2 \times 36.2 \times 36.2$ cm.)

COLLECTION: Israel Museum, Jerusalem, gift of Helen Hesse Charash, 1978

PROVENANCE: Ethelyn and Lester Honig, New York. Fourcade Droll, New York

Cutting gestures, surely not unrelated to Hesse's cutting her hair at this time, play a very important role in the series of *Accession* boxes, for which Hesse cut literally thousands of pieces of extrusion. *Accession I* is a rectangular box, open at the top, possibly a found object. Four other boxes in the series made subsequently are cubes that Hesse had fabricated for her. For each box she cut rubber extrusion into five-inch lengths and looped it through adjoining holes with the extrusion pointing inward, making a very simple and wholly successful three-dimensional elaboration of *Constant* (49). The inner space created by the extrusion is suggestively organic, the impression intensified by the sharp contrast with the ordered appearance of the box's exterior. A similar contrast is suggested in *Inside I* (53). Both the contrast of organic and geometric qualities and an opening toward the inside are characteristic of the work of Ruth Vollmer, with whom Hesse had become close. One strongly senses Hesse's striving to get away from the more "childish" materials and techniques of string, glue, and papier-mâché she had been using up to this point.

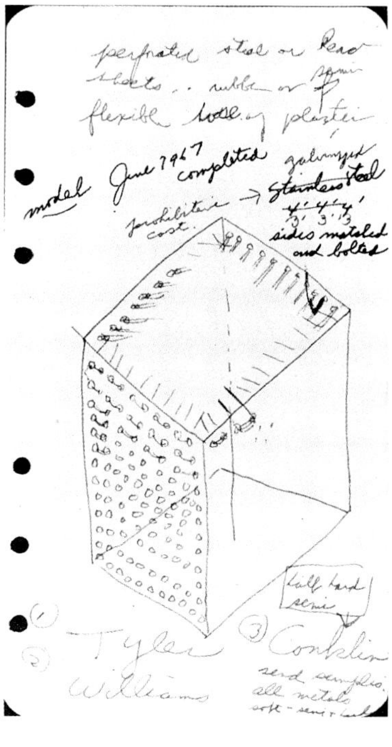

58 **Accession II**

1967

MATERIALS: Galvanized steel and plastic tubing

SIZE: 30¾ × 30¾ × 30¾ in. (78.1 × 78.1 × 78.1 cm.)

COLLECTION: Detroit Institute of Arts, Founders Society Purchase, Friends of Modern Art Fund, and Miscellaneous Gifts Fund (accession no. 79.34)

PROVENANCE: Aldrich Museum of Contemporary Art, Ridgefield, Connecticut. Droll/Kolbert Gallery, New York

Hesse realized that she was onto something with *Accession I,* and in the fall of 1967 she went to Arco Metals in Manhattan to have a 30-inch galvanized perforated steel cube fabricated. This was to become *Accession II.* She then cut and threaded many thousands of lengths of vinyl extrusion to make its bristling interior, a process that took her until the following January to complete. This was the first time Hesse had gone outside her circle of friends for help. (The success of her experience at Arco Metals led her to a collaboration with Doug Johns, a plastics fabricator on Staten Island, in June 1968.) The first version of *Accession II* was shown at the Milwaukee Art Center in an exhibition called "Directions 1: Options." A statement for the catalogue, dated June 21, 1968, says, "I don't ask that Accession be participated with other than thought. There is no option in arrangement in Accession. The structure has 50,670 holes filled with vinyl extrusion. Each piece of extrusion is necessary to complete the structure." (Hesse writes 50,670, but it is more likely that the number was 30,670, still a lot of extrusion.) The sculpture was badly damaged during the exhibition and another version, illustrated here, was refabricated and completed by the spring of 1969.

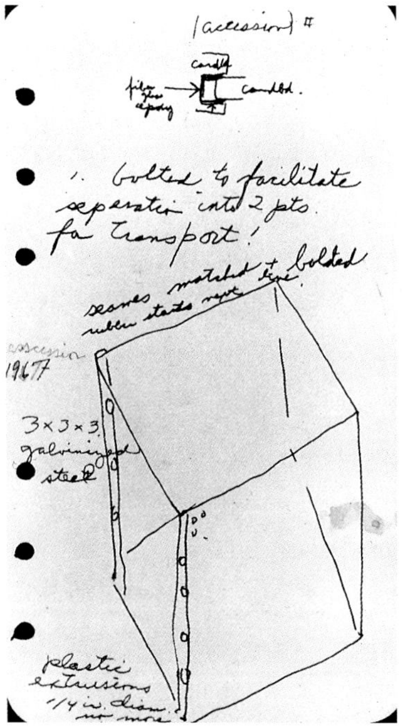

59 **Untitled ("LeWitt Glass Case")**

1967–1968

MATERIALS: Glass and metal case containing six units of latex, wire, rubber cords, plaster mold

SIZE: 14⅝ × 10¼ × 10¼ in. (37.1 × 26 × 26 cm.)

COLLECTION: LeWitt Collection, on loan to the Wadsworth Atheneum, Hartford, Connecticut (temporary loan no. 146.318.1976)

PROVENANCE: Acquired from the artist by Sol LeWitt

This is the earliest of the glass cases. In late August 1967 Hesse began experimenting with latex rubber, and a number of small test pieces that resulted from these experiments were given as gifts to Sol LeWitt. It was LeWitt's idea to isolate and display the test pieces in a pastry case he had found on the Bowery. Hesse liked the idea well enough to make two versions of her own in 1968 using similar groupings of test pieces and small works. This case contains six test units: one is a test piece for *Repetition Nineteen II* (64); one is a test piece for *7 Objects/69* (Tanglewood Press, 1969; see 87); one is a latex test piece; one unit is wire with rubber cords; and two are latex trays, one with a plaster mold.

60 Untitled ("Kardon Glass Case")

1968

MATERIALS: Mixed media, glass and metal case

SIZE: $14\frac{5}{8} \times 10\frac{1}{4} \times 10\frac{1}{4}$ in. ($37.1 \times 26 \times 26$ cm.)

COLLECTION: Janet and Robert Kardon, Philadelphia, Pennsylvania

PROVENANCE: Purchased from Fischbach Gallery, New York, July 22, 1969

See number 59.

61 Untitled ("Douglas Glass Case")

1968

MATERIALS: Glass and metal display case; metal, latex, plaster, paint, string, tape, and plastic

SIZE: $14\frac{1}{2} \times 10\frac{1}{2} \times 10\frac{1}{2}$ in. ($36.8 \times 26.7 \times 26.7$ cm.)

COLLECTION: Gustaf Douglas, location unknown

PROVENANCE: Purchased from Fischbach Gallery, New York, in 1968. Steve Antonakos and Naomi Spector, New York. Sold to Bonnier Gallery, Geneva

See number 59. This case contains one *Repetition Nineteen,* one *Repetition Nineteen* with a ball, four gray tubes with string, a gray pad with strings, a white hemisphere, metal numerals in a white plastic rectangle set in a latex "pie crust," a plaster and latex "sandwich," and grommets set in a plexiglass sheet.

62 **Repetition Nineteen I**

1967

MATERIALS: Aluminum screening, papier-mâché, Elmer's glue, polyester resin, and Dutch Boy Diamond Gloss paint

SIZE: Each of nineteen units: 9⅛–10½ × 6½–9⅛ in. (23.2–26.7 × 16.5–23.2 cm.)

COLLECTION: Museum of Modern Art, New York

PROVENANCE: Gift of Mr. and Mrs. Murray Charash

Repetition Nineteen I was finished in September 1967: it is the first of three versions Hesse did over a period of ten months. Here the artist began to dismantle the minimalist geometry that was so characteristic of her work in late 1966 and 1967, and the sculpture moves toward a more emotionally suggestive use of geometric form and space. Rather than present the idea of order opposing chaos, as she had done in *Metronomic Irregularity I* (37), *Addendum* (52), and *Inside I* (53), she introduced disorder into the geometric structures themselves by distorting the shapes and disposing them randomly in space. Disconnected and released from the grid, the circular forms are now made freestanding. They appear at first like discarded paint cans. And it takes a while to realize that there is in fact an order, a nuanced sequencing made by stressing the cans from nearly perfect to very warped. This sequenced shaping is a subtle, recurring theme that begins with "Purple Piece" (16) and is very clearly seen in "Model for Unrealized Sculpture" (70). Technically the first version of *Repetition Nineteen* is similar to early work, where the forms were built up by papier-mâché and enamel. *Repetition Nineteen I* is the last piece in which Hesse would use papier-mâché. Although she planned to make a second version of *Repetition Nineteen* from sheet metal coated with Sculp-Metal, she abandoned those materials in favor of latex as she began to work with rubber. A test piece for *Repetition Nineteen II* can be seen on the top shelf of the "Douglas Glass Case" (61).

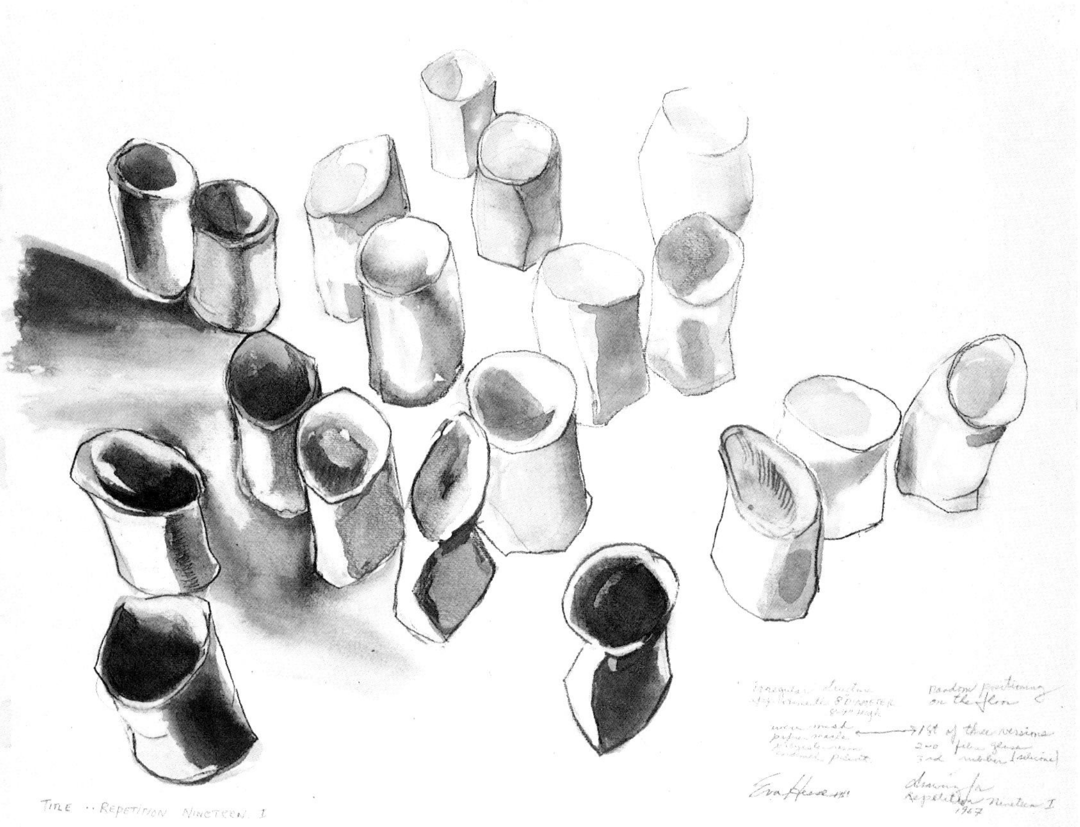
random positioning
on the floor
1st of three versions
Eva Hesse
drawing for
Repetition Nineteen I
1967
TITLE .. REPETITION NINETEEN I

1967

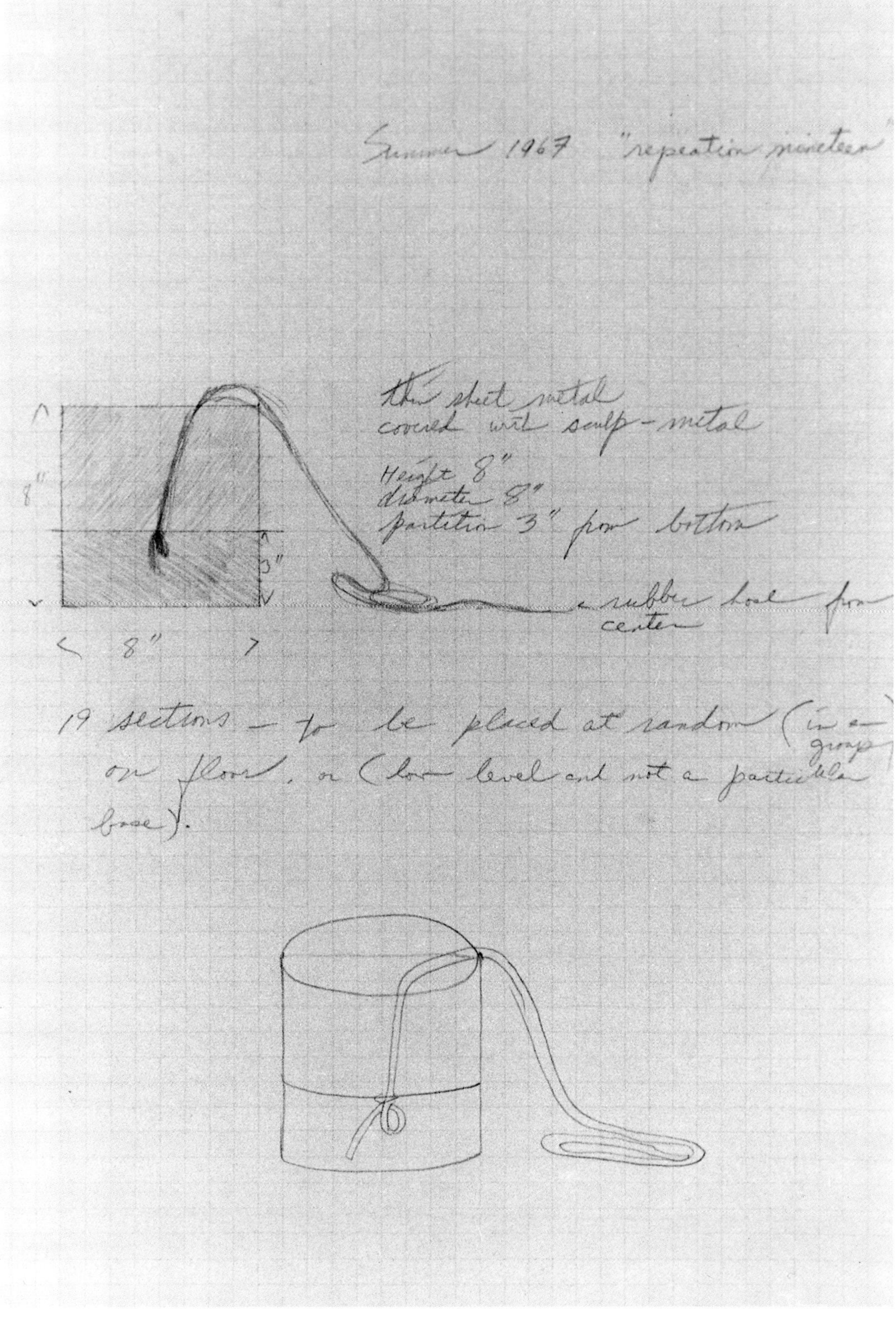
Summer 1967 "repeation nineteen"
thin sheet metal
covered with sculp-metal
Height 8"
diameter 8"
partition 3" from bottom
8"
3"
rubber hose from center
8"
19 sections — to be placed at random (in a group) on floor, or (low level and not a particular base).

63 Test Units for *Repetition Nineteen II*

1967

MATERIALS: Latex over cotton and surgical tubing

SIZE: Esman unit: 3 × 3½ in. (7.6 × 8.9 cm.); cord: 40 in. (101.6 cm.); inside depth: 2 in. (5.1 cm.); Lynn unit: 3¼ × 3½ in. (8.2 × 8 × 9 cm.); cord: 36½ in. (92.7 cm.); inside depth: ¾ in. (1.9 cm.)

COLLECTION: One unit, Dr. and Mrs. Aaron Esman, New York; one unit inside glass case (59), LeWitt Collection, Wadsworth Atheneum, Hartford, Connecticut (temporary loan no. 146.318.1976); one unit, Florette and Ronald B. Lynn, New Jersey; one unit inside glass case (60), Janet and Robert Kardon, Philadelphia, Pennsylvania

PROVENANCE: Esman unit, acquired from the artist in 1969; LeWitt unit, acquired from the artist; Lynn unit, acquired from the artist; Kardon unit, purchased from Fischbach Gallery, New York, 1969

CONDITION: Esman unit, darkened but still supple, cracked inside where cord protrudes; LeWitt unit, good; Lynn unit, darkened slightly, small crack underneath; Kardon unit, not seen

Hesse's original idea for *Repetition Nineteen II* was for a series of nineteen specially fabricated steel buckets (8 × 8 inches) that would then be coated with Sculp-Metal. A long gray rubber tube was to be threaded through the center of a false bottom in each bucket (see Lippard, *Eva Hesse,* page 111, figure 155, incorrectly captioned; see Hesse's label). The heights of the false bottoms were to vary from 1 to 7 inches from the floor, a continuation of Hesse's interest in serial arrangements. When she started experimenting with latex, however, the Sculp-Metal version was abandoned in favor of the new material. Hesse never completed the project in latex, but she did make this series of units and a second group (64) of latex buckets with false bottoms and protruding cords.

Hesse began to work with latex in August 1967 when she bought a small quantity of liquid casting rubber from Cementex on Canal Street. Her strong affinity for this material (see page 14 for a description) had an immediate effect on the course of her work. She stopped working with the materials and techniques she had slowly developed over the preceding two years—forms bound with cord, or built with papier-mâché and Sculp-Metal—and started to construct a large number of her pieces from this beautiful but unstable material. Much that was implicit in Hesse's art up to this point was to be released through the medium of latex. The distorted geometry that had been so laboriously achieved in *Repetition Nineteen I* now becomes built into the use of latex. The sensuous skinlike quality of the latex gives the sculpture an extremely organic appearance, an impression heightened by the way the bottom of each bucket swells and pushes out its rubber umbilical cords.

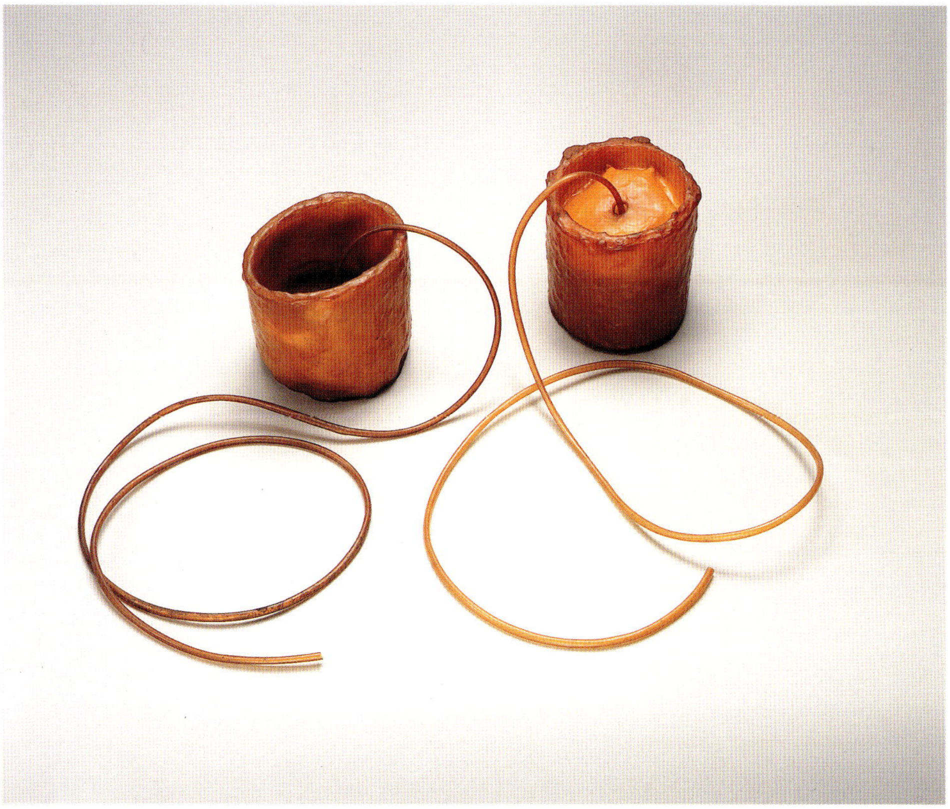

64 Test Pieces for *Repetition Nineteen II*

1967–1968

MATERIALS: Latex over cotton and surgical tubing

SIZE: Height of units: 5½–8 in. (14–20.3 cm.); width of units: 10½–11 in. (26.7–27.9 cm.); length of cords: 18–62 in. (45.7–157.5 cm.); inside depth varies

COLLECTION: Illustrated unit, Dr. and Mrs. Aaron Esman, New York; three other units, Estate of Eva Hesse

PROVENANCE: Esman unit, purchased from the artist in 1969

CONDITION: Esman unit, some cracking along folds in three places and some darkening with age, still supple; three estate pieces, some minor cracking but generally good

See number 63.

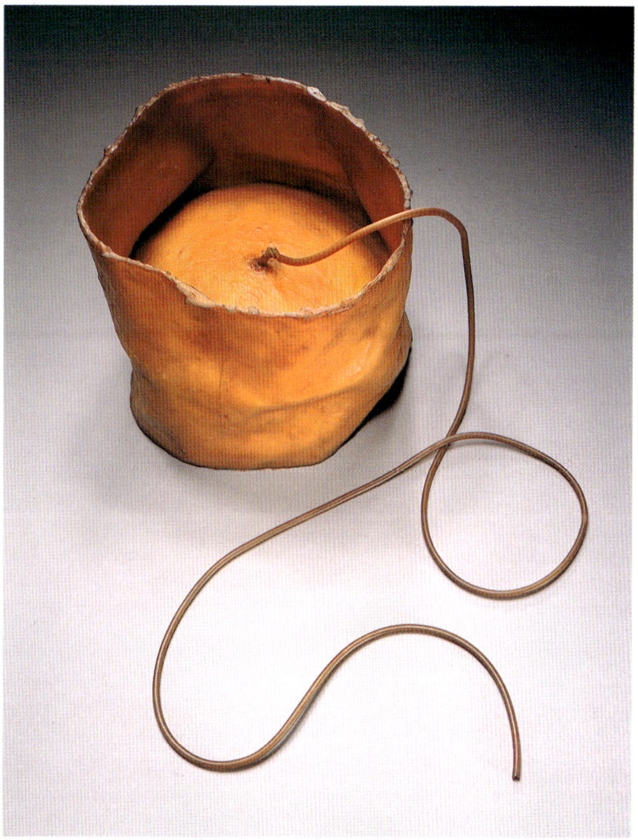

65 Study for *Schema*

1967

MATERIALS: Latex

SIZE: LeWitt model: 9½ × 9½ in. (24.1 × 24.1 cm.)

COLLECTION: One model (illustrated), LeWitt Collection, on loan to the Wadsworth Atheneum, Hartford, Connecticut (temporary loan no. 146.319.1976); second model, Marilyn Cole Fischbach Collection, New York

PROVENANCE: LeWitt model, acquired from the artist; Fischbach model, acquired from the artist

See number 66.

66 **Schema**

1967

MATERIALS: Latex

SIZE: 42 × 42 in. (106.7 × 106.7 cm.)

COLLECTION: Philadelphia Museum of Art, gift of Helen Hesse Charash, 1979 (accession no. 1979.185.1)

PROVENANCE: Estate of Eva Hesse

Hesse gave a definition for *Schema* in her notebook: "synopsis, outline, diagram. general type, essential form, conception of what is common to all members of a class." A drawing (see Lippard, *Eva Hesse,* page 114, figure 159) for this piece and its companion, *Sequel* (67), dated October 1967 indicates how carefully Hesse planned her first latex pieces. The drawing also indicates that *Schema* was originally planned to be on a low base, the same size as its latex mat. However, when the piece was exhibited at Fischbach in November 1968, it was placed directly on the floor, in a manner more consistent with the prejudice against pedestals in the late sixties. Hesse painted the latex in layers, ten to fifteen of them, for the flat sheet, and five to eight for each of the hemispheres cast over half of a rubber ball. Latex with its paintlike consistency and layered application brought Hesse back to the realm of painting and drawing. Only by the assertive placement on the floor is the sculptural quality of this piece revealed.

67 **Sequel**

1967

MATERIALS: Latex

SIZE: 30 × 32 in. (76.2 × 81.3 cm.)

COLLECTION: Saatchi Collection, London

PROVENANCE: Purchased from the Estate of Eva Hesse through either Droll/Kolbert Gallery, New York, or Metro Pictures, New York

To the translucent taffy-colored latex she used for *Schema* (66) Hesse added a powdered white pigment to create the opaque white *Sequel.* Here she formed full irregular spheres and then dispersed them randomly on a sheet. This random placement is similar to *Repetition Nineteen I* (62). The precise, somewhat mathematical titling of these pieces (66, 67, 68), recalls the titles Ruth Vollmer was using at the time *(Biconcavity, Interstitial Form),* and the two artists were certainly very close. Vollmer was concerned with the sphere, and her piece "Skewed Spheres" suggests a further connection with Hesse. Hesse's use of spheres may also have been influenced by Lucio Fontana's bronze spheres with gashes exhibited in a show at the Marlborough Gallery in winter 1967 that Hesse saw and liked.

68 **Stratum**

1967–1968

MATERIALS: Latex with white pigment, string, and grommets

SIZE: 42 × 42 in. (106.7 × 106.7 cm.)

COLLECTION: Piece no longer exists

PROVENANCE: Fischbach Gallery, New York. Mrs. Sidney Gerber, Seattle, Washington

The idea of using latex as paint is especially noticeable in this piece. While the progress of Hesse's sculpture in 1967 is resolutely toward greater three-dimensionality and use of space, *Stratum*—flat and hung on the wall—is something of an anomaly in this sequence, although it does anticipate *Aught* (84). Here Hesse has combined a new material with an old form, as seen in the series of wall reliefs with protrusions (46–49). Robert Smithson titled a work of his *Glass Stratum,* also dated 1967.

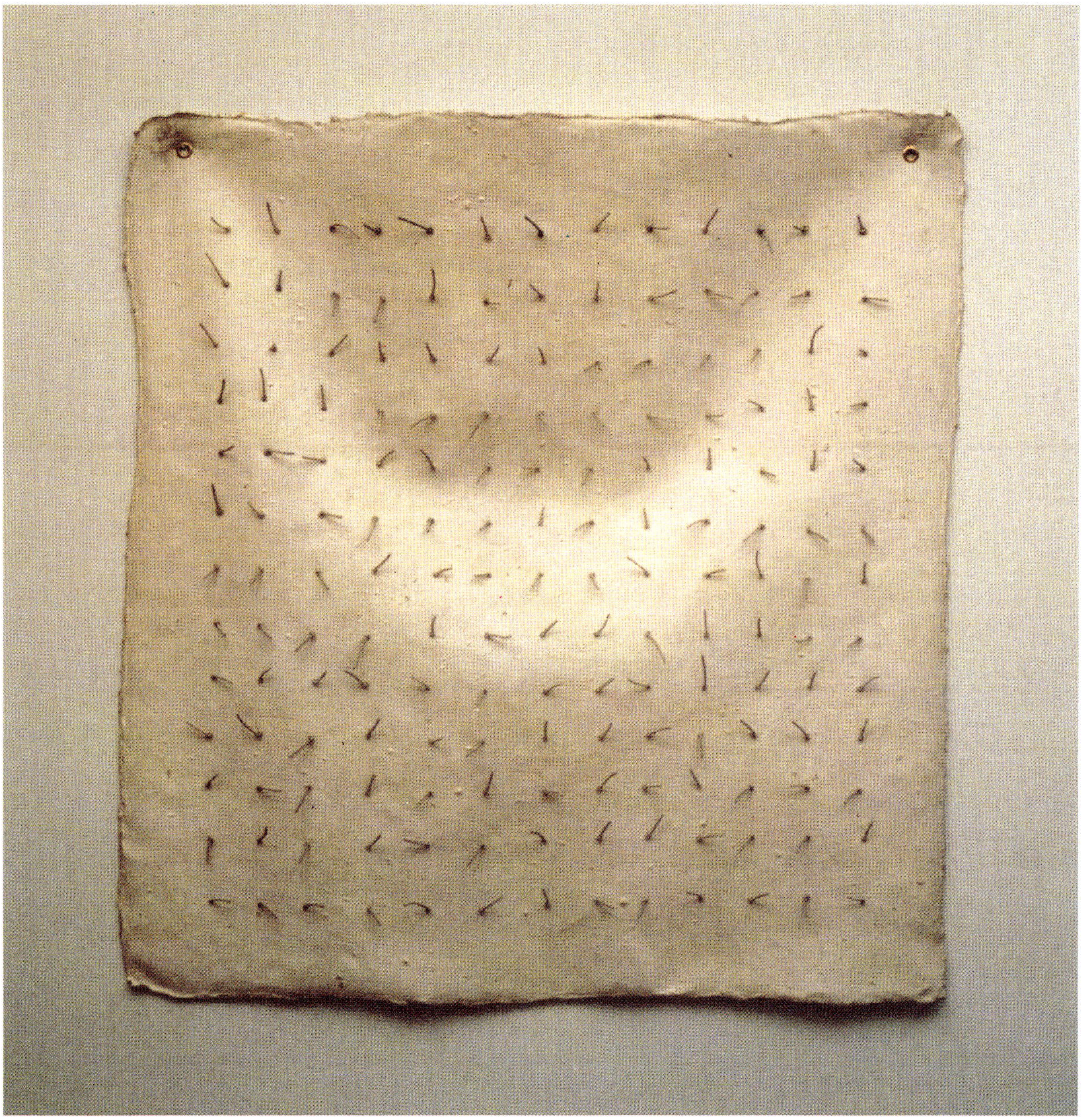

69 Sans I

1967–1968

MATERIALS: Latex and metal grommets

SIZE: 72 × 7 × 1 in. (182.9 × 17.8 × 2.5 cm.)

COLLECTION: Piece no longer exists

PROVENANCE: Fischbach Gallery, New York. Mrs. Sidney Gerber, Seattle, Washington

Hesse made *Sans I* by casting forty-eight rectangular units in latex over a simple plaster mold (see Berkeley test pieces in Appendix B) and then gluing them together with additional latex. By rubberizing and therefore deforming the grid structure, Hesse neatly altered the idea of the grid as a rigidly plotted field. She further emphasized the flexible nature of latex and the instability of the grid by hanging *Sans I* on the wall, with the lower section extending onto the floor. Hesse had connected the wall and the floor in earlier works by using hanging cords which appear to escape from two-dimensional or pictorial space into "real space" (see 32, 51, 52). In *Sans I* the emphasis is instead on an intentional display of the weakness inherent in the structure, opening the question of whether the piece occupies two- or three-dimensional space. *Sans I* is the prototype for a very large version, *Sans II* (79), cast in fiberglass, and *Sans III* (89), another latex version.

NEW YORK 1968

70 Untitled ("Model for Unrealized Sculpture")

1968

MATERIALS: Unfired clay on painted cardboard

SIZE: 13½ × 1¼ × 1¼ in. (34.3 × 3.2 × 3.2 cm.)

COLLECTION: Museum of Modern Art, New York

PROVENANCE: Bequest of Ruth Vollmer (gift of the artist)

This is a model for a large sculpture that was never built. It was made from clay that Hesse had been given by Ruth Vollmer. Curiously, this is the only time Hesse used clay. Like many artists of the late sixties she preferred nonorganic, industrial materials that did not have any aesthetic connotations or history. The model is an interesting combination of the sequencing of two earlier pieces—"Purple Piece" (15) and *Addendum* (52), with the variously deformed buckets of *Repetition Nineteen I* (62). The persistence and variety of sequencing in Hesse's work indicate that these ideas were more than just the passing influence of minimalist thinking.

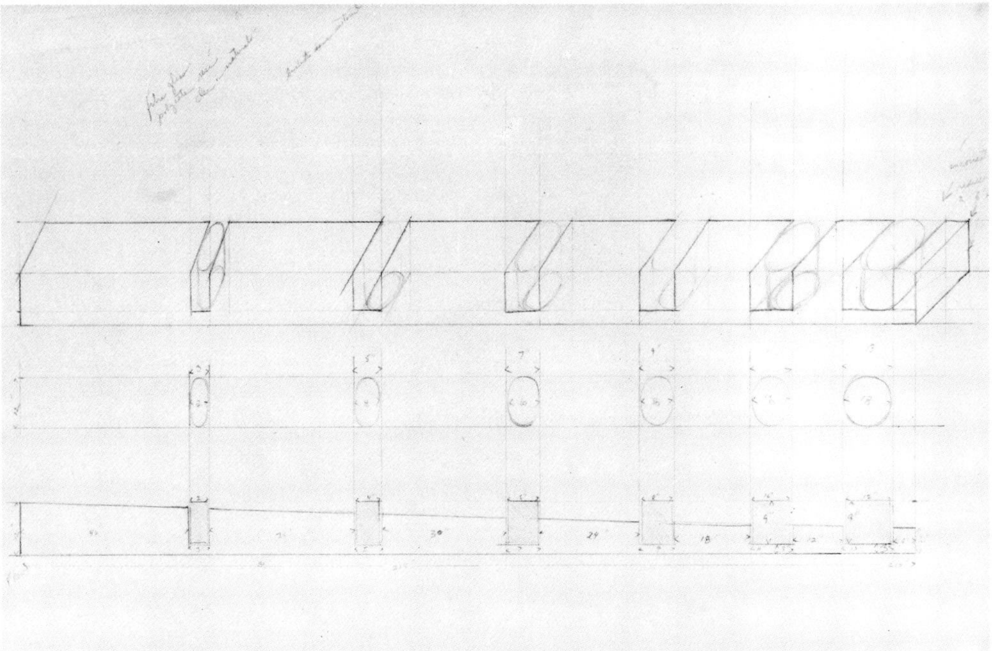

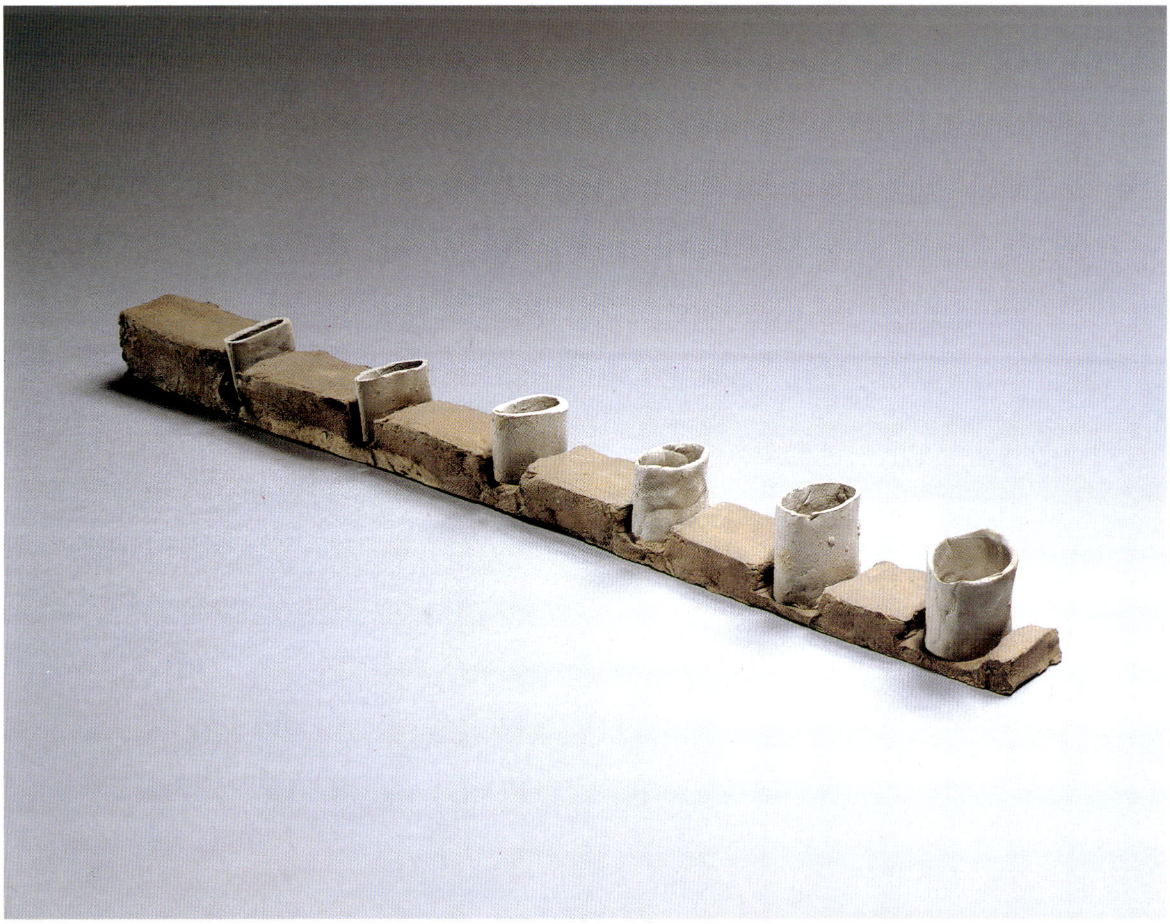

71 **Untitled ("Ruth Vollmer Boat Bumper")**

1968

MATERIALS: Epoxy paint and string on stuffed canvas

SIZE: 10⅞ × 13 × 5 in. (27.6 × 33 × 12.7 cm.)

COLLECTION: Museum of Modern Art, New York

PROVENANCE: Bequest of Ruth Vollmer (gift of the artist)

This and number 72 are minor pieces made from boat bumpers purchased at a marine supply store where Hesse had been taken by Ruth Vollmer. She added string to all three. She then painted and epoxied one piece and gave it to Vollmer, leaving the other two unpainted. The Vollmer piece has more sculptural presence than the Berkeley pair and is closer in form and feeling to *Vertiginous Detour* (28). The shagginess and suggestive disposition of the Berkeley pieces give them a more humorous quality.

72 **Untitled ("Berkeley Boat Bumpers")**

1968

MATERIALS: String on stuffed canvas

SIZE: Each of two units: 12 × 12 × 5 in. (30.5 × 30.5 × 12.7 cm.)

COLLECTION: University Art Museum, University of California, Berkeley (accession no. 1979.17.2), gift of Helen Hesse Charash, 1979

PROVENANCE: Estate of Eva Hesse

See number 71.

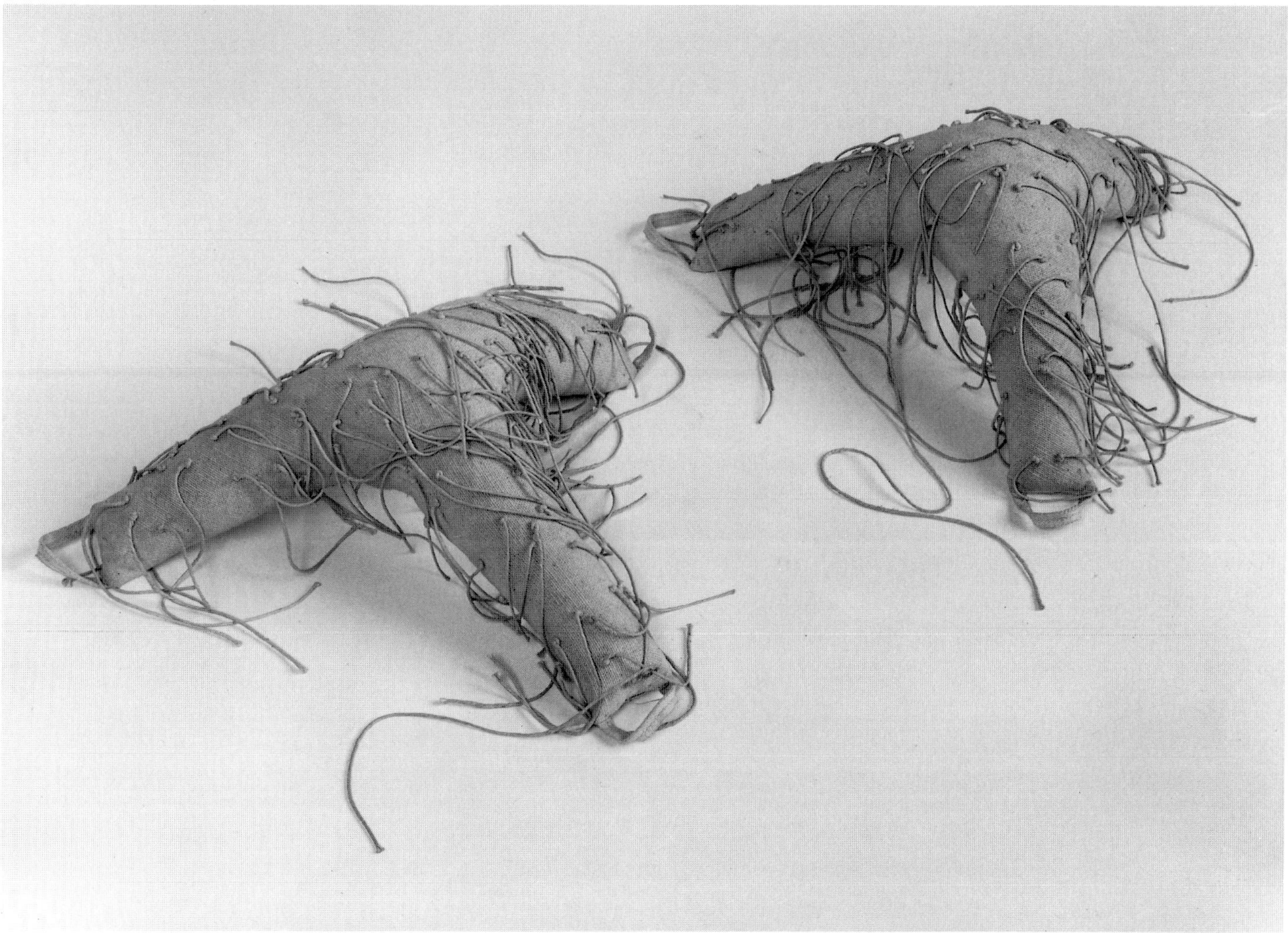

73 **Repetition Nineteen III**

1968

MATERIALS: Fiberglass and polyester resin

SIZE: Height of each of nineteen units: 19–20¼ in. (48.3–51.4 cm.); diameter of each unit: 11–12¾ in. (27.9–32.4 cm.)

COLLECTION: Museum of Modern Art, New York

PROVENANCE: Gift of Anita and Charles Blatt

Repetition Nineteen III was the first piece that Hesse had fabricated in fiberglass at Aegis Reinforced Plastics on Staten Island. Doug Johns, one of the owners of Aegis, recalls that Hesse brought him a drawing with specifications calling for nineteen units with false bottoms, each at a different height and with rubber tubing protruding from the center, like the test pieces for *Repetition Nineteen II* (63, 64). Johns, who was already making pieces for Robert Smithson and Robert Morris, assumed that Hesse wanted the same kind of precise, clean, mechanical finish to her pieces; and because Hesse was not directly involved with the manufacture, she was quite unhappy with the result. She rejected the piece, but the learning experience was valuable for both her and Johns, and they worked closely together on the next attempt. She eliminated the false bottoms when she realized they would be visible through the translucent fiberglass, and she abandoned the idea of rubber cords since they did not seem to look right with the resin. As she had done with latex, Hesse began to allow the material to play a greater role in determining the form of her work. Once Johns knew the effect that Hesse was after, completing this piece was relatively easy. The papier-mâché-and-wire forms were coated with parting compound and then covered with pieces of fiberglass material soaked with resin. After the resin had cured, the forms were carefully picked out. The result was a definite success.

Repetition Nineteen III was the beginning of a fruitful collaboration between Johns and Hesse that lasted until her death. Johns advised Hesse on technical matters, and either fabricated or helped her to fabricate all the major pieces—seventeen of them—that were completed after June 1968. The collaboration was extended and complicated when it turned into a romantic involvement as well; Johns lived in Hesse's studio and devoted himself exclusively to the production of her pieces after Aegis went out of business in the fall of 1968.

In a statement regarding the installation of *Repetition Nineteen III*, dated June 21, 1968, Hesse said, "I don't ask that the piece be moved or changed, only that it could be moved and changed. There is not one preferred format other than the specific idea inherent in the specific piece."

74 **Accession III**

1968

MATERIALS: Fiberglass and plastic tubing

SIZE: 30 × 30 × 30 in. (76.2 × 76.2 × 76.2 cm.)

COLLECTION: Ludwig Museum, Cologne, West Germany

PROVENANCE: Not provided, probably purchased from Fourcade/Droll, New York

The idea of making a fiberglass version of *Accession* was suggested to Hesse by Doug Johns after he saw the metal version, *Accession II* (58), in her studio. He showed her a piece of fiberglass threaded with clear vinyl extrusion that he had made (collection Antonakos/Spector, New York), and the fabrication of the piece was begun in the summer of 1968. It was not completed until the fall because it took a very long time to drill 28,000 holes and fill them with extrusion.

The box section of this piece was made over a collapsible wooden form covered with parting paper and parting compound before the resin and fiberglass were applied. The resin and fiberglass were built up in layers until they formed a coating a half-inch thick and quite heavy. A piece of perforated metal radiator cover was then clamped to the side of the box and used as a guide for drilling the holes: the clear vinyl tubing was cut and threaded through the holes. Hesse helped with the threading but was not otherwise involved with the fabrication.

Accession III gives quite a different impression from that of the other *Accession* boxes with their dark, dense interiors and strong contrast between interior and exterior. The fiberglass version, with translucent sides and tubes, holds light instead of absorbing it. This box was never repeated in fiberglass, whereas Hesse made four versions in metal.

75 **Accession IV**

1968

MATERIALS: Galvanized steel and rubber tubing

SIZE: 8⅛ × 8 × 8¼ in. (20.6 × 20.3 × 20.9 cm.)

COLLECTION: Ethelyn and Lester Honig, New York

PROVENANCE: Acquired from the artist in exchange for medical care, circa 1968 (Ethelyn Honig shared a studio with Hesse, and her husband was Hesse's doctor.)

CONDITION: Some rubber tubing cracking where it is bent

According to Lippard, *Accession IV* and *V* were made sometime in 1968. They are both closer in concept to *Accession I* and *II* (57, 58) than to *Accession III*. Hesse returned to metal with rubber extrusion possibly as a reaction against what she described in the Cindy Nemser interview as the jewellike quality of *Accession III*.

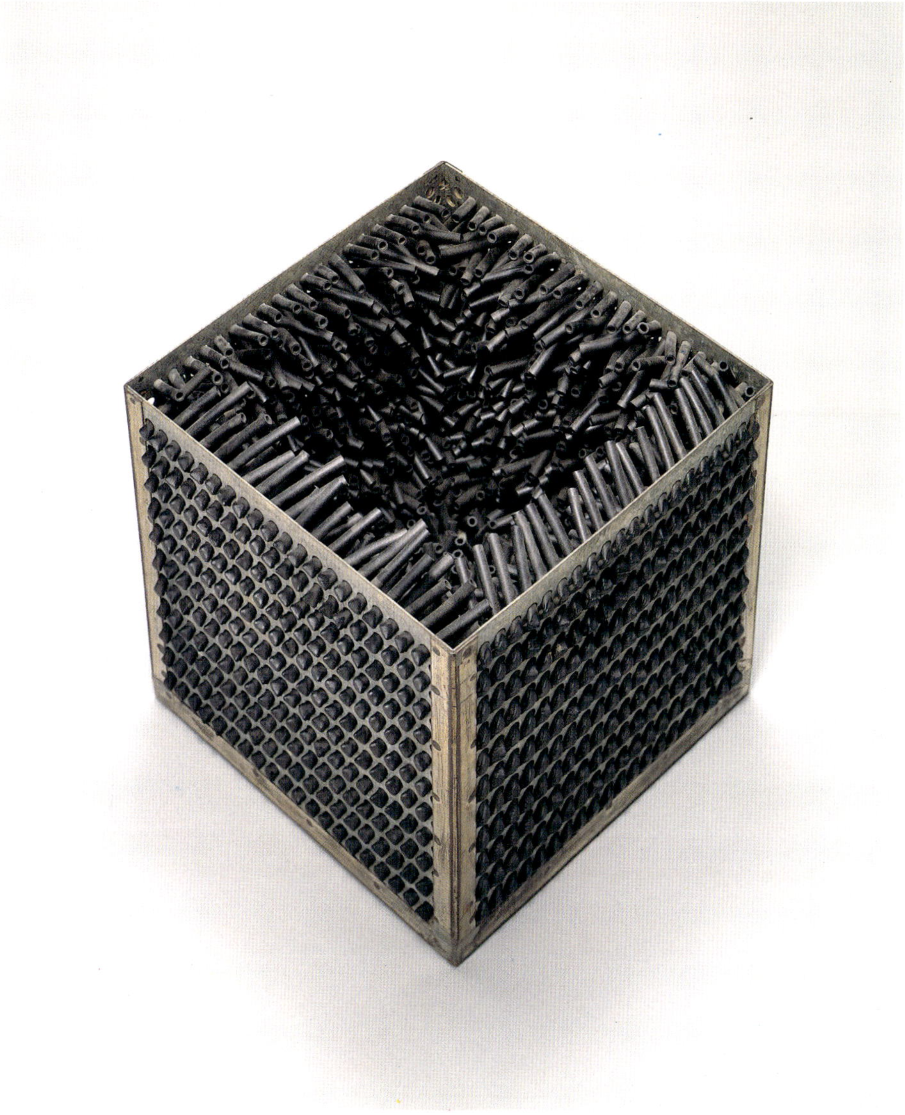

76 **Accession V**

1968

MATERIALS: Galvanized steel and rubber tubing

SIZE: 10 × 10 × 10 in. (25.4 × 25.4 × 25.4 cm.)

COLLECTION: LeWitt Collection, on loan to the Wadsworth Atheneum, Hartford, Connecticut (temporary loan no. 146.320.1976)

PROVENANCE: Acquired from the artist by Sol LeWitt

See number 75.

77 Model for *Accretion*

1968

MATERIALS: Cardboard tubes, metal washers, Sculp-Metal, and vinyl cords

SIZE: Length of tubes: 20 in. (50.8 cm.); diameter of tubes: 1 in. (2.5 cm.); length of extrusions from six units: 110 in. (279.4 cm.)

COLLECTION: Weatherspoon Art Gallery, University of North Carolina, Greensboro (accession no. 83.3528), gift of Helen Hesse Charash, 1983

PROVENANCE: Estate of Eva Hesse

Made in 1967, this piece consists of nineteen or twenty cardboard tubes covered with Sculp-Metal and capped at each end with metal washers. (There are twenty tubes, but one of them has such a different surface that it may well be an experimental unit that was added to the piece only after Hesse died.) Lengths of gray vinyl extrusion are strung through six of the tubes.

Hesse seems never to have resolved how she intended this piece to be displayed; a number of drawings indicate different possibilities (see Lippard, *Eva Hesse,* pages 124–125). It seems certain that the units should be grouped on a high base, with the cords hanging to the floor, as in *Ingeminate* (18). In a film of Hesse made by Dorothy Beskind in the winter of 1967–1968, the units are laid on a tabletop with the cords hanging over the side. However, the cords were not used in the larger version of this piece, and so the issue of placement and base disappeared when Hesse decided to lean the tubes against the wall

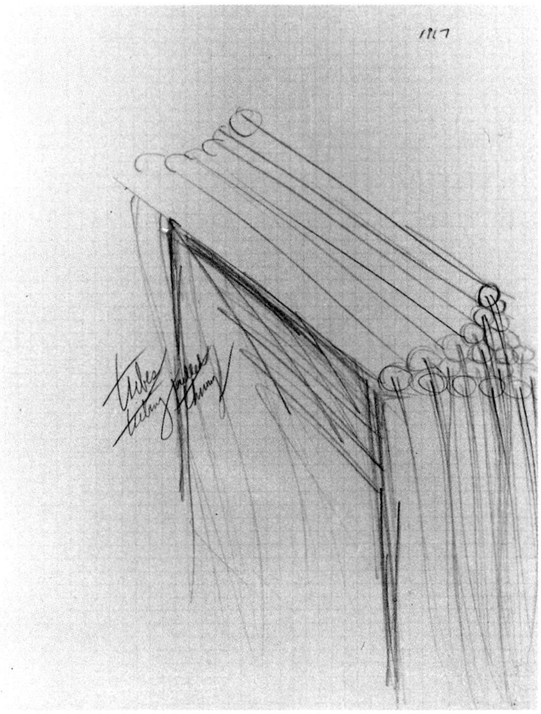

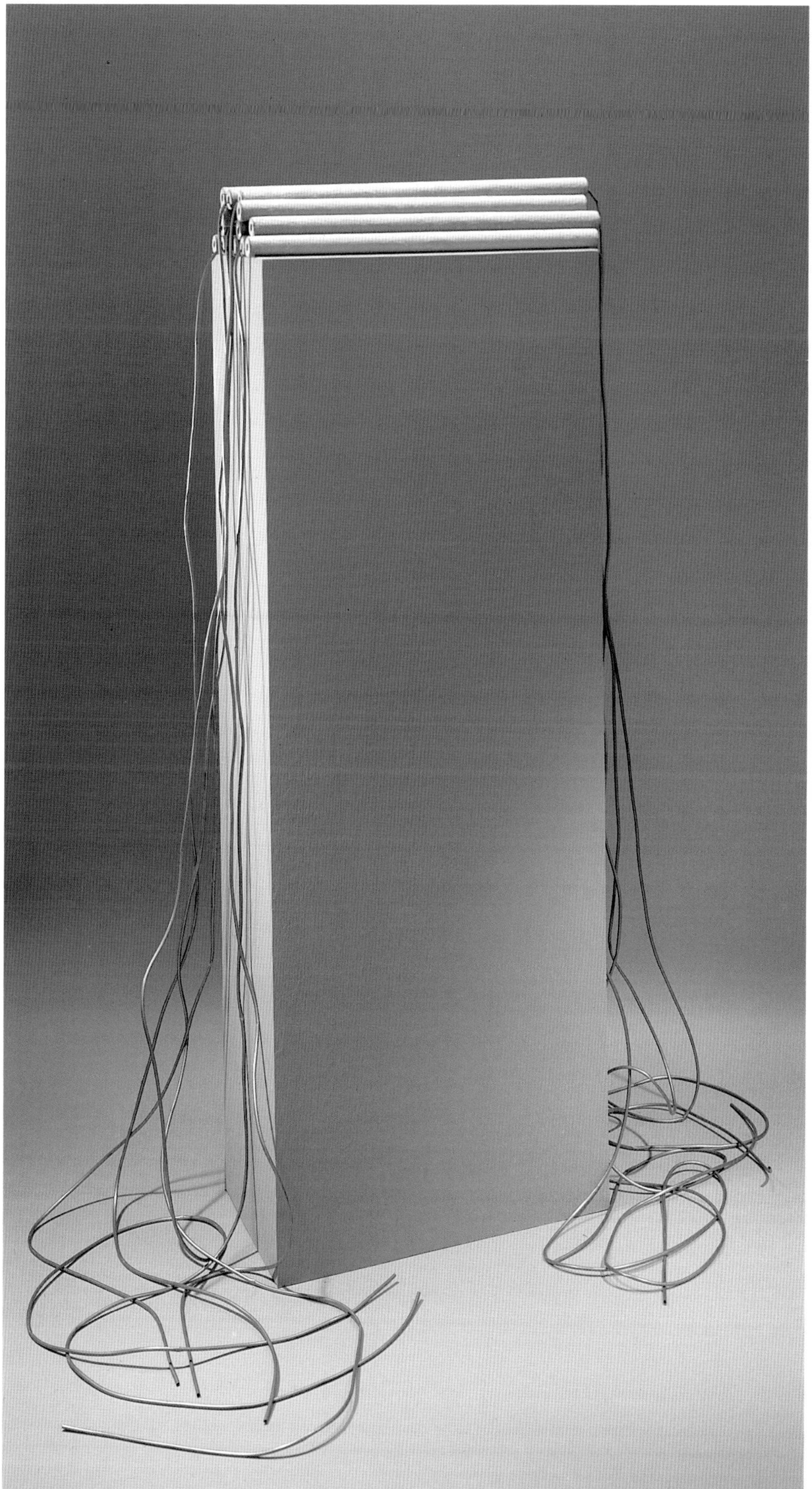

78 **Accretion**

1968

MATERIALS: Fiberglass

SIZE: Length of each of the fifty units: 58 in. (147.3 cm.); diameter of each unit: 2½ in. (6.3 cm.)

COLLECTION: Rijksmuseum Kröller-Müller, Otterlo, The Netherlands (inventory no. 2197–77 KMS)

PROVENANCE: Purchased from Droll/Kolbert Gallery, New York, in 1977

Accretion was the second piece made at Aegis in the summer of 1968. Hesse expanded the number and size of the units in the model so that the piece could span the entire wall (39 feet) at Fischbach, where she would show the fiberglass pieces in November. The sculpture could be fabricated rapidly because all the forms were regular and the workmen at Aegis were more familiar with the technique. To make this piece, a mandrel, or rotating tube, was covered with parting paper, and a sheet of fiberglass cloth was cut to size to fit the circumference of the tube. A coat of resin was then applied, and when it cured, the paper-wrapped tube was removed and additional resin was applied to increase the translucency. The units vary slightly in texture, thickness, and color (from the different batches of resin), but the overall impression is of a group of fifty almost identical units. This regularity was the very quality that Hesse had objected to so strongly in the initial attempts at making *Repetition Nineteen III.* Here she introduced randomness by placing the units against the wall in an irregularly spaced row. They can expand or contract according to the amount of space available for their display.

79 **Sans II**

1968

MATERIALS: Fiberglass and polyester resin

SIZE: Each of five units: 38 × 36 × 6⅛ in. (96.5 × 91.4 × 15.5 cm.); width of entire piece: 430 in. (1092.2 cm.)

COLLECTION: Two units, Whitney Museum of American Art, New York (accession no. 60.105); one unit, Saatchi Collection, London; one unit, Dr. Norman Messite, New York; one unit, Refco Group Ltd., Chicago

PROVENANCE: Whitney units, purchased from Fischbach Gallery, New York, in 1969, with funds from Ethelyn and Lester Honig and the Albert List Family; Saatchi unit, ex-collection Jared Sable, Toronto; Messite unit, acquired from the artist by exchange; Refco unit, ex-collection Ellen V. Amel, Nyack, New York, purchased from Rosa Esman Gallery, New York, in 1988

Sans II was the last and most important of the four pieces fabricated at Aegis for Hesse's exhibition at Fischbach. It was completed shortly before the show opened on November 6, 1968. The model for this piece was the latex *Sans I* (69), which Hesse had made almost a year before, and the process for making the two pieces was in principle identical: repeated casts were made of the same module and then linked together in a long chain. Hesse had titled her Fischbach show "Chain Polymers," underscoring the fact that the materials she was using—latex and polyester resin—were polymers. The title also refers to the organizing principles of both *Sans I* and *Sans II* and recalls the chemical reaction by which a large number of simple molecules are combined to form a chainlike macromolecule during the process of polymerization.

Hesse began by making a boxlike plaster negative mold of the module to be repeated. Johns then made a positive urethane rubber mold from it which was used to cast all sixty modules. For each cast the rubber mold was covered with parting compound and parting paper before applying fiberglass and resin. When the resin cured, the cast was removed and the top edges were broken off so that they would be irregular. The sixty modules were then assembled into five groups of twelve modules, tied together with a rope, and joined by applying a continuous layer of fiberglass and resin to the backs of the pieces. Hanging devices were also added at this time. When the back cured, the front edges were joined with small pieces of fiberglass and resin, and an additional coat of resin was applied to consolidate and even out the appearance of the surface. Hesse hung the five sections together horizontally and the sculpture thus took up 35 feet of the 39 feet of wall available in the gallery. The exaggerated horizontality of *Sans II* recalls *Metronomic Irregularity II* (38), *Addendum* (52), and *Accretion* (78) and was to culminate in *Expanded Expansion* (92).

Johns's ability to translate the model into a huge fiberglass version while retaining the idiosyncratic touch of the Hesse original is astounding. In part this can be attributed to his growing understanding of Hesse's intentions, an understanding that was intensified by the intimacy that existed between them at the time.

80 **Area**

1968

MATERIALS: Latex on wire mesh and metal wire

SIZE: 240 × 36 in. (609.6 × 91.4 cm.)

COLLECTION: Wexner Center for the Visual Arts, Ohio State University, Columbus, purchased in part with designated funds from Helen Hesse Charash (accession no. 1977.001)

PROVENANCE: Jan Runquist, Geneva. Purchased from Droll/Kolbert Gallery, New York, in 1976

Area was made in the summer of 1968 for Lucy Lippard's exhibition "Soft and Apparently Soft Sculpture." The latex material suited Hesse at this point because it offered a way of working against the beauty and perfection of the fiberglass pieces concurrently being made in Staten Island, and of counteracting the loss of control that the new means of production inevitably entailed. Hesse's intention was that *Area* would have nineteen sections. However, the pressure of the deadline and the extreme July heat in the studio caused her to stop work after ten sections were made. The process of fabrication here was similar to that for the *Sans* series (69, 79, 89), that is, a module was repeated over and over until the sculpture was "finished." The implication of this process is that the piece can be stopped at any point or continued to accommodate the amount of space available.

In the Nemser interview, Hesse emphasized that for her the importance of *Area* derived from the work's hidden relationship to *Repetition Nineteen III*. "*Area* is made out of the mold of another piece, *Repetition Nineteen III*. It is the insides that we took out. And then I made it into another piece. I mean there is no connection whatsoever except if you saw it, it is very clear. . . . I rubberized the forms, attached them and sewed them together with wire and that is the piece. . . . I have a personal attachment because it comes from another piece. I take a piece from one piece and make it totally another one. *Repetition Nineteen III* was made of empty containers and there was that sexual connotation. It is anthropomorphic. *Area* isn't, or is in a totally different way. It is used as a flat piece with a suggestive three-dimensionality. *Area* is so ugly, I mean the color. *Repetition Nineteen III* is clear fiberglass." In fact, the charged relationship between the two pieces—created by reusing the parts of one in the other—was an intellectual idea, but one that is not visually apparent.

81 **Seam**

1968

MATERIALS: Latex on wire mesh and metal wire

SIZE: 108 × 48 in. (274.3 × 121.9 cm.)

COLLECTION: Kaiser Wilhelm Museum, Krefeld, West Germany

PROVENANCE: Not provided

CONDITION: Fair; darkened, dirty, still flexible in 1986; displayed flat on the wall

Seam was made in summer 1968 and exhibited in "Anti-Form" at the John Gibson Gallery in October. The technique was similar to that used in *Area*, and consisted of attaching two sections of wire mesh and coating them with latex mixed with filler. By this time Hesse was using latex as a coating rather than a casting material. She experimented with a variety of supports for the latex—such as wire mesh, canvas, and cheesecloth—to give it some rigidity so that she could make the pieces larger. *Seam* is related to both *Sans I* (69) and *Area* (80) in the use of the grid structure and the placement between wall and floor. However, the grid structure in *Seam* is greatly deformed here, obscured within the folds of rubberized mesh. Hesse's definition for *seam*, from a notebook entry—"a line of junction between two edges"—can apply equally to the two joined rectangles of the L and to the junction of wall and floor reinforced by the placement of the sculpture.

82 **Model for *Augment* and *Aught***

1968

MATERIALS: Latex on cotton

SIZE: Each of the twenty-nine units: 4½ × 8½ in. (11.4 × 21.6 cm.); height of stacked piece: 2¾ in. (7 cm.)

COLLECTION: Stephen Antonakos and Naomi Spector, New York

PROVENANCE: Fischbach Gallery, New York, 1968

CONDITION: Good, but some darkening and brittleness at edges

Augment (83) and *Aught* (84) were made in the summer of 1968 and shown at an exhibition curated by Robert Morris at the Leo Castelli Warehouse the following December. The show, "Nine at Leo Castelli," sought to define "anti-form" and "process" as trends in a movement away from minimalism. Both works were also included in Harold Szeeman's exhibition "When Attitudes Become Form," which opened at the Bern Kunsthalle in March 1969; this exhibition had a similar agenda but was international in scope. Hesse's inclusion in these important shows indicates how quickly her career was accelerating after the 1968 Fischbach exhibition. Although *Augment* and *Aught* are two separate pieces, they are often mistaken as one piece because they were shown together at both exhibitions. The stacked arrangement of the model differs from that in *Augment* and *Aught*.

83 **Augment**

1968

MATERIALS: Latex over canvas

SIZE: Each of nineteen units: 78 × 40 in. (198.1 × 101.6 cm.)

COLLECTION: Kaiser Wilhelm Museum, Krefeld, West Germany

PROVENANCE: Not provided

CONDITION: Unexhibitable (already damaged in 1969)

Augment is made of sheets of rubberized canvas (78 by 40 inches) placed on the floor and overlapping one another with the final sheet folded over on itself. Hesse's definition of the title in a notebook as "increase, make greater," refers to the repetition and accumulation of the units. However, an underlined definition for *Stratum* from the same notebook would seem to describe *Augment* even better: "horizontal layer or section of material, especially any of several lying one upon the other." The idea of the endlessly repeatable module found in the *Sans* series (69, 79, 89), *Accretion* (78), and much of her work in 1968 is expressed in *Augment* as thin units lying on top of each other. The effect of the accumulation of layers is more noticeable in the photograph of the model for *Augment* (82).

84 **Aught**

1968

MATERIALS: Double sheets of latex stuffed with polyethylene, metal grommets

SIZE: Each of four units: 78 × 40 in. (198.1 × 101.6 cm.)

COLLECTION: University Art Museum, University of California, Berkeley, gift of Helen Hesse Charash, December 1979

PROVENANCE: Estate of Eva Hesse

Aught is made of four units that are the same size as those of *Augment* but are constructed quite differently. Double sheets of rubberized canvas have been stuffed with polyethylene drop cloths, causing the surface of each unit to bulge in a different way. Normally the polyethylene—used to prevent the rubber from sticking to the floor during fabrication—would have been discarded after the latex was dry. The idea of reusing a rejected part of the process is reminiscent of the reuse of the old molds of *Repetition Nineteen III* in making *Area* (80). The four units here hang side by side from grommets at the top corners, and their consequent buckling further disturbs the regularity of the surface. In both this effect and its rather painterly quality *Aught* most closely resembles *Stratum* (68). Hesse had used polyethylene drop cloths in "Nine Nets" (30) and would later incorporate them into her two last pieces, an untitled wall piece and *Seven Poles* (100, 103).

85 **Untitled ("Clothespin Piece")**

1968

MATERIALS: Rubberized cheesecloth with plastic clothespin added by the artist for display purposes

SIZE: 42½ × 6–7 × ¾ in. (107.9 × 15.2–17.8 × 1.9 cm.)

COLLECTION: Estate of Eva Hesse

CONDITION: Rubber discolored, flattened; top two units considerably darker and less flexible than lower three units

Hesse continued to experiment with latex over cheesecloth and other fabrics. The result was a number of sleeve pieces late in 1968. None is a major work, but all relate to important works and say something about her approach to form, process, and materials during this period. Most of the pieces were made in the same way. A piece of fabric was looped and joined to form an open cylinder and then coated with latex. The open cylinder form, which began with *Repetition Nineteen I* (62), went through many stages of transformation (see 63, 70, 73) in addition to these rubberized versions. The use of latex for the sleeves gives an extremely organic and sexual quality to these pieces. Hesse is photographed wearing one of the sleeves on page 164.

87 **Untitled ("Wapner Sleeve")**

1967

MATERIALS: Rubberized cheesecloth

SIZE: Height of units: 1–2 in. (2.5–5.1 cm.); width of units: 7 in. (17.8 cm.); depth of units: 5½–6½ in. (14–16.5 cm.)

COLLECTION: Grace and Jerry Wapner, Woodstock, New York

PROVENANCE: Acquired from the artist

CONDITION: Units darkened considerably, especially on the outside, and stiff and brittle in some areas

Hesse made many of these sleeves (see Berkeley test pieces, page 247, photograph 2, for other examples), and they were sold in groups of four or five at the Fischbach show in 1968. The sleeves were stacked in a pile like the units in the model for *Aught* and *Augment* (82). Many artists at the time were experimenting with limited editions of small works using unorthodox materials and procedures, and it is possible that Hesse had something similar in mind. Hesse's concept of a repeated module was easily translated to the form of a multiple and she did make a multiple of similar pieces for Tanglewood Press in 1969 (*Enclosed*, 88). Because of the oxidation of the latex, the sleeves in this piece have darkened considerably; originally they would have been a light yellow ocher as in *Enclosed*.

88 **Enclosed**

1969

MATERIALS: Latex over cloth tape and balloon

SIZE: Each of the eight units: 8¾–10¼ × 3½–5¾ × 2–3 in. (22.2–26 × 8.9–14.6 × 5.1–7.6 cm.)

COLLECTION: Dr. and Mrs. Aaron Esman, New York

PROVENANCE: Acquired from the artist by commission

Hesse was commissioned by Rosa Esman to make a multiple consisting of 100 sleeves to be included in the edition 7 *Objects/69*. This edition was put together using multiples made by seven process artists (David Bradshaw, Hesse, Stephen Kaltenbach, Bruce Nauman, Alan Saret, Richard Serra, Keith Sonnier) and was produced by Tanglewood Press. Hesse first describes the process for making this multiple in a note dated November 2, 1968: "Observations. small wrinkled all rubber (with wallpaper tape) over balloons. 1. —Leave balloon inside (attached) this causes wrinkles 2. —cut only at ends 3. —for extreme crumbled, wrinkles—cut when wet. 4. —larger ones that come out flat. All inside balloon removed 5. not too much filler 3 to 1 or 4 to 1." A drawing at Oberlin illustrates the steps described by Hesse and gives a date of February 8, 1969, indicating that she was still making these pieces three months later. The sources for the multiple, as for the other sleeves, were *Repetition Nineteen III* (73) and *Area* (80). In this sleeve multiple, because it is made over a balloon instead of a fabric cylinder, there is also a connection to the earlier balloon pieces of 1965–1966 (18, 19, 24–27). However, while the process is similar, the effect is entirely different. In part this is a result of the different media: papier-mâché dries hard and forms a rigid shell, while the flexible latex does not hold the original shape and tends to collapse when it dries. This collapsing was a quality that Hesse now deliberately sought. Moreover, by cutting off the ends of the balloons Hesse transformed what had been an emphatically male shape into one that is clearly female.

NEW YORK 1969

89 **Sans III**

Completed January 1969

MATERIALS: Latex and metal grommets

SIZE: 156 × 3 × 2 in. (396.2 × 7.6 × 5.1 cm.); inside dimensions of each of forty-nine units: 1⅞ × 2⅞ × 2 in. (4.8 × 7.3 × 5.1 cm.)

COLLECTION: Estate of Eva Hesse

CONDITION: Poor; unexhibitable

Hesse made this final version of the *Sans* series for an exhibition at the Bern Kunsthalle, "When Attitudes Become Form." Completed in January 1969, it was the last latex sculpture she made. *Sans III* is a variation of the polymer-chain concept first expressed in *Sans I* (69) and extends the idea by aligning the modules end to end. In *Sans I* Hesse had placed the forty-eight units in two rows of twenty-four. The individual units themselves were divided in half by a barely visible raised line that mirrors the binding of the two chains. *Sans II* (79) is an expanded but direct translation of the structure of *Sans I* but was cast in reinforced fiberglass. In *Sans III* Hesse joins the forty-nine modules into a 13-foot-long chain.

Sans III is a logical development of the ideas of sequenced, repeated forms that Hesse had been working on since 1967. However, the skeletal thinness and exaggerated verticality of the piece give a disturbing impression and are reminiscent of the severe reductiveness of earlier sculptures such as *Cool Zone* (9) and "Spoke Piece" (15). According to Doug Johns, Hesse had begun exhibiting symptoms of illness in late summer 1968—sleepiness, headaches, nausea—and by January of the following year when she made this piece she was very sick. Other pieces done at this time (90, 94) have the same tenuous reductive quality and should certainly be viewed in the context of Hesse's failing health.

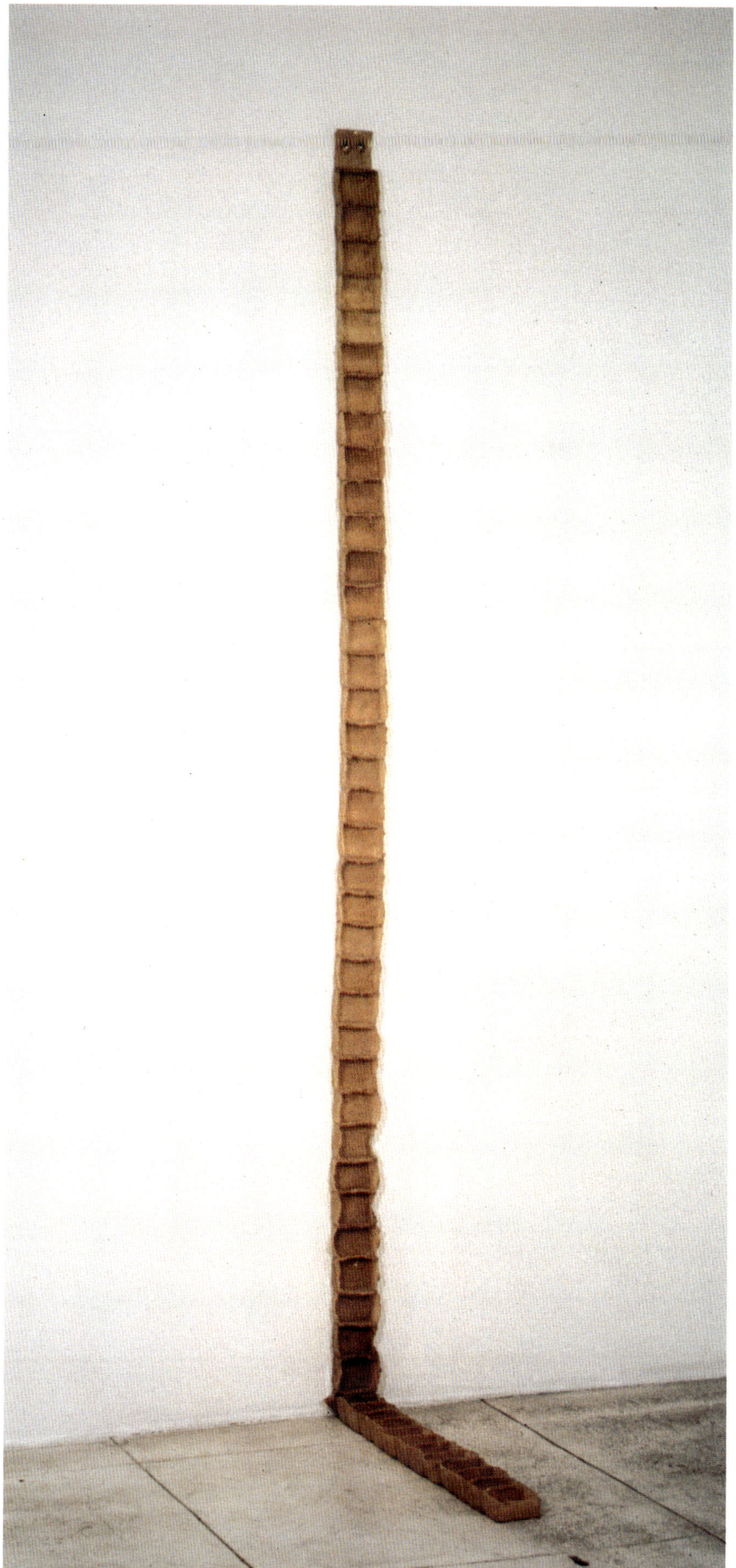

90 **Vinculum II**

1969

MATERIALS: Twenty-three latex-on-wire-mesh plaques stapled to shielded wire, rubber extrusion

SIZE: Height of installed piece: ca. 117 in. (297.2 cm.); width: 2½ in. (6.3 cm.); depth: ca. 115½ in. (293.4 cm.); length of extrusions: 7–62 in. (17.8–157.5 cm.)

COLLECTION: Museum of Modern Art, New York, Gilman Foundation Fund

PROVENANCE: Purchased from Fourcade Droll, New York, 1975

CONDITION: Latex amber-colored and brittle; plaques no longer movable; rubber extrusion replaced with vinyl in 1972

Vinculum II, like *Sans III*, was completed in January 1969 for the show at the Bern Kunsthalle. Hesse discussed the relationship between this work and *Vinculum I* (91; actually completed two months after *Vinculum II*) in her interview with Cindy Nemser. "*Vinculum II* is connected to the ladder piece in that is made with the same rubber hosing. But *Vinculum I* is solid and staid and inflexible, except for the hose, while *Vinculum II*, though very similar, is totally flexible. There isn't anything that can be staid or put. All these parts can be moved. Every connection is movable. So it has a very fragile, tenuous quality. It is very, very taut as it is attached from two angles. There is lots of tension, yet the whole thing is flexible and moves. It's made of wire mesh with latex and the parts are just stapled so they can really go up and down. They are positioned so that they can be moved. And through the wire and fiberglass [Hesse says "fiberglass" but must mean "latex," as there is no fiberglass in this piece] is a hole and these irregular rubber hoses go through them. They're all different lengths. Everything is tenuous because the hoses are not really knotted very tight and they can change and I don't mind it, within reason."

In fact Hesse has taken the structure of *Sans III* and stretched it almost to the breaking point in *Vinculum II*, while introducing the possibility of moving the modules along the guide wires. The dangling cords that were so conspicuous in her work before 1968 are reintroduced here to give this sculpture its emotive charge. At the same time they accentuate the aura of radical fragility that surrounds the piece.

91 **Vinculum I**

Completed March 1969

MATERIALS: Reinforced fiberglass, vinyl tubing, and metal screen

SIZE: Each of two units: 104 × 8½ × 2 in. (264.2 × 21.6 × 5.1 cm.)

COLLECTION: Ganz Collection, New York

PROVENANCE: Purchased from Fischbach Gallery, New York, November 6, 1969

CONDITION: Rubber extrusion replaced with vinyl in 1979

Vinculum I was completed in March 1969 for inclusion in the Whitney Museum exhibition "Anti-Illusion: Procedures/Materials." It was made with the help of Doug Johns, who had been living in Hesse's studio since the fall, and her assistant, Martha Schieve. Hesse, who was now quite ill, both needed help and enjoyed the collaborative process and the freedom it allowed. In the Nemser interview she referred to *Vinculum I*: "Prior to that time the process of my work used to take a long time. First because I did most of it myself, and then when I planned the larger pieces and worked with someone, they were more formalistic. Then when we started working less formalistically or with greater chance, the whole process became speeded up. When we did one of the pieces at the Whitney that I loved the most, the ladderlike piece, *Vinculum I*, it took a very short time. It was a very complex piece, but the whole attitude was different, and that is more the attitude I want to work with now. . . . That was one of the last pieces I did before I got so ill. It was one of the pieces we started working with less plan. I just described the vague idea to two people I worked with and we went and just started doing it."

Despite this newfound collaborative spirit, *Vinculum I* is very closely tied to Hesse's other pieces at this time. The structure of the work derives from the *Sans* series, in particular *Sans I* (69), in which the two vertical chains are linked together. In *Vinculum I* the bonds between the modules and chains are completely loosened, a clear result of her collaboration with Johns and Schieve; and the ladder structure recalls *Laocoon*. *Vinculum I* and *Vinculum II* are a pair, as Hesse points out in the passage quoted with *Vinculum II*; they belong to a whole series of paired constructions (*Long Life*/"Moderna Museet" [17, 20]; *Repetition Nineteen III*/*Area* [73, 80]; and *Augment*/*Aught* [83, 84]) that Hesse made in order to underline the contradictory nature of her structures.

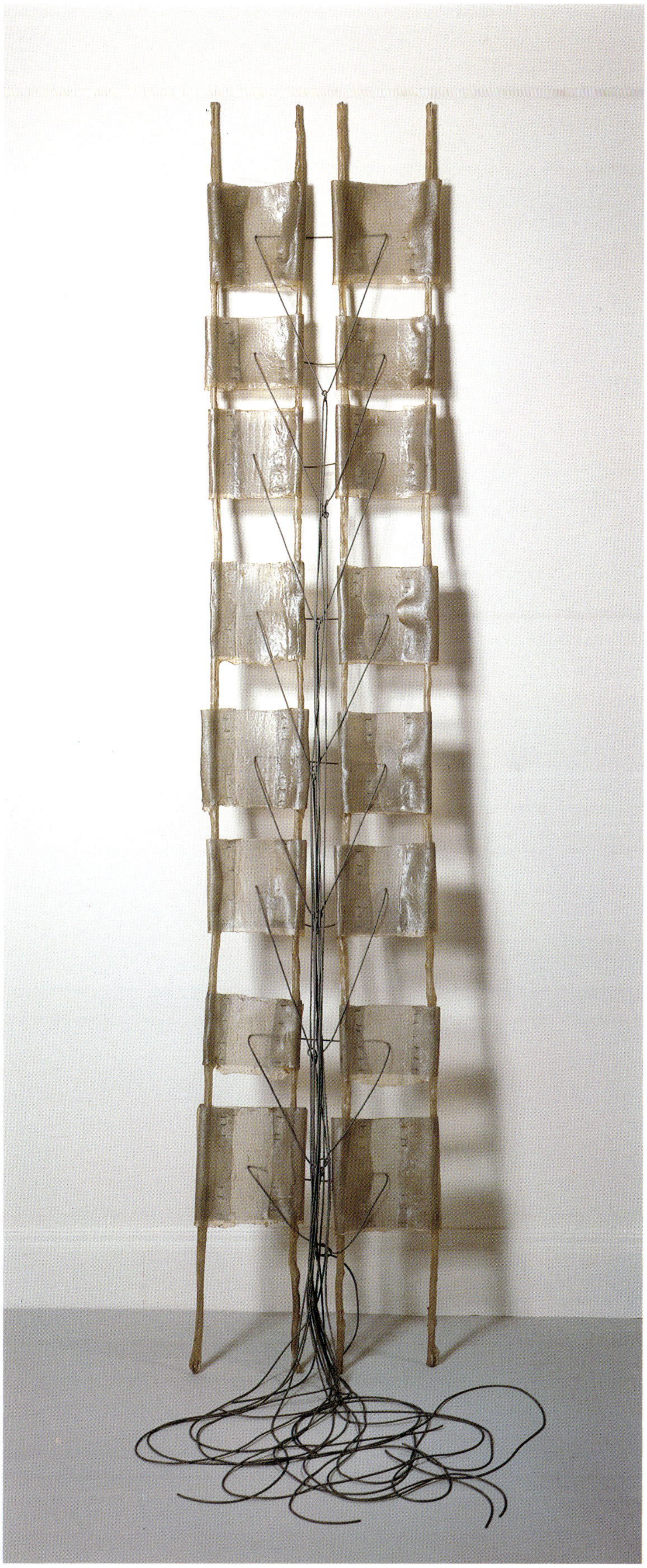

92 Expanded Expansion

Completed February 28, 1969

MATERIALS: Reinforced fiberglass poles and rubberized cheesecloth

SIZE: Three units of three, five, and eight poles, respectively; height: 122 in. (309.9 cm.); width: 60, 120, 180 in. (152.4, 304.8, 457.2 cm.)

COLLECTION: Solomon R. Guggenheim Museum, New York, gift of the Family of Eva Hesse, 1975 (accession no. FN 75.2138)

PROVENANCE: Estate of Eva Hesse

CONDITION: Has become less flexible and somewhat peach-colored with age; second unit from left noticeably discolored

Expanded Expansion, another collaboration with Johns and Schieve, was also made for the "Anti-Illusion: Procedures/Materials" exhibition at the Whitney. It was completed on February 28, 1969. One of Hesse's most monumental works, it is 10 feet high and when fully extended spans more than 30 feet. As suggested by the title, it is the cumulation of the horizontal development in her work which began with *Metronomic Irregularity II* (38), *Addendum* (52), and *Sans II* (79). As important to Hesse, however, was the notion of the sculpture's ability to shrink as well as expand so that the size of the work is defined by the requirements of its environment. This idea had particular currency among the "anti-form" and "process" sculptors with whom Hesse was sympathetic at the time. Hesse was more interested in the possibilities of expanding and shrinking giving the sense of absurdity and exaggeration.

In this work she combined two of her favorite materials, latex and fiberglass. Johns, who was well aware of the fugitive quality of latex, tried from the very beginning of his collaboration with Hesse to discourage her from using it. However, he recalls, Hesse lectured him on how important the instability of materials was to her process. "She was very aware that it was temporary. She was not defensive about it; she was offensive about it. She would say that it was an attribute. Everything was for the process—a moment in time, not meant to last." Curiously, however, Hesse was concerned about the permanence of reinforced fiberglass, according to Johns. By contrasting enduring fiberglass with ephemeral latex and cheesecloth, Hesse was to further her continuing dialogue of paired opposites, and to subvert the idea of the monumental by implying that the forms were only momentarily stable.

There are three rough sketches at Oberlin that show how this work evolved by combining the structure and positions of *Accretion* (78) and *Vinculum I* (91) with the rubberized sheets used for *Aught* (84). Johns fabricated sixteen 10-foot poles from woven fiberglass material reinforced with polyester resin. The thirteen rubberized sections were made individually by laying cheesecloth onto plastic and then coating it with latex. When the sheets were dry they were attached to the poles with additional flaps of fiberglass resin. The sculpture was then organized into three

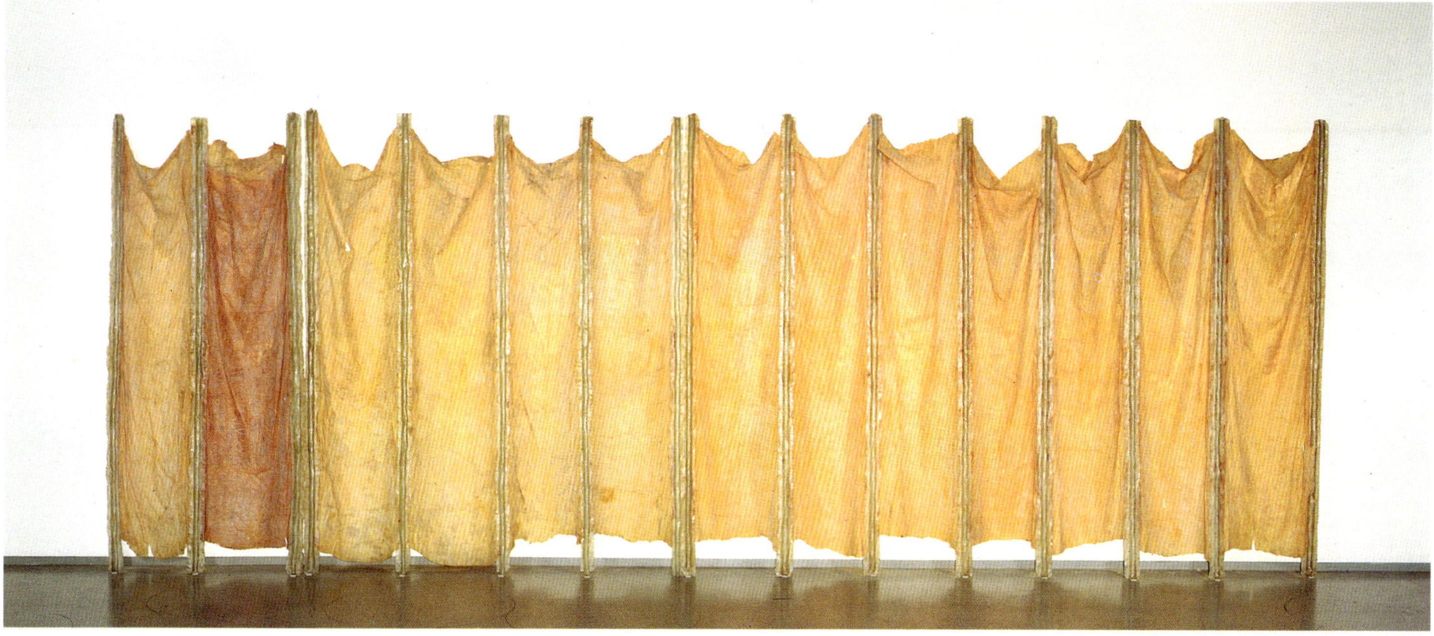

sections of three, five, and eight poles. (The modular structure is so subsumed into the expanse of the piece that it is only a vestigial reminder of what had once been a major concern for Hesse.) A photograph shows a section under construction in Hesse's studio; the sculpture was made on the floor and Hesse liked the way it looked there. A second photograph shows the work installed, continuing around a corner in Hesse's studio and giving a good idea of the ability of the sculpture both to adapt to and to define space. Both photographs show how much lighter and more flexible the latex was at that time. In the twenty years since the piece was made, the latex has oxidized considerably, becoming quite brittle. It has turned from a light yellow to a deep peach color. The second panel from the left is a much deeper pink than the other panels, suggesting that when the work was folded for storage this unit was on top and more exposed to oxygen than the underlying units were. The fragility and stiffness of the latex panels make it impossible to exercise the many options for placement that were originally inherent to the sculpture. However, despite these changes *Expanded Expansion* is still a powerful presence.

93 Connection

1969

MATERIALS: Reinforced fiberglass over cloth-covered wire

SIZE: Each of twenty units: 16–65 × 1–3 in. (40.6–165.1 × 2.5–7.6 cm.)

COLLECTION: Ganz Collection, New York

PROVENANCE: Purchased from Fourcade Droll, New York, July 10, 1972

Connection consists of at least twenty units Hesse worked on with Johns and Schieve in February and March 1969. The units constructed over the course of a few sessions were never installed during the artist's lifetime, and according to Gioia Timpanelli Hesse considered the piece unfinished. After her death the executors of her estate assembled the twenty units found in her studio into a single piece, and it is normally installed as a random cluster hanging from the ceiling, more or less re-creating the relationship of the units when they were made. Originally there were at least twenty-one sections; she gave one to Johns as a gift. The artist explained her intentions for this piece to Johns by saying that she wanted the process of making it to be very simple and free. They were to construct the piece with no preconceived plan, but rather to let the work develop spontaneously. Johns put nails randomly into the ceiling approximately a foot apart, and twisted wires of different lengths were hung from them. Small irregular pieces of fiberglass soaked with resin were then wrapped around the wire armatures. The shapes were formed by the action of gravity on the fiberglass resin and the addition of more pieces on top of the initial core.

The resulting units have a strangely organic quality that is visceral yet bloodless and anticipates Hesse's last piece, *Seven Poles* (103). Most of the units have loops at either end. The title suggests the possibility of connecting these modules to the ceiling or to each other. Hesse did allow some of the units to be exhibited for sale as multiples during an exhibition in late 1969 at the Jewish Museum, "A Plastic Presence." This would indicate that while she might have been pleased with the individual units she was certainly ambivalent about how the piece worked as a whole. *Connection* was the first sculpture since *Vertiginous Detour* (28), of early 1966, that hung from the ceiling. This orientation remained important to Hesse; six of her last eight works are suspended from the ceiling.

94 **Untitled ("Ice Piece")**

1969

MATERIALS: Reinforced fiberglass over cloth-covered wire

SIZE: Varying lengths for each of twenty-two units; total length: 62 ft. (18. 9 m.); irregular width, ca. 1 in. (2.5 cm.)

COLLECTION: Estate of Eva Hesse

CONDITION: Three units cracked

"Ice Piece" was made for the Whitney Museum exhibition "Anti-Illusion: Materials/Procedures," along with *Vinculum I* (91) and *Expanded Expansion* (92). In a loose page in the Hesse archive at Oberlin, she compares this piece with *Expanded Expansion* and establishes a relationship that is not readily apparent to the viewer. "Intentionally two pieces of great contrast in form but similar in thought and extreme position. Both are endless. If the ceiling were higher or space on the floor larger it could as well be continued and exaggerate its position more. The rubberized cheesecloth also could continue. Both take a stand on absurdity. Both by means of form as well. One is endless and yet a thin longish substance that is linked together and one feels the infinity to which it could extend. The other is opposite in form, large looming, powerful, yet precarious. Its positioning as a unit or sectional units could take many stands. The flexible and also inflexible quality is there and in contrast."

The twenty-two units that make up this work were fabricated using the same techniques as for *Connection*. Twisted wire armatures with loops at either end are coated with torn pieces of fiberglass and resin. The work differs from *Connection*, however, in that the units are much thinner and more uniform in thickness, and have much less character as individual modules. The problem of their display was resolved by linking the units together into one very long chain (62 feet). The resulting segmented line rises vertically to the full height of the space it occupies, while the remainder lies stiffly coiled on the floor in an irregular spiral. "Ice Piece" is without doubt one of Hesse's most radically reduced sculptures in a family of pieces that includes *Cool Zone* (9), "Spoke Piece" (15), *Sans III* (89), and *Vinculum II* (90). The protruding cord, which was to become a signature element in her work, has been internalized to take on a supporting function. Encased in a transparent sheath of resin, it threatens to dissolve in space as it ascends toward the ceiling.

95 **Tori**

1969

MATERIALS: Reinforced fiberglass over wire mesh

SIZE: Each of nine units: 30–47 × 12½–17 × 10¼–15 in. (76.2–119.4 × 31.7–43.2 × 26–38.1 cm.)

COLLECTION: Judge Steven D. Robinson, Miami, Florida

PROVENANCE: Purchased from Donna Schneier, Inc., New York, October 1973

Tori was made by Hesse, Johns, and Schieve. Six of the units were completed by early April 1969, when Hesse finally collapsed. On April 18 she underwent an operation for a brain tumor. The three remaining units of *Tori* were completed by Johns sometime in late July or early August, when Hesse returned to her studio before undergoing a second operation on August 18.

The nine units that make up *Tori* were made, like *Vinculum I* (91), by coating wire mesh with fiberglass and resin. Each form was made by looping a piece of mesh into an open cylinder and joining it at two points with staples in such a way that a gashlike opening was formed along the side of each unit. Formally this is the last of the open cylinder pieces that began with *Repetition Nineteen III* (73), *Area* (80), and the rubber sleeve pieces (85–88). With *Tori* Hesse invokes the battered appearance of the *Repetition Nineteen III* molds and disperses them in a random pile on the floor. By splitting open each form and exposing the inside she intensifies the impression of objects that have been used up and rejected.

The sculpture was not titled until the fall of 1969. The working title had been "mesh pillows." Johns had fabricated a piece for Robert Morris called *Torus* and felt there was an affinity between the circular forms of the two sculptures. Hesse then decided to title the work with the plural of the word *torus*.

96 **Right After**

1969

MATERIALS: Casting resin over fiberglass cord and wire hooks

SIZE: 78 × 180 × 120 in. (198.1 × 457.2 × 304.8 cm.)

COLLECTION: Milwaukee Art Center, Milwaukee, Wisconsin, gift of Friends of Art

PROVENANCE: Not available

Right After was started in late 1968 but was not completed until July or August 1969. The title refers to the fact that it was the first piece Hesse returned to after her first operation. It was completed for the exhibition "A Plastic Presence," which opened at the Jewish Museum in New York in November 1969. The technique for making *Right After* was simple and Johns recalls that it came together very quickly. Many hooks were suspended from the ceiling by wires, then 100- to 200-foot lengths of fiberglass roving (woven cord) were dipped into the resin in sections. Hesse then draped the wet roving over the hooks. As the resin cured, the transparent webs of cord hardened permanently in place. An undated loose page in the Hesse archive at Oberlin describes the process: "Climbing around, getting things up, moved about, around and hung. Four hands changing, manipulating, changes, things to allow things to happen. Suspended hangings, enabling themselves to continue, connect and multiply."

The idea of connecting a chaotic network of cords to a system of fixed points recalls *Laocoon* (31) and *Metronomic Irregularity* (37–39). But with *Right After* the web of gluey-looking cords is allowed to encroach into the room, and like the spider web the work resembles, it manages to be both beautiful and repellent at the same time. Hesse, however, expressed reservations about the beauty of *Right After* in the Nemser interview. She felt that in completing the piece the translucent beauty of the fiberglass dominated and that it left "the ugly zone and went to the beauty zone": the strangeness and simplicity of the work were compromised. Hesse's mistrust of the decorative and the beautiful was well-known. Having erred in the direction of beauty, she then proceeded to make an ugly version of the piece (101). A similar relationship exists between *Repetition Nineteen III* (73) and *Area* (80), as well as among *Accession III, IV,* and *V* (74, 75, 76).

97 Test Piece for *Contingent*

1969

MATERIALS: Latex over cheesecloth

SIZE: 144 × 44 in. (365.8 × 111.8 cm.)

COLLECTION: Stephen Antonakos and Naomi Spector, New York

PROVENANCE: Gift of the artist

This test piece is important because its condition is very close to that of *Contingent* itself when it was first exhibited. The test piece was given by Hesse to Naomi Spector and has been carefully stored away from light and heat and never exhibited. As a result, the latex has oxidized very little. The color and flexibility have remained stable and therefore the unit gives an excellent idea of what most of Hesse's latex pieces looked like when they were first made.

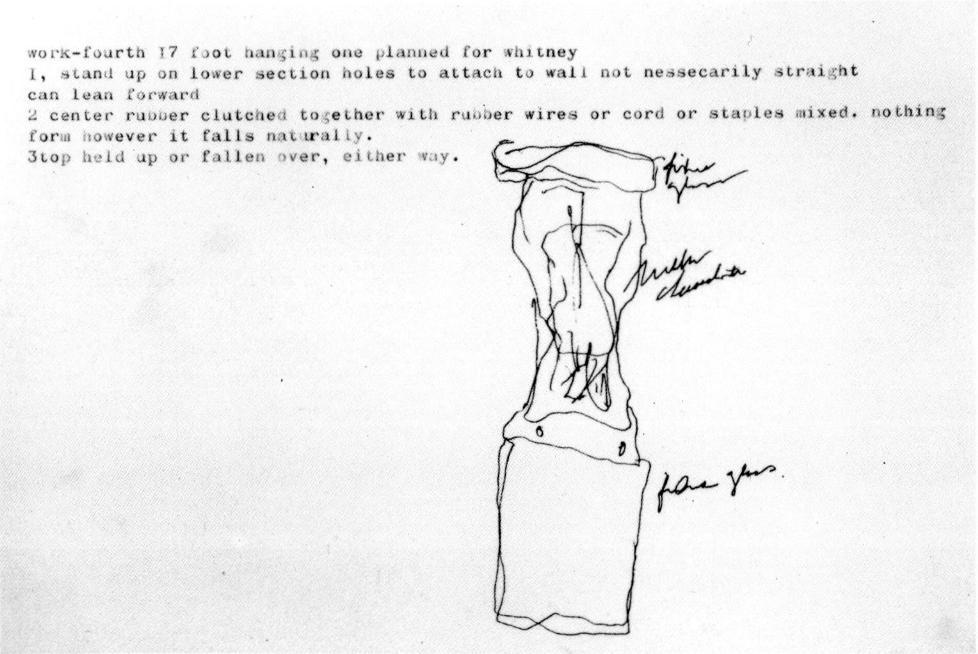

98 **Contingent**

Completed November 16, 1969

MATERIALS: Reinforced fiberglass and latex over cheesecloth

SIZE: Height of each of eight units: 114–168 in. (289.6–426.7 cm.) width: 36–48 in. (91.4–122 cm.)

COLLECTION: National Gallery of Australia, Canberra

PROVENANCE: Estate of Eva Hesse. Purchased from Fourcade Droll, New York, 1973

CONDITION: Latex darkened and brittle

Hesse's last five pieces, beginning with *Contingent*, were made by Jonathan Singer and myself, working under the supervision of Doug Johns. After a second operation in August 1969 and subsequent chemotherapy, Hesse could do very little work herself. She would plan the pieces, and Johns would figure out how they could be made. He would then show us how to do the work and Hesse would supervise, often from her bed. At this time Johns ceased to be as actively involved in the fabrication of Hesse's work as he had been during 1968 and 1969. Certainly this change is evident in the technical quality of the last pieces. Singer and I had never worked with fiberglass, resin, or latex before, nor did we have the close working relationship that had developed between Johns and Hesse. As a result, the execution and finish of the last works are crude by comparison to the Hesse/Johns collaborations. The focus changed to process and moment, "letting things happen." Hesse did not care as much now about the niceties of planning and execution, and she allowed more irregularities as well as a greater sense of emotion to be incorporated into the work.

Contingent was finished on November 16, 1969, and exhibited in "Art in Process IV" at Finch College. Hesse's statement about the piece, a long stream-of-consciousness poem, was included in the catalogue. She had planned to have the work consist of at least nine irregular sheets of rubberized cheesecloth and fiberglass, but there was only enough latex for eight. The catalogue description, written under the weight of her illness, speaks of contradiction and a desire to push the work as far as it would go to achieve something that is "not yet known." "I remember I wanted to get into non art, nonconnotive [*sic*], non anthropomorphic, non geometric, non, nothing, everything, but of another kind, vision, sort. from a total other reference point."

More than any other of Hesse's sculptures, *Contingent* successfully synthesizes the qualities of painting and sculpture. Light, color, and gravity are merged and activated in a way that is possible only in a hybrid form. The eight bannerlike units appear as skins lifted off the surface of a painting and allowed to hang, magically suspended in midair. At the same time the light-absorbing qualities of the latex are played off against the light-transmitting qualities of the fiberglass. The fragile latex midsections are pulled taut by the heavier fiberglass attachments, imparting a palpable tension to the piece; and this tension is exaggerated by the poignant contrast of the ephemeral and enduring qualities of the two materials.

NEW YORK 1970

99 Model for One Unit of *Untitled* ("Wall Piece")

1970

MATERIALS: Reinforced fiberglass over wire mesh, and latex over cloth over wire

SIZE: 12 × 9 × 4½ in. (30.5 × 22.9 × 11.4 cm.); length of cord: 78 in. (198.1 cm.)

COLLECTION: Albright-Knox Art Gallery, Buffalo, New York (inventory no. 1978.5)

PROVENANCE: Estate of Eva Hesse. Purchased from Droll/Kolbert Gallery, New York, June 1978, with funds from Elisabeth H. Gates and Sherman S. Jewett

See number 100. This small fiberglass and wire mesh piece was made at the same time as "Wall Piece," and as with that sculpture a rubber-coated, cloth-covered wire was added later. However, unlike "Wall Piece," this model is a single unit. The drawing illustrated below is one of three Hesse made for "Wall Piece," each indicating a different arrangement of the cords that were subsequently attached to the fiberglass plaques.

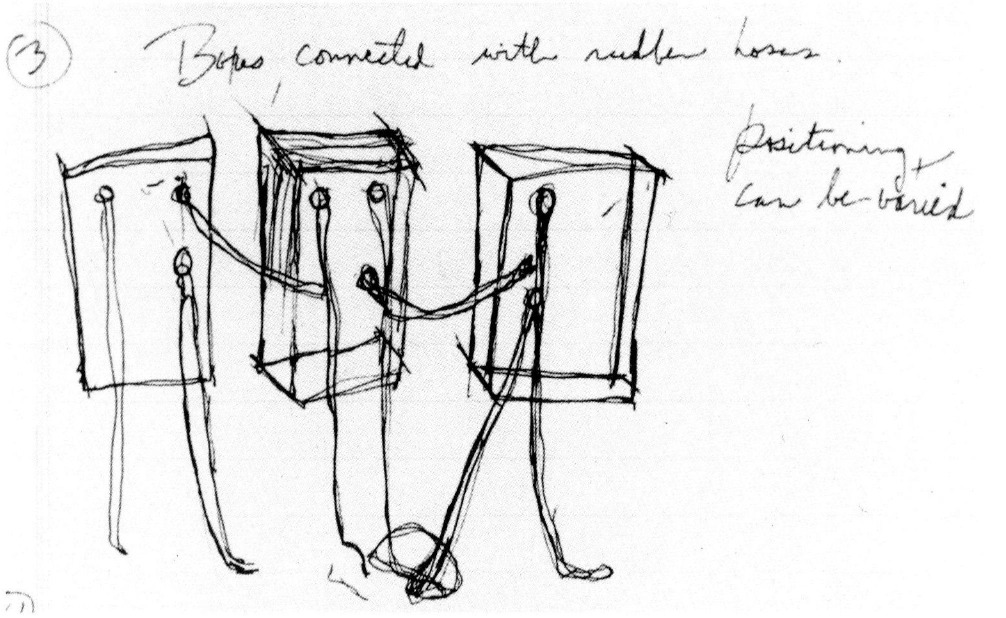

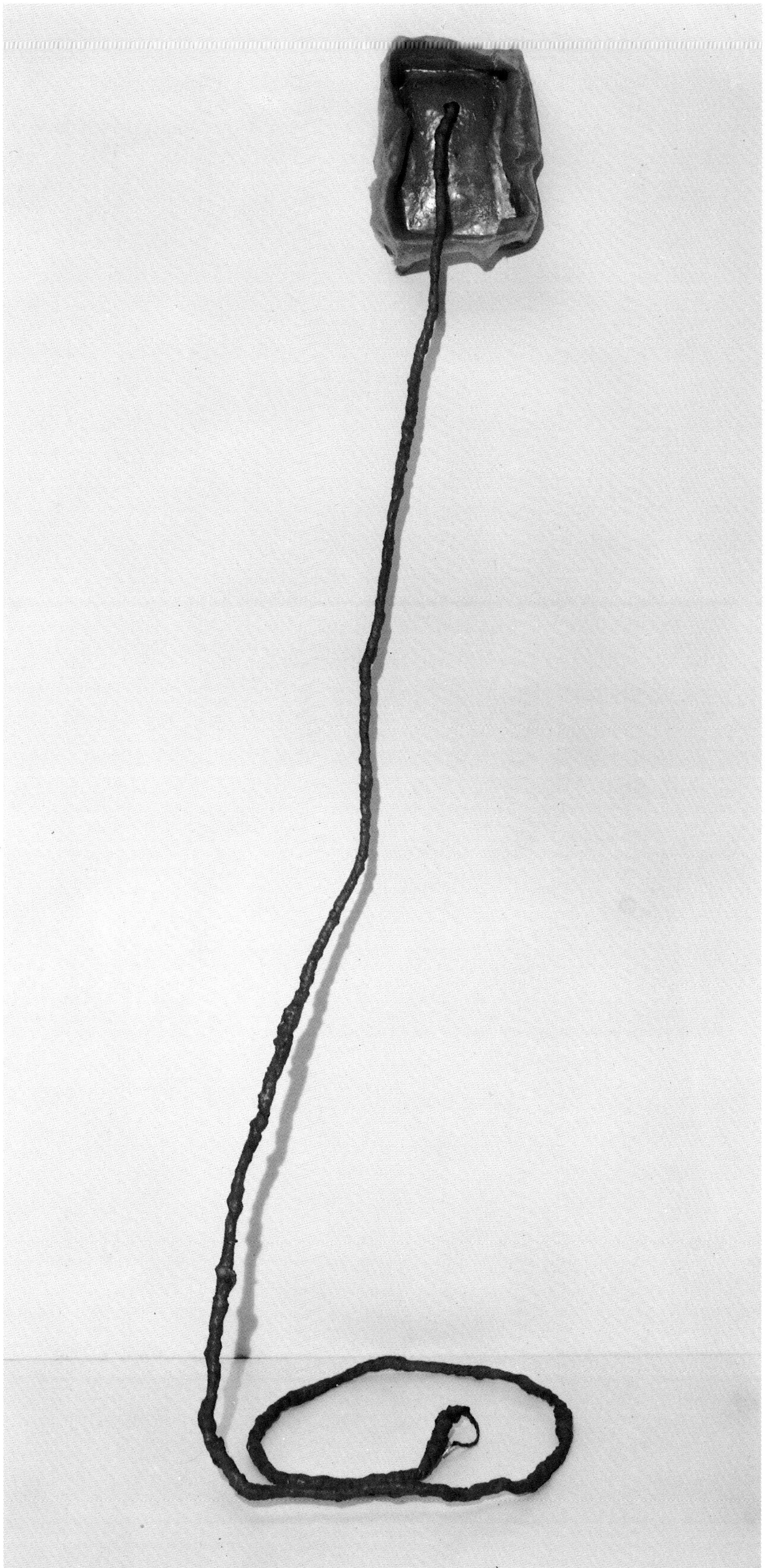

100 **Untitled ("Wall Piece")**

1970

MATERIALS: Reinforced fiberglass over wire mesh and polyethylene, and latex over cloth over wire

SIZE: Each of four units: 34–42¾ × 23–34 × 2–6 in. (86.4–108.6 × 58.4–86.4 × 5.1–15.2 cm.)

COLLECTION: Ganz Collection, New York

PROVENANCE: Purchased from Fourcade Droll, New York, July 10, 1972

The four irregular shallow boxes of this work were to be a kind of trial piece for Singer and me to help us learn the techniques of working with fiberglass and resin. The piece was actually started late in 1969 but was interrupted by Hesse's return to the hospital between Christmas and January 1970. We resumed work on it in late January. The four units are each a different size and depth, and act as a kind of disconnected version of the *Sans* sculptures (69, 79, 89). Hesse wanted the surfaces to be active and varied; the two units on the right have polyethylene drop cloths inserted between the mesh and the fiberglass for this purpose. The concern for luminous, active surfaces in both this piece and *Contingent* (98) stems from a series of wash drawings, often referred to as "Window" drawings, that Hesse had done in Woodstock, New York, the previous summer.

After the boxes were finished we were asked to make ten or eleven long rubberized cords. The process for making them was simple and consisted of wrapping cheesecloth tightly around long aluminum wires. Hesse wanted the surface of these cords to be irregular and roughly textured; often it was necessary to rewrap a section in order to obtain just the right result. In the end we applied a coat of latex; the cords that resulted were quite similar to the snake elements of *Laocoon*. It is possible that Hesse intended these cords to be joined together as in "Ice Piece" (94), or that she intended them for yet another piece. However, eventually she decided to use them with the four fiberglass trays, and two holes were drilled toward the top of each unit so that they could be attached at the rear with a pin. A drawing (page 230) indicates that Hesse originally intended that the trays be connected with rubber hoses. The awkward relationship between the latex cords and the fiberglass units makes this work quite moving.

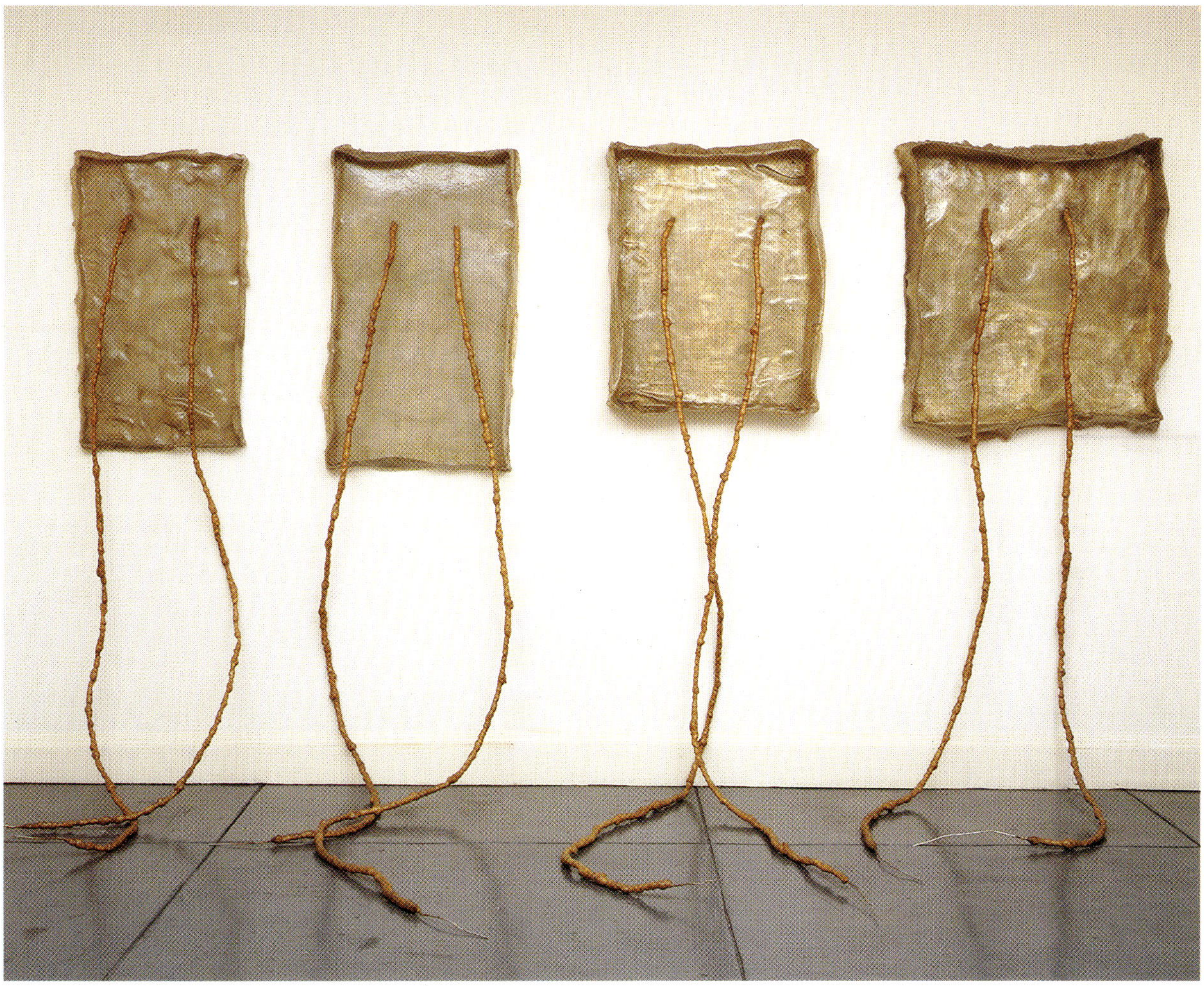

101 **Untitled ("Rope Piece")**

1970

MATERIALS: Latex over rope, wire, and string

SIZE: Height of three units: 144, 126, 90 in. (365.8, 320, 228.6 cm.); width varies with installation

COLLECTION: Whitney Museum of American Art, New York

PROVENANCE: Purchased from Fourcade Droll, New York, July 10, 1972. Purchased from the Estate of Victor Ganz, April 1988

Hesse made one section of this piece in January 1970, working with a friend, David Magasis, who had brought her a large quantity of rope and twine. She was photographed with this part of the work in a *Life* magazine article of February 27, 1970, entitled "Fling, Dribble, and Drip." In the article she is quoted saying: "This piece is very ordered. Maybe I'll make it more structured, maybe I'll leave it changeable. When it is completed its order could be chaos. Chaos can be structured as non-chaos. That we know from Jackson Pollock."

Hesse and I made another section together in early March. The process was simple and quick. We dipped the ropes into a bucket of latex, knotted and tangled them, and hung them from wires attached to the ceiling. The work was then put aside to make room for the fabrication of what turned out to be her last piece.

Although it is possible that Hesse might have done more with this piece had she lived, the scale, complexity, and manner in which the piece hangs from the ceiling do correspond closely with *Right After* (96). And when the two are seen together it is "Rope Piece" that is the stronger. In fact the real question of this piece is the issue of its installation. After Victor Ganz purchased it in 1972, he asked me to install it on more than a dozen different occasions. I have come to the conclusion that there is no "right" way to install the work. An annotated drawing from November 1969 (Timpanelli collection) supports this conclusion. There are two notebook entries—written three years earlier, when she finished *Laocoon* (31)—that point to Hesse's interest in a work of this type: "Rope irregular (like a snake hung while working on Laocoon. Hang from the ceiling to floor ad infinitum (room) . . . will do one that does not come from a form, that is endless, totally encroaching and irrational. With its own rationale even it looks chaotic." This gives at least the spirit if not the letter of Hesse's intentions regarding the display of what she called the "knot piece."

While "Rope Piece" is undeniably chaotic in appearance, it has an underlying order imposed by the latex that glues the ropes together and the points by which the ropes are attached to the ceiling. While the ropes are flexible and can be expanded and contracted in an infinite variety of ways, the integrity and structure of the tangled web remain forever unchangeable. Like Pollock, Hesse seemed to have realized what "chaos theorists" have more recently put forth: that chaos indeed possesses a structure and that all systems of order are temporary.

102 **Model for *Seven Poles***

1970

MATERIALS: Plaster over wire and cloth-covered wire

SIZE: Each of seven units: 4¾–6¾ × 5 × 5 in. (12.1–17.1 × 12.7 × 12.7 cm.)

COLLECTION: Ganz Collection, New York

PROVENANCE: Gift of Helen Hesse Charash, 1974

Hesse made a drawing in the fall of 1969 of three L-shaped bent or broken elements (see illustration). That December when she was in the hospital she made a second drawing, according to Gioia Timpanelli, which expanded this idea, for a piece to be exhibited at Owens-Corning Fiberglas Center the next spring. Another drawing (see Lippard, *Eva Hesse*, figure 222) shows tall, slender bent units bound together with cords and standing in a semicircle; this third idea was translated into the small plaster, cloth, and wire model here, which Hesse submitted to Corning for a commission, the L-shaped poles turned inward in a circle. Corning commissioned a large version for $4,000. The actual sculpture (103) was not purchased by Corning because Hesse abandoned the interconnected arrangement in favor of a random displacement of the units.

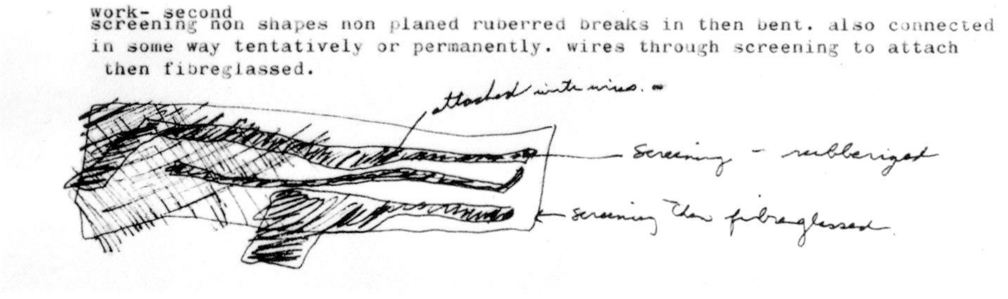

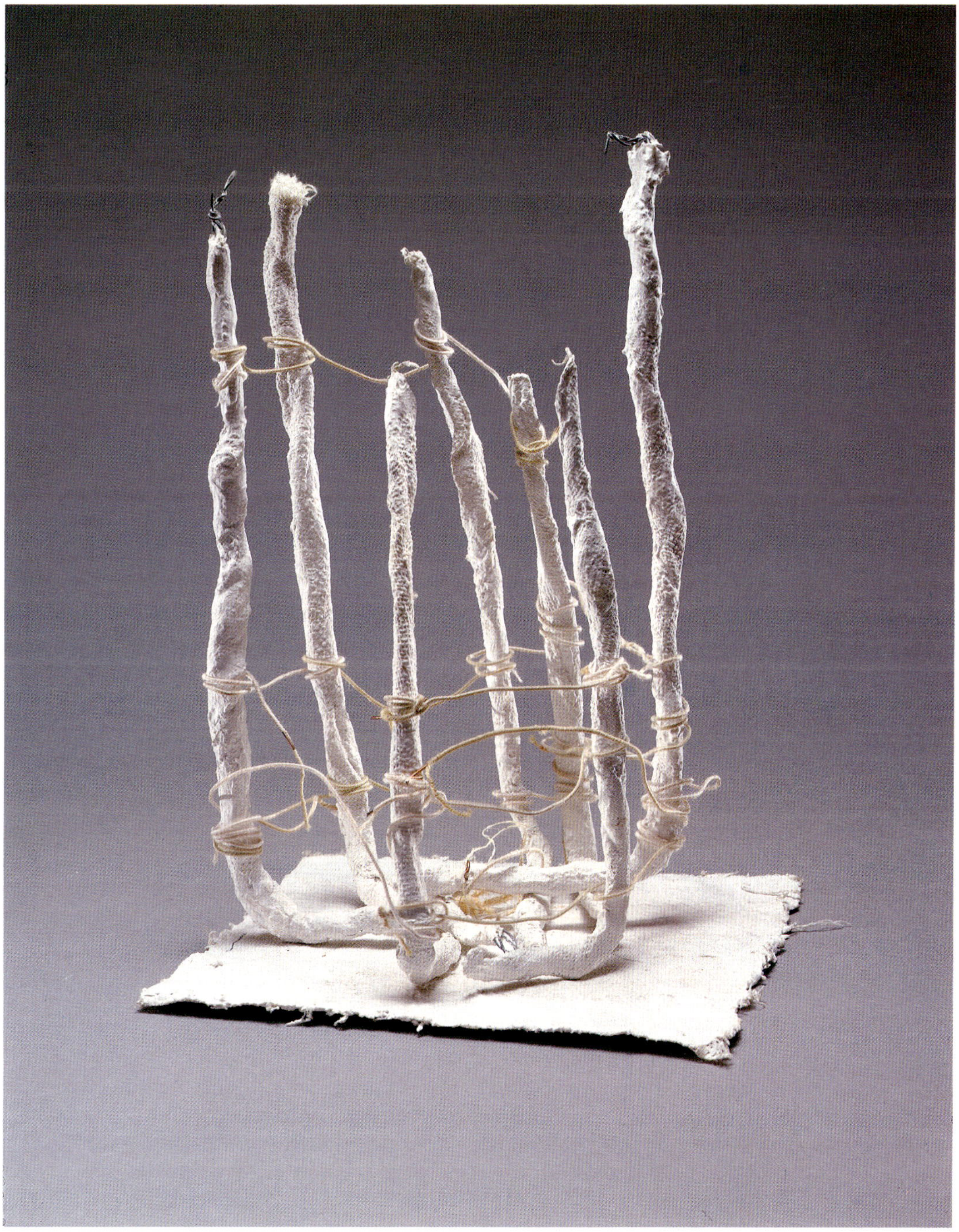

103 **Seven Poles**

1970

MATERIALS: Reinforced fiberglass over polyethylene over aluminum wire

SIZE: Height of each of seven units: 74–111 in. (188–281.9 cm.); circumference of each unit: 10–16 in. (25.4–40.6 cm.)

COLLECTION: Centre Georges Pompidou, Musée National d'Art Moderne, Paris

PROVENANCE: Purchased from Fourcade Droll, New York, by Victor Ganz, July 10, 1972. On loan to the Philadelphia Museum of Art, July 1977–July 1987. Purchased from Ganz in 1986

In early 1970 Hesse showed the model (102) to Doug Johns and asked him to determine how it could be translated into a large-scale fiberglass version. By early March they had agreed on a method for fabricating seven L-shaped units. The technique was an elaboration of the method first used for *Connection* (93) and "Ice Piece" (94). A length of 3/16-inch aluminum wire was twisted so that loops were formed on either end. Sheets of clear polyethylene were then wrapped around the spinal cord–like armature and held in place by coils of thinner wire. This wrapping of wire with softer materials had been used to form the "snakes" of *Laocoon* (31) and the rubberized "cords" of "Wall Piece" (100). Once the height and proportions of each of the seven L-shaped armatures were determined, they were hung from the ceiling by wire. The polyethylene was then coated with many small pieces of resin-soaked fiberglass. The resin was allowed to cure, and the process was repeated until a kind of transparent skin formed around each unit. Soon it became obvious that because of the height of the units, as well as the intention of joining them together on a mat as they were in the model, we would not be able to move the piece out of Hesse's studio. Johns, Singer, and I then persuaded Hesse to abandon the base and the connecting elements in favor of a random arrangement of the units. She was pleased by the way the individual units were turning out and, in her very weakened state, accepted our idea. When she went into the hospital again on March 21, work on the sculpture stopped.

When it became clear that Hesse would not survive a third brain operation, Johns could not bring himself to continue working on the piece, and Singer and I were urged to complete it. The opening of the Corning exhibit was delayed to give us time to finish. Lacking direction from either Johns or Hesse, we installed the piece as best we could for the opening on May 14. Hesse was shown photographs and we were told that she was pleased with the result. She died on May 29.

If she had been in better health, Hesse would most probably have insisted on maintaining the arrangement of the model. After installing this piece on numerous occasions I have come to favor an arrangement that approximates the orientation of the model as closely as possible. Had the piece been built like the model, its poles

would have been supported by cords linking the units; being freestanding, it would have differed from all of Hesse's late works, hanging as they do from the ceiling or attached to the wall.

The L-shaped units of *Seven Poles* are not unique in Hesse's works and are a conflation of the shape of *Sans III* (89) and the technique of "Ice Piece" (94); the forms echo the seven gangly bent tubes of *Several* (19). As for the inspiration of the piece, various proposals have been made. The most probable suggestion and the one that seems most to match the spirit of the model was Ruth Vollmer's: *Seven Poles* was inspired by a group of Olmec standing figurines. Hesse and Vollmer had visited Mexico City in January 1968, and the Olmec group they would have seen in the National Museum of Anthropology is a ritual cache of sixteen figurines, 8 inches high, partially enclosed by long slender "celts" (blade-shaped uprights) placed in a semicircle outside the group of figurines. Hesse's model particularly recalls the Olmec group not, however, as a reference to personage, as has been suggested, but rather in the way the L-shaped units are organized. Hesse had earlier abstracted highly schematized formal features from other sculptures, that is, the "snakes" of *Laocoon* (31) and the "breasts" of *Ishtar* (21).

HESSE'S STUDIO, 1970

Appendix A Missing Sculptures

A1 **Oomamaboomba**

Because we have a good color photograph, this piece has been given a regular catalogue entry even though its location is unknown. See number 5.

A2 **Untitled**

1966

MATERIALS: Papier-mâché over balloon

SIZE: 23 × 20 in. (58.4 × 51.8 cm.)

PROVENANCE: Robert Ryman, New York. Fourcade Droll, New York

A3 **Untitled**

1966

MATERIALS: Wood shavings, glue, and rubber tubing

SIZE: 9 × 9 × 1 in. (22.9 × 22.9 × 2.5 cm.); attached cord: 84 in. (213.4 cm.)

PROVENANCE: Stolen from Droll/Kolbert Gallery, New York, circa 1984

Frame is not part of the sculpture.

A3

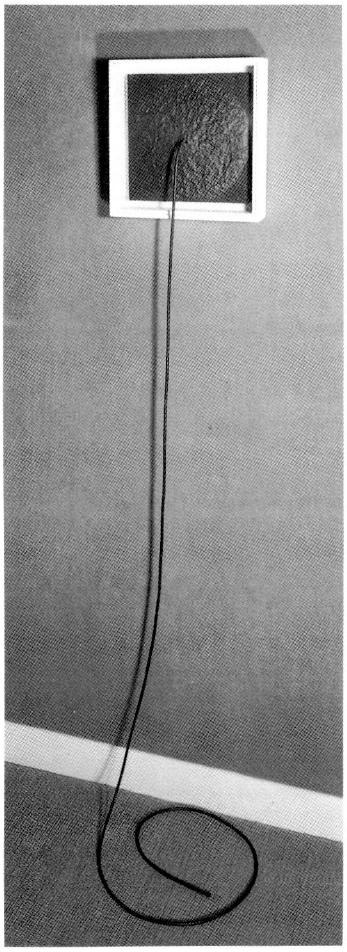

A4 **Untitled**

1967

MATERIALS: Sculp-Metal over steel washers and wood

SIZE: 8 × 8 in. (20.3 × 20.3 cm.)

COLLECTION: Present owner unknown

PROVENANCE: Dr. Helene Papanek, New York (According to Dr. Papanek's heirs, this piece was either sold or given away to someone caring for Dr. Papanek shortly before her death.)

A5 **Untitled**

1967

MATERIALS: Foam rubber, papier-mâché, and metal springs

SIZE: Each unit: 3 × 4 × 1 in. (7.6 × 10.2 × 2.5 cm.); height of each unit with spring: 9½ in. (24.1 cm.)

COLLECTION: Given by Lippard as that of Robert J. Berenson, New York (It has not been possible to locate Mr. Berenson to verify that the piece is still in his collection.)

Note: A1 and A3 were recovered in October 1988 as this book was going to press. They are now in the estate of Eva Hesse.

A4

A5

Appendix B Berkeley Test Pieces

1966

MATERIALS: See below.

SIZE: See below.

COLLECTION: University Art Museum, University of California, Berkeley, gift of Helen Hesse Charash, 1979

PROVENANCE: Estate of Eva Hesse

Photograph 1	nos. 18a, 18b	Two plaster tiles, 8 × 8 × 3/8 in., 8 × 8 × 1 in.
	nos. 17a, 17b	Two unfired clay blocks, 3 5/8 × 2 1/4 × 7/8 in. (possibly test pieces for *Sans I*)
	nos. 23a, 23b	Two plaster blocks, 3 1/2 × 3 1/8 × 1/2 in., 3 3/4 × 2 7/8 × 1 7/8 in. (possibly mold for *Sans III*)
	no. 15	Latex wire screen, 3 1/2 × 4 5/8 × 2 3/8 in. (test piece for *Sans* series)
	nos. 6a, 6b, 6c	Wax and latex units, 4 × 3 × 2 1/4 in.
Photograph 2	no. 12	Ten black wax squares in slanted stack configuration, variable dimensions, ca. 1 × 1 in.
	no. 9	Nine wax discs, irregular, 1 in. thick, 3 in. in diameter
	no. 24	Thirteen latex-over-cheesecloth units, each 7 × 4 1/2 × 1 in. (similar to no. 87)
	no. 3	Ten circular latex units, 2 3/4 in. in diameter
Photograph 3	no. 11	Latex and staples forming a ring; each unit, 3/8 × 5 1/2 in.; entire piece, 7 1/2 × 6 3/4 × 1 1/2 in.
	no. 16	Latex-and-cloth rectangle, 3 3/4 × 7 1/2 in.
	no. 10	Cloth-covered latex folded over and wrapped with narrow cloth strips, 9 5/8 × 2 1/2 × 1 in.
	no. 8	Folded metal screen covered with latex, pins, 5 1/8 × 3 1/2 × 1 1/4 in.
	no. 4	Latex, 8 × 2 3/8 × 7/8 in.

1

2

3

Photograph 4	no. 5	Two units, wood, gray paint, papier-mâché, nuts, and bolts, $4 \times 3\frac{3}{4} \times 1\frac{5}{8}$ in.
	nos. 26a, 26b	Two units, molded paper; one an irregular hemisphere, ca. 6 in. in diameter; one elliptical, $12\frac{3}{4} \times 3\frac{1}{2} \times 1\frac{3}{8}$ in.
	no. 21	Cardboard and gray paint cylinder, $3\frac{1}{4}$ in. in diameter, 3 in. high
	no. 22	Irregular latex cylinder, $3\frac{3}{8}$ in. in diameter, $3\frac{1}{8}$ in. high (test piece for *Repetition Nineteen I*)
Photograph 5	nos. 27a–i	Ten hemispherical pieces, latex, metallic pigment, and paint, varying in diameter, $2\frac{1}{4}$–$3\frac{1}{4}$ in.
	no. 28	Roughly textured latex hemisphere, $4\frac{5}{8} \times 2\frac{7}{8} \times 1\frac{3}{4}$ in.
	no. 29	Collapsed latex hemisphere, $6 \times 3 \times 1\frac{5}{8}$ in.

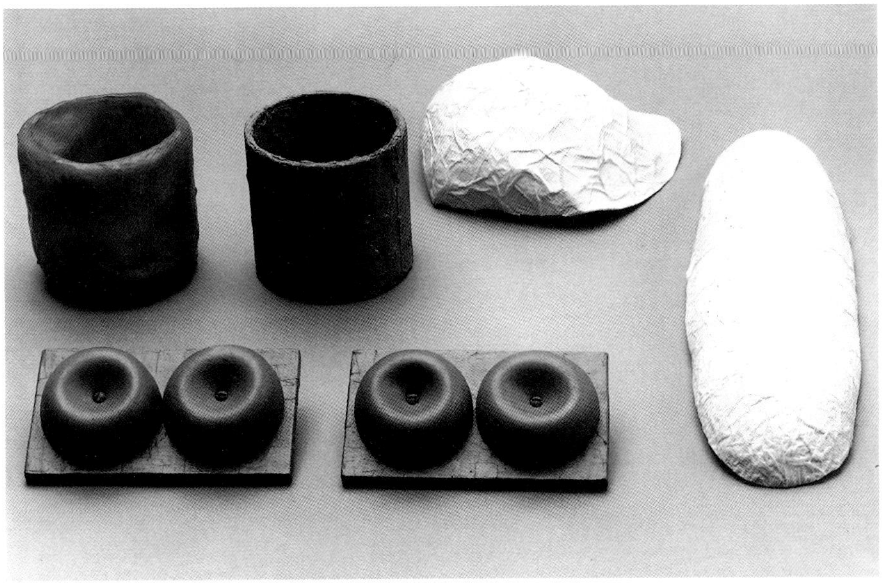
4

5

Appendix C Eva Hesse Archive

This information, from the Eva Hesse Archive at the Allen Memorial Art Museum, Oberlin College, Oberlin, Ohio, has been compiled by the Allen Memorial Art Museum.

DRAWINGS

1 Study for *Laocoon*, 1965–1966
Pen, ink, and pencil on paper, 77.52.1

2 Untitled (after *Laocoon*), 1968
Gouache and pencil on paper, 77.52.2

3 Study for *Contingent*, 1969
Pencil on yellow lined paper, 77.52.3

4 Study for *Contingent*, 1969
Pencil on yellow lined paper, 77.52.4

5 Study for *Contingent*, 1969
Pencil on yellow lined paper, 77.52.5

6 Study for *Contingent*, 1969
Pencil on yellow lined paper, 77.52.6

7 Study for *Contingent*, 1969
Pencil on yellow lined paper, 77.52.7

8 Study for *Repetition Nineteen*, 1967
Pencil on graph paper, 77.52.8

9 Study for *Repetition Nineteen*, 1967
Pencil on graph paper, 77.52.9

10 Untitled, 1967
Pencil on graph paper, 77.52.10

11 Untitled (after *Accretion*), 1967
Pencil on graph paper, 77.52.11

12 Untitled (after *Accretion*), 1967
Pencil on graph paper, 77.52.12

13 Untitled, 1967
Ink on graph paper, 77.52.13

14 Untitled, 1969
Pencil on yellow lined paper, 77.52.14

15 Untitled, 1968
Ink on stationery, 77.52.15

16 Untitled, 1967–1968
Pen and ink on unlined notebook paper, 77.52.16

17 Untitled, 1967–1968
Pen and ink on unlined notebook paper, 77.52.17

18 Untitled, 1967–1968
Pen and ink on unlined notebook paper, 77.52.18

19 Untitled, ca. 1967–1968
Pen and ink on lined notebook paper, 77.52.19

20 Study for *Expanded Expansion*, 1969
Pen and ink on white paper, 77.52.20

21 Study for *Tori*, 1969
Pen and ink on white paper, 77.52.21

22 Untitled, 1967–1968
Pen and ink on white paper, 77.52.22

23 Study for *Untitled*, 1970
Pen and ink on white lined paper, 77.52.23

24 Study for *Untitled*, 1970
Pen and ink on white notebook paper, 77.52.24

25 Four notebook pages, 1966
Pen, ink, and pencil on white lined notebook paper, 77.52.25a–d

26 Four notebook pages, 1966
Pen and ink on white unlined notebook paper, 77.52.26a–d

27 Untitled, n.d.
Wax crayon and pencil, 82.102.10

28 Untitled, n.d.
Ballpoint pen, 82.102.12

29 Untitled, n.d.
Graphite pencil, 82.102.13

30 Untitled, n.d.
Wax crayon and pencil, 82.102.15

31 Untitled, n.d.
Collage with crayon and pencil, 82.102.25

32 Untitled, 1963
Pen and ink, wash, and watercolor on perforated sketchbook paper, 82.105.1

33 Untitled, 1960–1961
Ink with wash, pastel, crayon, and graphite, 82.105.2

34 Untitled, 1963
Gouache and watercolor, 82.105.3

35 Untitled, ca. 1962
Graphite pencil and wax crayons on white wove paper, 82.105.4

36 Untitled, 1960
Gouache and inks on white wove paper, 82.105.5

37 Untitled, 1960
Gouache and ink on white wove paper, 82.105.6

38 Untitled, 1960
Gouache and ink on white wove paper, 82.105.7

39 Untitled, 1960–1961
Gouache and inks on white wove perforated sketchbook paper, 82.105.8

40 Untitled, ca. 1961
Ink with wash and watercolor, 82.105.9

41 Untitled, ca. 1961
Pen and ink with wash on white wove paper, 82.105.10

42 Untitled, 1960–1961
Ink with wash on white wove paper, 82.105.11

43 Untitled, ca. 1961
Pen and inks with wash on white wove paper, 82.105.12

44 Untitled, 1960–1961
Ink with washes and crayon on white wove paper, 82.105.13

45 Untitled, ca. 1961
Ink with wash on white wove paper, 82.105.14

46 Untitled, ca. 1961
Pen and ink on white wove paper, 82.105.15

47 Untitled, ca. 1961
Ink with washes on white wove paper, 82.105.16

48 Untitled, ca. 1961
Ink with wash and watercolor on white wove paper, 82.105.17

49 Untitled, 1960–1961
Inks with wash on white wove paper, 82.105.18

50 Untitled, 1960–1961
Inks with wash on white wove paper, 82.105.19

51 Untitled, ca. 1961
Pen and ink with washes on white wove paper, 82.105.20

52 Untitled, ca. 1961
Pen and ink with wash and crayon on white wove paper, 82.105.21

53 Untitled, ca. 1961
Pen and ink with wash on white wove paper, 82.105.22

54 Untitled, ca. 1961
Inks with wash on white wove paper, 82.105.23

55 Untitled, ca. 1961
Inks with wash on white wove paper, 82.105.24

56 Untitled, ca. 1961
Recto: Ink with wash on white wove paper
Verso: Graphite pencil on white wove paper, 82.105.25

57 Untitled, ca. 1961
Ink, wash, and watercolor on white wove paper, 82.105.26

58 Untitled, ca. 1961
Recto: Ink with wash and traces of crayon on white wove paper
Verso: Ink with wash and crayon on white wove paper, 82.105.27

59 Untitled, 1963
Collage of pen and inks with wash, wax crayon, watercolor, and gouache on white wove paper, 82.105.28

60 Untitled, ca. 1961
Ink with washes and wax crayon on white wove paper, 82.105.29

61 Untitled, 1960
Watercolor and ink with wash on white wove paper, 82.105.30

62 Untitled, 1960
Ink with washes on white wove paper, 82.105.31

63 Untitled, 1960–1961
Ink with washes on white wove paper, 82.105.32

64 Untitled, 1960
Pen and ink with wash on white wove paper, 82.105.33

65 Untitled, 1960–1961
Watercolor and ink with wash on white wove paper, 82.105.34

66 Untitled, 1960–1961
Ink with wash on white wove paper, 82.105.35

67 Untitled, ca. 1961
Ink with washes on white wove paper, 82.105.36

68 Untitled, 1963
Gouache, watercolor, pen and ink, ballpoint pen, and wax crayon on white wove perforated sketchbook paper, 82.105.37

69 Untitled, 1960–1961
Inks with wash and watercolor on white wove paper, 82.105.38

70 Untitled, 1963
Collage with felt-tip pen, gouache, wax crayon, and graphite pencil on white wove paper, 82.105.39

71 Untitled, 1963
Collage with graphite pencil, watercolor, wax crayon, and felt-tip pen on white wove paper, 82.105.40

72 Untitled, late 1950s
Pen and ink and watercolor on white wove paper, 82.105.41

73 Untitled, ca. 1960
Inks with wash on white wove paper, 82.105.42

74 Untitled, ca. 1961
Ink with washes on white wove paper, 82.105.43

75 Untitled, 1960
Gouache and pen and ink with washes on white wove paper, 82.105.44

76 Untitled, 1964
Pen, watercolor, and gouache, 83.106.1

77 Untitled, n.d.
Watercolor and pen, 83.106.2

78 Untitled, n.d.
Watercolor and pencil on paper, 83.106.3

79 Untitled, 1964
Watercolor and graphite pencil on green card, 83.106.4

80 Untitled, n.d.
Ink stamp, watercolor, gouache, pencil, and silver paint, 83.106.5

81 Untitled, 1964
Watercolor and gouache collage, 83.106.6

82 Untitled, 1962
Graphite pencil and crayon collage mounted on board, 83.106.7

83 Untitled, n.d.
Watercolor and crayon, 83.109.1

84 Untitled, 1963
Graphite pencil, crayon, and gouache collage, 83.109.2

85 Untitled, 1963
Graphite pencil, gouache, and felt-tip pen, 83.109.3

86 Untitled, n.d.
Pen, ink, watercolor, gouache, and crayon, 83.109.4

87 Untitled, n.d.
Graphite pencil, ink, gouache, and felt-tip pen, 83.109.5

88 Untitled, n.d.
Gouache, 83.109.6

89 Untitled, n.d.
Watercolor, 83.109.7

90 Untitled, n.d.
Graphite pencil, 83.109.8

91 Untitled, n.d.
Ink, gouache, and watercolor, 83.109.9

92 Untitled, 1962
Pencil, gouache, and crayon, 83.109.10

93 Untitled, n.d.
Pencil and crayon collage, 83.109.11

94 Untitled, n.d.
Graphite pencil and crayon, 83.109.12

95 Untitled, n.d.
Watercolor and graphite pencil, 83.109.13

96 Untitled, n.d.
Graphite pencil, ink, watercolor, and gouache, 83.109.14

97 Untitled, 1962
Graphite pencil, crayon, felt-tip pen, and gouache collage, 83.109.15

98 Untitled, n.d.
Pen and ink, 83.109.16

99 Untitled (Two Figures), n.d.
Graphite pencil, 83.109.17

100 Untitled (Two Figures), n.d.
Graphite pencil, 83.109.18

101 Untitled, n.d.
Graphite pencil, 83.109.19

102 Untitled ("About Boxes and Arrows"), n.d.
Ink and gouache collage, 83.109.20

103 Untitled, n.d.
Pen, gouache, and watercolor, 83.109.21

104 Untitled, n.d.
Woodblock, 83.109.22

105 Untitled, n.d.
Gouache, 83.109.23

106 Untitled, n.d.
Ink, crayon, and gouache on unlined notebook paper, 83.109.24

107 Untitled, n.d.
Graphite pencil and felt-tip pen, 83.109.25

108 Untitled, n.d.
Gouache, 83.109.26

109 Untitled (Standing Figure), n.d.
Pen and ink, 83.109.27

110 Untitled (Seated Woman), n.d.
Graphite pencil and charcoal, 83.109.28

111 Untitled (Standing Nude), n.d.
Graphite pencil, 83.109.29

112 Untitled (Seated Nude), n.d.
Charcoal, 83.109.30

113 Untitled (Figure Studies), n.d.
Pen and ink, 83.109.31

114 Untitled, n.d.
Pen and ink, 83.109.32

115 Untitled, 1952
Watercolor, 83.109.35

116 Untitled (Still Life), n.d.
Watercolor, 83.109.36

117 Untitled (Two Figures), n.d.
Graphite pencil, 83.109.37

118 Untitled (Female Torso), n.d.
Graphite pencil, 83.109.38

119 Untitled (Female Nude in Studio), n.d.
Ink on paper, 83.109.39

120 Untitled, 1962
Graphite pencil and felt-tip pen, 83.109.40

121 Untitled (Still Life), n.d.
Watercolor, 83.109.41

122 Untitled (Still Life), n.d.
Watercolor, 83.109.42

123 Untitled (Standing Nude), n.d.
Pen and ink, 83.109.43

124 Untitled (Landscape), n.d.
Watercolor, 83.109.44

125 Untitled, n.d.
Graphite pencil on paper, 83.109.46

126 Untitled, n.d.
Ballpoint pen on paper, 83.109.47

127 Untitled, n.d.
Ballpoint pen on paper, 83.109.48

128 Untitled ("Bob"), n.d.
Graphite pencil on paper, 83.109.49

129 Untitled, 1962
Graphite pencil and Conté crayon collage, 83.109.50

130 Untitled, n.d.
Ballpoint pen and crayon collage, 83.109.51

131 Untitled, n.d.
Ballpoint pen and crayon, 83.109.52

132 Untitled, n.d.
Graphite pencil, 83.109.53

133 Untitled, n.d.
Graphite pencil, 83.109.54

134 Untitled (Female Nude), n.d.
Ink on paper, 83.109.55

135 Drawing tablet cover with pencil sketch, n.d.
Graphite pencil, 83.109.56

136 Untitled (Female Nude), n.d.
Graphite pencil, 83.109.57

137 Untitled, n.d.
Diluted ink, 83.109.58

138 Untitled (Nude), n.d.
Ink on paper, 83.109.59

139 Untitled (Female Torso), n.d.
Ink on paper, 83.109.60

140 Untitled, n.d.
Crayon and watercolor, 83.109.61

141 Untitled (Figure Studies), n.d.
Sanguine, 83.109.62

142 Untitled (Nude), n.d.
Graphite pencil, 83.109.63

143 Untitled (Walking Figure), n.d.
Charcoal on paper, 83.109.64

144 Untitled, n.d.
Graphite pencil on paper, 83.109.65

145 Untitled, n.d.
Ink on paper, 83.109.66

146 Untitled (Recto: Study of Hand; verso: Study of Foot), n.d.
Charcoal on paper, 83.109.68

147 Untitled (Two Figures), n.d.
Graphite pencil on paper, 83.109.69

148 Untitled (Nude), n.d.
Graphite pencil, 83.109.70

149 Untitled, n.d.
Graphite pencil on paper, 83.109.71

150 Untitled, n.d.
Ink on paper, 83.109.72

151 Untitled, n.d.
Ink on paper, 83.109.73

152 Untitled, n.d.
Gouache on paper, 83.109.77

153 Untitled, n.d.
Graphite pencil on paper, 83.109.78

154 Untitled, n.d.
Ink on paper, 83.109.79

155 Untitled, n.d.
Graphite pencil on paper, 83.109.80

156 Untitled, n.d.
Graphite pencil on paper, 83.109.81

157 Untitled, n.d.
Graphite pencil on paper, 83.109.82

158 Untitled, n.d.
Pen on paper, 83.109.83

159 Untitled, 1962
Felt-tip pen, graphite pencil, ink, and crayon collage, 83.109.84

160 Untitled (Landscape), n.d.
Watercolor on paper, 83.109.86

161 Untitled, n.d.
Pen on paper, 83.109.87

162 Untitled, n.d.
Pen on paper, 83.109.88

163 Untitled, n.d.
Graphite pencil on paper, 83.109.89

164 Untitled (Female Nude), n.d.
Ink on paper, 83.109.90

165 Untitled, n.d.
Ink on paper, 83.109.91

166 Untitled, n.d.
Graphite pencil on paper, 83.109.92

167 Untitled, n.d.
Watercolor on paper, 83.109.93

168 Untitled, n.d.
Graphite pencil on paper, 83.109.95

169 Untitled, n.d.
Gouache and charcoal drawing laid on board, 83.109.96

170 Untitled (Still Life), n.d.
Charcoal and white chalk on board, 83.109.97

171 Untitled, n.d.
Ink and gouache on paper, 83.109.98

172 Unidentified pieces (miscellaneous fragments) 83.109.99

173 Untitled (Flower Still Life), n.d.
Graphite pencil and pastel on paper, 83.109.100

174 Untitled (Flower Still Life), n.d.
Tempera on paper attached to board, 83.109.101

175 Untitled, 1967
Ink on graph paper, 84.48

176 Untitled, 1965
Black and colored inks on white paper, 86.27

1–31, 76–174: Gift of Helen Hesse Charash; 32–75: Gift of Philip Droll through Donald Droll; 175: Friends of Art Endowment Fund; 176: Gift of Ellen H. Johnson in Memory of Chloe Hamilton Young

BOX 2*

1 Diary, 1969: Datebook

2 Notebook, 1969 (postal coupon in back cover): Addresses, appointments, party list, materials list

3 Datebook/Diary, 1967: Addresses, appointments, doodles

4 Datebook/Diary, 1970: Appointments, notes written at Christmas in hospital (loose pages clipped to pages for March)

5 Spiral notebook, April 1966: Journal/diary, addresses, sketches, newspaper clipping

6 Bound notebook, 1964–1965: Diary (Kettwig-am-Ruhr, West Germany), sketches/doodles, show list

7 Small diary/datebook, 1964: Diary/journal

8 Small diary/datebook, 1965: Diary/journal

9 Large diary, "Record 1967," gift from Sol LeWitt, December 1966: Mostly unused, introduction in front by Hesse, two notes for pieces on inside back cover

10 Bound notebook, September 1958: Diary, small sketches for paintings

11 Folder, "Fischbach Gallery": Notes on materials and methods marked "Teaching Notes," letter of 1966

12 Diary, 1969: Diary entries, notes, reminders

13 Looseleaf binder, 1969 (?): Addresses, party lists, materials lists

14 Datebook/diary, 1955: Diary entries, lists, appointments

15 Datebook, 1968: Appointments, phone numbers

**There is no Box 1.*

16 University notebook, late 1966–early 1967: Diary entries, sketches, inserted letter to Tom Doyle (never sent?)

17 University notebook, late 1966: Diary entries, phone numbers, list of works (on back cover), list of journal articles, sketches

18 Bound notebook (German), 1965: Inserted notes (about Tom Doyle), drawings (inside back cover), diary entries

19 Manila envelope: transcripts of Cindy Nemser interview, correspondence concerning it

20 Manila folder: School papers

BOX 3

1 Folder: Memorabilia, first money earned for artwork, Paul Klee quotes from Victor Moscoso, Mother's Day cards

2 Manila envelope, "Eva's Students," 1969: "What is art?" assignment

3 Spiral notebook: Yale class notes (Italian), book list, pages headed "dream nite March 23 to 24," figure sketch, paper on painting

4 Spiral notebook: Yale class notes (history of art—Italian Renaissance)

5 Spiral notebook: Artist quotes (Maillol, Matisse, Picasso, et al.), notes on nature of art and problem of aesthetic form

6 Spiral notebook: Yale class notes (Greek art), loose pages of writing about a dream

7 Scrapbook: correspondence with *Seventeen* magazine, clippings of Hesse's artwork published in the magazine (with accompanying brief interview), 1954; clippings and commencement material from Yale University, 1959

8 Manila folder: "Officialdom": report cards and diplomas from junior high (1951) through Cooper Union (1957)

9 Notebook, 1956: English class notes and paper drafts from Cooper Union; doodles

10 Yale notebook: October 1958–May 1959: Painting class notes, notes on plays, diary entries, poetry (haikus), inserted class handouts, calligraphy examples

BOX 4

1 Catalog, "Something Else Press, 1969–70"

2 Yearbook, *The Palette, 1952*, from the School of Industrial Art; photograph of Hesse on page 47 in the "Window Display" section

3 Collage-covered notebook, 1954(?): Camp Lebanon memorabilia

4 Red plastic notebook, "Scribbles": Business cards of suppliers, contractors, etc., miscellaneous phone numbers

5 Slide envelope, 1967 (?): Slides of works by Hesse, Donald Graham, one Sol LeWitt piece

6 Slide box, 1958–1959: Slides of paintings

7 Brown folder: Journal articles, newspaper clippings, reviews; letters to and from other artists; exhibition announcements; one slide and one photograph

BOX 5

1 Manila envelope: 189 postcards, February 1957–May 1970; most from Lucy Lippard and Sol LeWitt; others from Carl Andre, Gioia Timpanelli, Mel Bochner, Dan Graham; most from 1969 to Hesse in the hospital

2 Folder, "Correspondence": bills, empty envelope from F. Arnhard Scheidt, tea bag labeled "Consumable Art Event"

3 Manila folder: 189 postcards, February 1957–May 1970; most from Lucy Lippard and Sol LeWitt; many from Bob and Nancy Smithson, Mel Bochner, Dan Graham, and Hesse's father and stepmother

BOX 6

1 Folder (C): Business correspondence

2 Folder (D): Business correspondence, latest dated September 6, 1970 (addressed to Mrs. Helen Charash)

3 Correspondence folder (#12), 1957–1959: Letters, mostly from "Mark"

4 Correspondence folder (A), 1969: Letters

5 Correspondence folder (#13): Letters

6 Letter: From Hesse to the assistant director of the Milwaukee Art Center, Jack Taylor, January 24, 1970

7 *Idem*, December 27, 1968

8 *Idem*, April 4, 1969

9 *Idem*, 1969

10 *Idem*, May 17, 1968

11 *Idem*, April 30, 1969

12 *Idem*, June 18, 1969

13 Wax-paper envelope: Correspondence between Hesse and Jack Taylor

14 Manila folder, "Correspondence: Dorothy James," 1967–1968: Letters from James to Hesse

15 Brown folder, "Postcards": Empty

16 Brown folder (F): Assorted late letters

17 Folder, "B, Correspondence," 1960–1966: Thirty-six items, including many letters from F. Arnhard Scheidt

18 Folder, "C, Business Correspondence,": June 1951–November 1968: Thirty-two items, including several undated pieces and some responses from Hesse penciled onto some of the pieces

19 Folder, "D, Correspondence, Undated": Twenty-nine assorted items

20 Folder, "E, Correspondence," 1969: Twenty items

21 Folder, "11, Correspondence, Undated," up to 1967: Thirty-three items, including eighteen pieces from Rosalyn (Rosie) Goldman at Woodstock, 1961, and elsewhere

22 Folder, "16, Correspondence," 1944–1956: Twenty-three items, including letter from Hesse to her mother, letters from her mother, 1944–1945 (in both English and German)

BOX 7

1 Manila folder, "Photographs of Drawings," 1966–1970: Photographs of drawings

2 Brown folder ("Photographs"): Photographs of friends, work

3 Brown folder (H): Notes, drawings, unmailed letters

4 Manila folder ("E.H. primarily her letters to Papanek"): Letters from Hesse to Dr. Helene Papanek

5 Blue graph notebook: One or two pages of drawings/doodles

6 Large German artist's notebook: Work in pencil, crayon, and paint; probably the work of children

7 Folder: Sketches, notes for sculptures

8 Folder, "Personal Writings"

9 Folder, "Essays by Lucy Lippard": "Tom Doyle" preface for Düsseldorf exhibition, 1965; "Eros Presumptive," 1967

10 Folder, "Correspondence": Letters, 1966–1968, including pieces from F. Arnhard Scheidt, Dorothy James, Grace Wapner

11 Folder, "Exhibition Catalogs and Announcements"

12 Folder, "Medical Info."

13 Folder, "Eva Hesse Bibliography, Lucy Lippard": Museum and gallery biographies (Museum of Modern Art, Fischbach, et al.)

14 Five-inch reel tape, "Acoustic Guide for Finch College 'Art in Process IV,' " 1969

15 Foam-core flats: drawings, sketches

BOX 8

Assorted catalogues

BOX 9

Assorted publications on Hesse

BOX 10

1 Assorted catalogues, posters, gallery announcements, and invitations mentioning Hesse, some of them reproducing her sculpture

2 Photographs: Twenty-three photographs of paintings and drawings at Yale; twenty-seven used in Lucy Lippard, *Eva Hesse* (1976); four of sculpture; thirteen of Hesse

3 Clippings, reviews, posthumous articles

BOX 11

1 Unmatted drawings: Three sheets, one with text "New Year's, 1970 in hospital . . ."

2 Unmatted drawings: Nine pieces

3 Unmatted works: Drawings and prints

4 Unmatted lithographs

5 Folder, "Unmatted Drawings": Nine works on paper in pencil, crayon, marker, and paint

6 Folder, "Unmatted works": Thirty-six still lifes, landscapes, nudes, abstract works in pen and ink, pencil, and watercolor

7 *Idem*

Exhibition and Publication History for Catalogue Entries

Full citations of publications and exhibitions can be found in the Bibliography and the Exhibitions section, respectively, beginning on pages 264 and 268. There as here, all entries are listed chronologically. "[Gr]" indicates a group exhibition, for which the corresponding full citation is in the Group Exhibitions section beginning on page 268. Exhibition catalogues are cited in the Exhibitions section rather than the Bibliography. For works mentioned in an exhibition catalogue but not shown, the citation below is under "Publication History," with the corresponding full citation in the Exhibitions section.

1 EXHIBITION HISTORY:
Kunstverein, 1965, no. 1
Guggenheim, 1972, no. 3, ill.
Whitechapel, 1979, no. 1, ill.
Rose Art Museum, 1985, no. 30
PUBLICATION HISTORY:
Lippard, 1976, cat. no. 1, p. 38, fig. 46

2 EXHIBITION HISTORY:
Kunstverein, 1965, no. 2
Moderna Museet, 1984, no. 40, p. 211 [Gr]
PUBLICATION HISTORY:
Lippard, 1976, cat. no. 2, p. 40, fig. 48

3 EXHIBITION HISTORY:
Kunstverein, 1965, no. 3
PUBLICATION HISTORY:
Lippard, 1976, cat. no. 3, p. 40, fig. 49

4 EXHIBITION HISTORY:
Kunstverein, 1965, no. 4
Rose Art Museum, 1985, no. 31
PUBLICATION HISTORY:
Lippard, 1976, cat. no. 4, p. 41, fig. 51
Moderna Museet, 1984, p. 122, ill. [Gr]

5 EXHIBITION HISTORY:
Kunstverein, 1965, no. 5
PUBLICATION HISTORY:
Lippard, 1976, cat. no. 5, p. 41, fig. 52 (printed in reverse)

6 EXHIBITION HISTORY:
Kunstverein, 1965, no. 6
Guggenheim, 1972, no. 4, ills.
Mayor Gallery, 1974
Whitechapel, 1979, no. 2, ill.
PUBLICATION HISTORY:
Shearer, catalogue foreword in Mayor Gallery, 1974
Lippard, 1976, cat. no. 6, p. 42, fig. 53
Hill, July 1979, p. 41

7 EXHIBITION HISTORY:
Kunstverein, 1965, no. 7
Moderna Museet, 1984, no. 38 [Gr]
PUBLICATION HISTORY:
Lippard, 1976, cat. no. 7, p. 42, fig. 54 (printed in reverse)

8 EXHIBITION HISTORY:
Kunstverein, 1965, no. 8
PUBLICATION HISTORY:
Lippard, 1976, cat. no. 8, p. 43, fig. 55

9 EXHIBITION HISTORY:
Kunstverein, 1965, no. 9
Kent Fine Art, 1987, pl. 15 [Gr]
PUBLICATION HISTORY:
Lippard, 1976, cat. no. 8, p. 43, fig. 56

10 EXHIBITION HISTORY:
Kunstverein, 1965, no. 10
Moderna Museet, 1984, no. 39 [Gr]
Kunstmuseum, 1987, p. 225, ill. (mistakenly titled *C-Clamp Blues*) [Gr]
PUBLICATION HISTORY:
Lippard, 1976, cat. no. 10, p. 44, fig. 58 (mistakenly titled *C-Clamp Blues*; printed in reverse)

11 EXHIBITION HISTORY:
Kunstverein, 1965, no. 11
Guggenheim, 1972, no. 1, ill.
Moderna Museet, 1984, no. 36 [Gr]
Kunstmuseum, 1987, p. 226, ill. (mistakenly titled *Pink*) [Gr]
PUBLICATION HISTORY:
Lippard, 1976, cat. no. 11, p. 44, fig. 57 (mistakenly titled *Pink*)

12 EXHIBITION HISTORY:
Kunstverein, 1965, no. 12
Guggenheim, 1972, no. 2, ill.
PUBLICATION HISTORY:
Lippard, 1976, cat. no. 12, p. 45, fig. 59 (printed in reverse)

13 EXHIBITION HISTORY:
Kunstverein, 1965, no. 13
Moderna Museet, 1984, no. 41.
Rose Art Museum, 1985, no. 32
Kent Fine Art, 1987, pl. 16 [Gr]
PUBLICATION HISTORY:
Lippard, 1976, cat. no. 13, p. 45, fig. 60

14 EXHIBITION HISTORY:
Kunstverein, 1965, no. 14
Moderna Museet, 1984, no. 37 [Gr]
Pat Hearn Gallery, 1987
PUBLICATION HISTORY:
Lippard, 1976, cat. no. 14, p. 46, fig. 61

15 PUBLICATION HISTORY:
Lippard, 1976, cat. no. 15, p. 50, fig. 64

16 EXHIBITION HISTORY:
Guggenheim, 1972, no. 5, ill.
Whitechapel, 1979, no. 3, ill.
Pat Hearn Gallery, 1987
PUBLICATION HISTORY:
Lippard, 1976, cat. no. 16, p. 51, fig. 66

17 EXHIBITION HISTORY:
Graham Gallery, 1966 [Gr]
PUBLICATION HISTORY:
Lippard, 1976, cat. no. 17, p. 50, fig. 65

18 EXHIBITION HISTORY:
Fischbach Gallery, 1966 [Gr]
PUBLICATION HISTORY:
Lippard, 1976, cat. no. 18, p. 52, fig. 67
Schjeldahl, 1984, pl. 18

19 EXHIBITION HISTORY:
Fischbach Gallery, 1966 [Gr]
Guggenheim, 1972, no. 7, ill.
Whitechapel, 1979, no. 5, ill.
PUBLICATION HISTORY:
Lippard, 1976, cat. no. 19, p. 53, fig. 68
Schjeldahl, 1984, pl. 19

20 EXHIBITION HISTORY:
Guggenheim, 1972 (not in catalogue)
Storm King, 1978 [Gr]
Whitechapel, 1979, no. 6, ill.
Moderna Museet, 1984, no. 42, p. 126, ill. [Gr]
PUBLICATION HISTORY:
Lippard, 1976, cat. no. 20, p. 54, fig. 69

21 EXHIBITION HISTORY:
Graham Gallery, 1966 [Gr]
Guggenheim, 1972, no. 6, ill.
PUBLICATION HISTORY:
Lippard, 1976, cat. no. 21, p. 55, fig. 70
Rubin, 1984, p. 673, ill.

22 EXHIBITION HISTORY:
Graham Gallery, 1966 [Gr]
Detroit Institute, 1972, no. 4, ill.
Guggenheim, 1972, no. 8, ill.
Droll/Kolbert Gallery, 1977
Vancouver Art Gallery, 1977, pl. 13 [Gr]
Stedelijk Museum, 1978, no. 1, ill. [Gr]
Whitechapel, 1979, no. 7, ill.
Yale University, 1981, p. 45, ill. [Gr]
Centre Georges Pompidou, 1986, pp. 225, 243, ill. [Gr]
Museum of Contemporary Art, 1986–1988, pp. 138, 345, ill. [Gr]
PUBLICATION HISTORY:
Gruen, March 13, 1966, p. 32
Lippard, May 1966, p. 64
Nemser, May 1970, pp. 59–60, ill.
Pincus-Witten, November 1971, pp. 40, 42, 44, ill.
Hughes, January 1, 1973, p. 37, ill.
Lippard, 1976, cat. no. 22, p. 57, fig. 71
Parker and Pollock, 1981, pp. 153, 156, fig. 92
Johnson, in Allen Memorial Art Museum, 1982, p. 14, ill.

23 PUBLICATION HISTORY:
Lippard, 1976, cat. no. 23, p. 60, fig. 76

24 PUBLICATION HISTORY:
Lippard, 1976, p. 69, visible in fig. 88

25 PUBLICATION HISTORY:
Lippard, 1976, cat. no. 87, p. 101, visible in fig. 88

26 PUBLICATION HISTORY:
Lippard, 1976, cat. no. 35, p. 67, fig. 87

27 EXHIBITION HISTORY:
Storm King, 1978 [Gr]
Wesleyan University, 1981 [Gr]
Rose Art Museum, 1985, no. 34
David Winton Bell Gallery, 1987 [Gr]
PUBLICATION HISTORY:
Lippard, 1976, cat. no. 34, p. 67, fig. 86

28 EXHIBITION HISTORY:
Guggenheim, 1972, no. 10, ill. (exhibited only in New York)
PUBLICATION HISTORY:
Lippard, 1976, cat. no. 26, p. 60, fig. 78; also visible in photograph of Hesse's studio, fig. 88

29 EXHIBITION HISTORY:
Fitzwilliam Museum, 1977, no. 10 [Gr]
Whitechapel, 1979, no. 8
PUBLICATION HISTORY:
Lippard, 1976, cat. no. 27, p. 60, fig. 77

30 EXHIBITION HISTORY:
Whitechapel, 1979, no. 9, ill.
Museum of Contemporary Art, 1986–1988, p. 345 [Gr]
PUBLICATION HISTORY:
Lippard, 1976, cat. no. 28, pp. 6, 61, 216, fig. 79; also visible in photograph of Hesse's studio, fig. 88

31 EXHIBITION HISTORY:
Guggenheim, 1972, no. 11, ill. (exhibited only in New York and Buffalo)
Allen Memorial Art Museum, 1980, no. 25, pl. 12 [Gr]
PUBLICATION HISTORY:
Art Journal, Fall 1970, p. 6
Allen Memorial Art Museum Bulletin, Spring 1971, p. 239
Art Quarterly, Spring 1971, p. 139
Lippard, May–June 1971, p. 68
Levin, February 1973, pp. 71–73
Lippard, 1976, cat. no. 25, pp. 58–59, fig. 75
Apollo, February 1976, p. 131, fig. 6
Holt, 1979, p. 35, no. 25, ill.

32 EXHIBITION HISTORY:
Sidney Janis Gallery, 1970, no. 26, ill. [Gr]
Guggenheim, 1972, no. 14, ill.
Salem Fine Arts Center, 1972, no. 85, p. 54, ill. [Gr]
Whitechapel, 1979, no. 12, ill.
Grey Art Gallery and Study Center, New York, 1983 (exhibited only in New York; not part of the traveling exhibition that originated at the Allen Memorial Art Museum in 1982)

PUBLICATION HISTORY:
Nemser, May 1970, p. 59, ill.
Pincus-Witten, November 1971, pp. 37, 40, ill.
Baker, February 1973, p. 57, ill.
Shapiro, February 1973, p. 40, ill.
Lippard, 1976, cat. no. 31, pp. 62, 63, 216 (n. 13), figs. 80, 88

33 EXHIBITION HISTORY:
Whitechapel, 1979, no. 10, ill.
PUBLICATION HISTORY:
Lippard, 1976, cat. no. 29, p. 64, fig. 81

34 EXHIBITION HISTORY:
Whitechapel, 1979, no. 11
Moderna Museet, 1984, no. 46
PUBLICATION HISTORY:
Lippard, 1976, cat. no. 30, p. 64, fig. 82

35 EXHIBITION HISTORY:
Guggenheim, 1972, no. 9
Lippard, 1976, cat. no. 24, p. 65, fig. 83

36 EXHIBITION HISTORY:
Storm King, 1978 [Gr]
Wesleyan University, 1981 [Gr]
PUBLICATION HISTORY:
Lippard, 1976, cat. no. 32, p. 65, fig. 84

37 EXHIBITION HISTORY:
Guggenheim, 1972, no. 12, ill.
Whitechapel, 1979, no. 13, ill.
Pat Hearn Gallery, 1987
PUBLICATION HISTORY:
Lippard, 1976, cat. no. 37, p. 79, fig. 107

38 EXHIBITION HISTORY:
Fischbach Gallery, 1966 (made specifically for this exhibition and dismantled afterward) [Gr]
Moderna Museet, 1984, no. 47 (reconstruction of the piece made by Sol LeWitt and David Higgenbotham for this exhibition) [Gr]
PUBLICATION HISTORY:
Lippard, 1976, cat. no. 38, pp. 80–81, fig. 108

39 EXHIBITION HISTORY:
Guggenheim, 1972, no. 13, ill.
List Visual Arts Center, 1986, p. 15, fig. 16 [Gr]
PUBLICATION HISTORY:
Lippard, 1976, cat. no. 39, p. 81, fig. 109

40 EXHIBITION HISTORY:
Whitechapel, 1979, no. 19, ill.
Städtische Kunsthalle, 1987, p. 43, ill. [Gr]
PUBLICATION HISTORY:
Lippard, 1976, cat. no. 48, p. 90, fig. 121

41 EXHIBITION HISTORY:
Whitechapel, 1979, no. 20
Städtische Kunsthalle, 1987 [Gr]
PUBLICATION HISTORY:
Lippard, 1976, cat. no. 49, p. 90, fig. 122

42 EXHIBITION HISTORY:
Whitechapel, 1979, no. 21, ill.
PUBLICATION HISTORY:
Lippard, 1976, cat. no. 50, p. 90, fig. 123

43 EXHIBITION HISTORY:
Guggenheim, 1972, no. 16
PUBLICATION HISTORY:
Lippard, 1976, cat. no. 45, p. 90, fig. 124
Whitechapel, 1979, no. 18, ill. (not exhibited)

44 EXHIBITION HISTORY:
Grey Art Gallery, 1985–1986 [Gr]
Institute of Contemporary Art, 1987 [Gr]
Wallach Art Gallery, Columbia University, New York, 1987 (exhibited only in New York, not at the Städtische Kunsthalle, Düsseldorf, where the show originated) [Gr]
PUBLICATION HISTORY:
Lippard, 1976, cat. no. 51, p. 91, fig. 126

45 EXHIBITION HISTORY:
Guggenheim, 1972, no. 22, ill.
Vancouver Art Gallery, 1977 [Gr]
PUBLICATION HISTORY:
Lippard, 1976, cat. no. 58, p. 97, fig. 130

46 EXHIBITION HISTORY:
Guggenheim, 1972, no. 15
Whitechapel, 1979, no. 14, ill.
Pat Hearn Gallery, 1987 [Gr]
PUBLICATION HISTORY:
Lippard, 1976, cat. no. 40, p. 88, fig. 118

47 EXHIBITION HISTORY:
Vancouver Art Gallery, 1977 [Gr]
Whitechapel, 1979, no. 15
Sidney Janis Gallery, 1984 [Gr]
Moderna Museet, 1984, no. 54
PUBLICATION HISTORY:
Lippard, 1976, cat. no. 41, p. 88, fig. 119

48 EXHIBITION HISTORY:
Guggenheim, 1972, no. 20, ill.
Vancouver Art Gallery, 1977 [Gr]
PUBLICATION HISTORY:
Lippard, 1976, cat. no. 46, p. 88, fig. 117

49 EXHIBITION HISTORY:
Guggenheim, 1972, no. 19, ill.
PUBLICATION HISTORY:
Lippard, 1976, cat. no. 47, p. 89, fig. 120
Whitechapel, 1979, ill.

50 EXHIBITION HISTORY:
Guggenheim, 1972, no. 17, ill.
Whitechapel, 1979, no. 17
PUBLICATION HISTORY:
Lippard, 1976, cat. no. 44, p. 86, fig. 114

51 EXHIBITION HISTORY:
Fischbach Gallery, 1968
Guggenheim, 1972 (not in catalogue)
Whitechapel, 1979, no. 16
Moderna Museet, 1984, no. 51 [Gr]
Rose Art Museum, 1985, no. 35
Pat Hearn Gallery, 1987
PUBLICATION HISTORY:
Lippard, 1976, cat. no. 43, p. 87, fig. 116

52 EXHIBITION HISTORY:
Finch College, 1967–1968 [Gr]
Guggenheim, 1972, no. 18, ill.
Whitechapel, 1979, no. 25, ill.
Museum of Contemporary Art, 1986–1988, p. 345 [Gr]
PUBLICATION HISTORY:
Bochner, December 1967, p. 33
Lee, December 1967, p. 44
Lippard, May–June 1971, p. 159
Lippard, 1976, cat. no. 59, pp. 94–95, fig. 129
Hill, July 1979, pp. 42–43, ill.

53 EXHIBITION HISTORY:
Vancouver Art Gallery, 1977, p. 11, ill. [Gr]
Whitechapel, 1979, no. 22
Moderna Museet, 1984, no. 52 [Gr]
PUBLICATION HISTORY:
Lippard, 1976, cat. no. 55, p. 99, fig. 134

54 EXHIBITION HISTORY:
Whitechapel, 1979
PUBLICATION HISTORY:
Lippard, 1976, p. 101, fig. 138 (lower left corner) and fig. 141 (upper right corner)

55 EXHIBITION HISTORY:
Vancouver Art Gallery, 1977, p. 11, ill. [Gr]
Whitechapel, 1979, no. 23
Moderna Museet, 1984, no. 53 [Gr]
PUBLICATION HISTORY:
Lippard, 1976, cat. no. 56, p. 99, fig. 134

56 EXHIBITION HISTORY:
Guggenheim, 1972, no. 21
PUBLICATION HISTORY:
Lippard, 1976, cat. no. 54, p. 99, fig. 135

57 EXHIBITION HISTORY:
Guggenheim, 1972, no. 23, ill. (labeled *Accession*)
Museum of Contemporary Art, 1977 [Gr]
PUBLICATION HISTORY:
Lippard, 1976, cat. no. 57, p. 104, fig. 145

58 EXHIBITION HISTORY:
Fischbach Gallery, 1968
Milwaukee Art Center, 1968, no. 39, p. 33, ill. [Gr]
Guggenheim, 1972, no. 24, ill.
Grand Rapids Art Museum, 1984 [Gr]
Whitney Museum at Philip Morris, 1985 [Gr]
Palacio de Velázquez, 1986 [Gr]
PUBLICATION HISTORY:
Lippard, 1976, cat. no. 70, p. 103, fig. 143

59 EXHIBITION HISTORY:
Guggenheim, 1972, no. 29, ill.
Storm King, 1978 [Gr]
Wadsworth Atheneum, 1987 [Gr]
PUBLICATION HISTORY:
Lippard, 1976, cat. no. 62, p. 98, fig. 132

60 PUBLICATION HISTORY:
Lippard, 1976, cat. no. 77, p. 98, fig. 131

61 EXHIBITION HISTORY:
Fischbach Gallery, 1968
Guggenheim, 1972, no. 28
PUBLICATION HISTORY:
Lippard, 1976, cat. no. 78, p. 98, fig. 133
Whitechapel, 1979, ill., and Kestner-Gesellschaft edition, 1979, p. 49, ill.

62 PUBLICATION HISTORY:
Lippard, 1976, cat. no. 60, p. 108, fig. 152

63 EXHIBITION HISTORY:
Pat Hearn Gallery, 1987 (Esman unit)
PUBLICATION HISTORY:
Lippard, 1976, cat. no. 61, p. 107, fig. 150

64 EXHIBITION HISTORY:
Fischbach Gallery, 1968 (all four units)
Guggenheim, 1972, no. 3, ill. (three estate units)
Droll/Kolbert Gallery, 1977 (three estate units)
Whitechapel, 1979, no. 26 (three estate units)
Pat Hearn Gallery, 1987 (Esman unit)
PUBLICATION HISTORY:
Lippard, 1976, cat. no. 69, p. 107, fig. 151 (three estate units)

65 EXHIBITION HISTORY:
Guggenheim, 1972, no. 26, ill. (LeWitt model)
Storm King, 1978 (LeWitt model) [Gr]
Wesleyan University, 1981 [Gr]
PUBLICATION HISTORY:
Lippard, cat. no. 64, p. 115, fig. 162 (Fischbach model)

66 EXHIBITION HISTORY:
Fischbach Gallery, 1968
Storm King, 1978 [Gr]
Pace Gallery, 1978–1979 [Gr]
PUBLICATION HISTORY:
Lippard, 1976, cat. no. 65, p. 112, fig. 157

67 EXHIBITION HISTORY:
Fischbach Gallery, 1968
Guggenheim, 1972, no. 27, ill.
Vancouver Art Gallery, 1977, p. 12, ill.
Whitechapel, 1979, no. 28, ill.
Moderna Museet, 1984, no. 55 [Gr]
Pat Hearn Gallery, 1987
PUBLICATION HISTORY:
Lippard, 1976, cat. no. 66, p. 113, fig. 158
Schjeldahl, 1984, vol. 1, no. 20, ill.

68 EXHIBITION HISTORY:
Fischbach Gallery, 1968
PUBLICATION HISTORY:
Lippard, 1976, cat. no. 68, p. 117, fig. 164

69 EXHIBITION HISTORY:
Fischbach Gallery, 1968
PUBLICATION HISTORY:
Lippard, 1976, cat. no. 67, p. 116, fig. 163

70 EXHIBITION HISTORY:
Guggenheim, 1972, no. 38, ill. (exhibited only in New York)
PUBLICATION HISTORY:
Lippard, 1976, cat. no. 86, p. 120, fig. 168

71 PUBLICATION HISTORY:
Lippard, 1976, cat. no. 87, p. 101, fig. 140

72 EXHIBITION HISTORY:
Whitechapel, 1979, no. 27
PUBLICATION HISTORY:
Lippard, 1976, cat. no. 88, p. 100, fig. 137

73 EXHIBITION HISTORY:
Fischbach Gallery, 1968
Flint Institute, 1968, no. 31 [Gr]
Institute of Contemporary Art, 1969 [Gr]
Guggenheim, 1972, no. 32, ill. (exhibited only in New York)
Museum of Contemporary Art, 1986–1988, pp. 139, 345, ill. [Gr]
PUBLICATION HISTORY:
Lippard, 1976, cat. no. 74, p. 109, fig. 153

74 EXHIBITION HISTORY:
Fischbach Gallery, 1968
Katonah Gallery, 1971, no. 2, cover ill. [Gr]
Stedelijk Museum, 1978, no. 2 [Gr]
Whitechapel, 1979, no. 29, ill.
Museum of Contemporary Art, 1983–1984, p. 230, ill. [Gr]
Merian-Park, 1984, pp. 171, 224, ill. [Gr]
PUBLICATION HISTORY:
Lippard, 1976, cat. no. 71, p. 130, fig. 177

75 EXHIBITION HISTORY:
Fischbach Gallery, 1968
Whitechapel, 1979, no. 30
PUBLICATION HISTORY:
Lippard, 1976, cat. no. 72, p. 103

76 EXHIBITION HISTORY:
Storm King, 1978 [Gr]
Grey Art Gallery, 1985 [Gr]
Wadsworth Atheneum, 1987 [Gr]
Städtische Kunsthalle, 1987 [Gr]
PUBLICATION HISTORY:
Lippard, 1976, cat. no. 73, p. 104, fig. 146

77 EXHIBITION HISTORY:
Weatherspoon Art Gallery, 1985 [Gr]
PUBLICATION HISTORY:
Lippard, 1976, cat. no. 81, p. 125, fig. 173

78 EXHIBITION HISTORY:
Vancouver Art Gallery, 1970, ill. [Gr]
Detroit Institute, 1972, no. 1, ill.
Guggenheim, 1972, no. 33, ill.
International Program, 1974, no. 15 (exhibited only in Melbourne) [Gr]
Stedelijk Museum, 1978, no. 4, ill. [Gr]
Whitechapel, 1979, no. 32, ill.
PUBLICATION HISTORY:
Lippard, May–June 1971, p. 71, ill.
Lippard, 1976, cat. no. 82, pp. 126–27, fig. 173

79 EXHIBITION HISTORY:
Fischbach Gallery, 1968 (all five units)
Whitney Museum, 1970 (two Whitney units) [Gr]
Whitney Museum, 1970–1971 (two Whitney units) [Gr]
Guggenheim, 1972, no. 34, ill. (two Whitney and Messite units)
Whitney Museum, 1975 (two Whitney units) [Gr]
Seibu Museum, 1976 (two Whitney units) [Gr]
Renaissance Society, 1977, no. 5, ill. (two Whitney units) [Gr]
Vancouver Art Gallery, 1977 (Messite unit) [Gr]
Storm King, 1978 (two Whitney units) [Gr]
Whitney Museum, 1982 (two Whitney units) [Gr]
Whitney Museum, 1983 (two Whitney units) [Gr]
Whitney Museum at Philip Morris, 1985 (two Whitney units) [Gr]
Whitney Museum, Stamford, 1985 (two Whitney units) [Gr]
Rose Art Museum, 1985 (two Whitney units)
Palacio de Velázquez, 1986 (two Whitney units) [Gr]
Pat Hearn Gallery, 1987 (Messite and Saatchi units)
PUBLICATION HISTORY:
Lippard, 1976, cat. no. 75, pp. 128–29, 133, figs. 176, 178

80 EXHIBITION HISTORY:
American Federation of Arts, 1968–1969 (piece created for this traveling exhibition) [Gr]
Fischbach Gallery, 1968
Aldrich Museum, 1969 [Gr]
Detroit Institute, 1972
Guggenheim, 1972, no. 37, ill.
Mayor Gallery, 1974
Columbus Museum, 1985 [Gr]
Hudson River Museum, 1985 [Gr]
PUBLICATION HISTORY:
Lippard, 1976, cat. no. 79, p. 122, fig. 171

65 EXHIBITION HISTORY:
Guggenheim, 1972, no. 26, ill. (LeWitt model)
Storm King, 1978 (LeWitt model) [Gr]
Wesleyan University, 1981 [Gr]
PUBLICATION HISTORY:
Lippard, cat. no. 64, p. 115, fig. 162 (Fischbach model)

66 EXHIBITION HISTORY:
Fischbach Gallery, 1968
Storm King, 1978 [Gr]
Pace Gallery, 1978–1979 [Gr]
PUBLICATION HISTORY:
Lippard, 1976, cat. no. 65, p. 112, fig. 157

67 EXHIBITION HISTORY:
Fischbach Gallery, 1968
Guggenheim, 1972, no. 27, ill.
Vancouver Art Gallery, 1977, p. 12, ill.
Whitechapel, 1979, no. 28, ill.
Moderna Museet, 1984, no. 55 [Gr]
Pat Hearn Gallery, 1987
PUBLICATION HISTORY:
Lippard, 1976, cat. no. 66, p. 113, fig. 158
Schjeldahl, 1984, vol. 1, no. 20, ill.

68 EXHIBITION HISTORY:
Fischbach Gallery, 1968
PUBLICATION HISTORY:
Lippard, 1976, cat. no. 68, p. 117, fig. 164

69 EXHIBITION HISTORY:
Fischbach Gallery, 1968
PUBLICATION HISTORY:
Lippard, 1976, cat. no. 67, p. 116, fig. 163

70 EXHIBITION HISTORY:
Guggenheim, 1972, no. 38, ill. (exhibited only in New York)
PUBLICATION HISTORY:
Lippard, 1976, cat. no. 86, p. 120, fig. 168

71 PUBLICATION HISTORY:
Lippard, 1976, cat. no. 87, p. 101, fig. 140

72 EXHIBITION HISTORY:
Whitechapel, 1979, no. 27
PUBLICATION HISTORY:
Lippard, 1976, cat. no. 88, p. 100, fig. 137

73 EXHIBITION HISTORY:
Fischbach Gallery, 1968
Flint Institute, 1968, no. 31 [Gr]
Institute of Contemporary Art, 1969 [Gr]
Guggenheim, 1972, no. 32, ill. (exhibited only in New York)
Museum of Contemporary Art, 1986–1988, pp. 139, 345, ill. [Gr]
PUBLICATION HISTORY:
Lippard, 1976, cat. no. 74, p. 109, fig. 153

74 EXHIBITION HISTORY:
Fischbach Gallery, 1968
Katonah Gallery, 1971, no. 2, cover ill. [Gr]
Stedelijk Museum, 1978, no. 2 [Gr]
Whitechapel, 1979, no. 29, ill.
Museum of Contemporary Art, 1983–1984, p. 230, ill. [Gr]
Merian-Park, 1984, pp. 171, 224, ill. [Gr]
PUBLICATION HISTORY:
Lippard, 1976, cat. no. 71, p. 130, fig. 177

75 EXHIBITION HISTORY:
Fischbach Gallery, 1968
Whitechapel, 1979, no. 30
PUBLICATION HISTORY:
Lippard, 1976, cat. no. 72, p. 103

76 EXHIBITION HISTORY:
Storm King, 1978 [Gr]
Grey Art Gallery, 1985–1986 [Gr]
Wadsworth Atheneum, 1987 [Gr]
Städtische Kunsthalle, 1987 [Gr]
PUBLICATION HISTORY:
Lippard, 1976, cat. no. 73, p. 104, fig. 146

77 EXHIBITION HISTORY:
Weatherspoon Art Gallery, 1985 [Gr]
PUBLICATION HISTORY:
Lippard, 1976, cat. no. 81, p. 125, fig. 173

78 EXHIBITION HISTORY:
Vancouver Art Gallery, 1970, ill. [Gr]
Detroit Institute, 1972, no. 1, ill.
Guggenheim, 1972, no. 33, ill.
International Program, 1974, no. 15 (exhibited only in Melbourne) [Gr]
Stedelijk Museum, 1978, no. 4, ill. [Gr]
Whitechapel, 1979, no. 32, ill.
PUBLICATION HISTORY:
Lippard, May–June 1971, p. 71, ill.
Lippard, 1976, cat. no. 82, pp. 126–27, fig. 173

79 EXHIBITION HISTORY:
Fischbach Gallery, 1968 (all five units)
Whitney Museum, 1970 (two Whitney units) [Gr]
Whitney Museum, 1970–1971 (two Whitney units) [Gr]
Guggenheim, 1972, no. 34, ill. (two Whitney and Messite units)
Whitney Museum, 1975 (two Whitney units) [Gr]
Seibu Museum, 1976 (two Whitney units) [Gr]
Renaissance Society, 1977, no. 5, ill. (two Whitney units) [Gr]
Vancouver Art Gallery, 1977 (Messite unit) [Gr]
Storm King, 1978 (two Whitney units) [Gr]
Whitney Museum, 1982 (two Whitney units) [Gr]
Whitney Museum, 1983 (two Whitney units) [Gr]
Whitney Museum at Philip Morris, 1985 (two Whitney units) [Gr]
Whitney Museum, Stamford, 1985 (two Whitney units) [Gr]
Rose Art Museum, 1985 (two Whitney units)
Palacio de Velázquez, 1986 (two Whitney units) [Gr]
Pat Hearn Gallery, 1987 (Messite and Saatchi units)
PUBLICATION HISTORY:
Lippard, 1976, cat. no. 75, pp. 128–29, 133, figs. 176, 178

80 EXHIBITION HISTORY:
American Federation of Arts, 1968–1969 (piece created for this traveling exhibition) [Gr]
Fischbach Gallery, 1968
Aldrich Museum, 1969 [Gr]
Detroit Institute, 1972
Guggenheim, 1972, no. 37, ill.
Mayor Gallery, 1974
Columbus Museum, 1985 [Gr]
Hudson River Museum, 1985 [Gr]
PUBLICATION HISTORY:
Lippard, 1976, cat. no. 79, p. 122, fig. 171

81 EXHIBITION HISTORY:
John Gibson Gallery, 1968 [Gr]
New Jersey State Museum, 1969, ill. [Gr]
Kunsthaus, 1972, no. 26, p. 33, ill. [Gr]
PUBLICATION HISTORY:
Lippard, 1976, cat. no. 80, p. 123, fig. 172

82 EXHIBITION HISTORY:
Fischbach Gallery, 1968
Guggenheim, 1972, no. 35, ill.
PUBLICATION HISTORY:
Lippard, 1976, cat. no. 85, p. 135, fig. 180

83 EXHIBITION HISTORY:
Galerie Ricke, 1968 [Gr]
John Gibson Gallery, 1968 [Gr]
Leo Castelli Warehouse, 1968 [Gr]
Kunsthalle, 1969, ill. [Gr]
PUBLICATION HISTORY:
Lippard, 1976, cat. no. 83, p. 134, fig. 179

84 EXHIBITION HISTORY:
Kunsthalle, 1969, ill. [Gr]
Detroit Institute, 1972, no. 2, ill.
Guggenheim, 1972, no. 36, ill.
Vancouver Art Gallery, 1977 [Gr]
Whitechapel, 1979, no. 33, ill.
University Art Museum, 1982 [Gr]
PUBLICATION HISTORY:
Lippard, 1976, cat. no. 84, p. 134, fig. 179

85 EXHIBITION HISTORY:
David Winton Bell Gallery, 1980 [Gr]
PUBLICATION HISTORY:
Lippard, 1976, cat. no. 76, p. 121, fig. 170

86 PUBLICATION HISTORY:
Lippard, 1976, cat. no. 89, p. 99, fig. 136

87 EXHIBITION HISTORY:
Fischbach Gallery, 1968
Weatherspoon Art Gallery, 1984–1985 [Gr]
PUBLICATION HISTORY:
Lippard, 1976, cat. no. 63, p. 130, fig. 177a

88 EXHIBITION HISTORY:
Pat Hearn Gallery, 1987
PUBLICATION HISTORY:
Lippard, 1976, cat. no. 92, p. 136, fig. 181

89 PUBLICATION HISTORY:
Guggenheim, 1972, no. 47 (not exhibited)
Lippard, 1976, cat. no. 90, p. 140, fig. 183

90 EXHIBITION HISTORY:
Guggenheim, 1972, no. 41, ill.
International Program, 1974, no. 17, p. 30, ill. [Gr]
Storm King, 1978, p. 11, ill. [Gr]
Pat Hearn Gallery, 1987
PUBLICATION HISTORY:
Nemser, May 1970, p. 62, ill.
Lippard, 1976, cat. no. 93, p. 148, fig. 194
Rubin, 1984, p. 673, ill.

91 EXHIBITION HISTORY:
Whitney Museum, 1969 [Gr]
Owens-Corning Fiberglas Center, 1970, ill. [Gr]
Guggenheim, 1972, no. 40, ill. (exhibited only in New York)
Stedelijk Museum, 1978, no. 4 [Gr]
Whitechapel, 1979, no. 35, ill.
Grey Art Gallery and Study Center, New York, 1983 (exhibited only in New York; not part of the traveling exhibition that originated at the Allen Memorial Art Museum in 1982)
List Visual Arts Center, 1986, p. 14, fig. 15 [Gr]
Museum of Contemporary Art, 1986–1988 [Gr]
PUBLICATION HISTORY:
Nemser, May 1970, p. 61, ill.
Rose, January 1, 1973, p. 60, ill.
Lippard, 1976, cat. no. 94, p. 149, fig. 195

92 EXHIBITION HISTORY:
Whitney Museum, 1969, ill. [Gr]
Katonah Gallery, 1971, no. 1, p. 2, ill. [Gr]
Guggenheim, 1972, no. 42, ill.
Guggenheim, 1977 [Gr]
Whitney Museum, 1978 [Gr]
Guggenheim, 1985–1986, no. 159, p. 222, ill. [Gr]
Guggenheim, 1987–1988, no. 116, ill. [Gr]
PUBLICATION HISTORY:
Lippard, 1976, cat. no. 95, pp. 150–51, fig. 196
Barnett, 1980, no. 247, pp. 514–15, ill.
Johnson, Summer 1983, p. 118, ill.

93 EXHIBITION HISTORY:
Guggenheim, 1972, no. 44, ill.
Whitechapel, 1979, no. 34, ill.
PUBLICATION HISTORY:
Lippard, 1976, cat. no. 91, p. 139, fig. 182

94 EXHIBITION HISTORY:
Whitney Museum, 1969 [Gr]
Whitechapel, 1979, no. 36, ill.
Grey Art Gallery and Study Center, New York, 1983 (exhibited only in New York; not part of the traveling exhibition that originated at the Allen Memorial Art Museum in 1982)
Moderna Museet, 1984, no. 64, p. 136, ill. [Gr]
Museum of Art, Fort Lauderdale, 1986, p. 265, pl. 83 (labeled "ice piece") [Gr]
Palacio de Velázquez, 1986 [Gr]
PUBLICATION HISTORY:
Lippard, 1976, cat. no. 96, p. 153, fig. 197

95 EXHIBITION HISTORY:
Art Museum, Princeton University, 1970, no. 14, ill. [Gr]
Guggenheim, 1972, no. 46, ill.
High Museum of Art, 1972 [Gr]
Wadsworth Atheneum, 1975 [Gr]
PUBLICATION HISTORY:
Lippard, 1976, cat. no. 97, p. 156, fig. 199

96 EXHIBITION HISTORY:
Jewish Museum, 1969–1970 [Gr]
Guggenheim, 1972, no. 43, ill. (exhibited only in New York)
PUBLICATION HISTORY:
Lippard, 1976, cat. no. 98, pp. 162–63, fig. 208

97 PUBLICATION HISTORY:
Lippard, 1976, cat. no. 99, p. 166, fig. 210

98 EXHIBITION HISTORY:
Finch College, 1969–1970 [Gr]
Fondation Maeght, 1970 [Gr]
Art Institute of Chicago, 1972, cat. no. 20, ill. (won the Logan Award) [Gr]
Detroit Institute, 1972
Guggenheim, 1972, no. 45, ill.
International Program, 1974 (exhibited only in Sydney and Adelaide) [Gr]
PUBLICATION HISTORY:
Leider, February 1970, p. 70
Nemser, May 1970, cover ill.
Baker, January 1971, pp. 47–48, 60–62, ill.
Lippard, May–June 1971, pp. 70, 72, ill.
Pincus-Witten, November 1971, p. 42
Pincus-Witten, November 1972, p. 74
Levin, February 1973, p. 73
Terbell, October 6, 1973, p. 16
Nemser, Winter 1973, p. 14, ill.

Nemser, 1975, pp. 201–24, 229, ill.
Lippard, 1976, cat. no. 101, pp. 4, 15, 56, 155, 155, 158, 164–67, 182, fig. 209
Krauss, 1977, pp. 272, 275, fig. 204 (incorrectly credited to the collection of Mr. and Mrs. Victor Ganz)
Brown, "Eva Hesse," in Mayor Gallery, 1979
Krauss, "Eva Hesse," in Whitechapel, 1979, ill.
Johnson, "Drawing in Eva Hesse's Work," in Allen Memorial Art Museum, 1982, p. 9
Waldman, in Guggenheim, 1985, p. 223, no. 160, ill. [Gr]

99 PUBLICATION HISTORY:
Lippard, 1976, cat. no. 103, p. 170, fig. 215
Spaulding, 1987, pp. 166–67, ill.

100 EXHIBITION HISTORY:
Owens-Corning Fiberglas Center, 1970 [Gr]
Guggenheim, 1972, no. 42, ill.
Extended loan to the Art Institute of Chicago, November 11, 1974–April 17, 1979
Whitechapel, 1979, no. 38, ill.
PUBLICATION HISTORY:
Shapiro, February 1973, p. 45, ill.
Boice, March 1973, p. 90, ill.
Nemser, Winter 1973, pp. 12–13, ill.
Lippard, 1976, cat. no. 104, p. 168, fig. 214

101 EXHIBITION HISTORY:
Institute of Contemporary Art, 1970 [Gr]
Corcoran Gallery, 1971, ill. [Gr]
Guggenheim, 1972, no. 52, ill.
Museum Fridericianum, 1972 [Gr]
Droll/Kolbert Gallery, 1977
Vancouver Art Gallery, 1977, p. 14, ill. [Gr]
Whitechapel, 1979, no. 37, ill.
Museen der Stadt Köln, 1981, no. 859, p. 494, ill. [Gr]
Wallach Art Gallery, Columbia University, New York, 1987 (exhibited only in New York, not at the Städtische Kunsthalle, Düsseldorf, where the show originated)
Whitney Museum, 1988 [Gr]
PUBLICATION HISTORY:
"Fling, Dribble, and Drip," February 27, 1970, ill.
Pincus-Witten, November 1971, p. 38, ill.
Lippard, 1976, cat. no. 102, p. 173, fig. 218

102 EXHIBITION HISTORY:
Guggenheim, 1972, no. 50, ill.
PUBLICATION HISTORY:
Lippard, 1976, cat. no. 105, p. 179, fig. 223
Spector, "A Selection from the Notebooks of Eva Hesse," in Whitechapel, 1979, ill.

103 EXHIBITION HISTORY:
Owens-Corning Fiberglas Center, 1970, ill. [Gr]
Guggenheim, 1972, no. 51, ill.
Whitney Museum, 1976, no. 99, pp. 205, 341, ill. [Gr]
Stedelijk Museum, 1978, no. 3, ill. [Gr]
Whitechapel, 1979, no. 39, ill.
Centre Georges Pompidou, 1986, no. 260, pp. 226, 243, ill. [Gr]
PUBLICATION HISTORY:
Pincus-Witten, November 1971, pp. 40–41, ill.
Kramer, December 17, 1972, ill.
Shapiro, February 1973, p. 44, ill.
Lippard, 1976, cat. no. 106, pp. 176–77, fig. 221

Bibliography

BOOKS AND PERIODICALS

"It's All Yours" (includes statement by Hesse). *Seventeen,* September 1954, pp. 140–41, 161.

D[onald] J[udd]. "Exhibition at Heller Gallery." *Arts Magazine,* vol. 35, no. 7 (April 1961), p. 60.

M[ark] R[oskill]. "Drawings by Three Young Americans at Heller." *ARTnews,* vol. 60, no. 2 (April 1961), p. 64.

Brian O'Doherty. Review of exhibition at Heller Gallery. *The New York Times,* April 18, 1961, p. 34.

V[alerie] P[etersen]. "Exhibition at Stone Gallery." *ARTnews,* vol. 62, no. 3 (May 1963), p. 19.

John Gruen. "Art: Young Americans." *New York Herald Tribune* (magazine section), March 13, 1966, p. 32.

Lucy R. Lippard. "An Impure Situation." *Art International,* vol. 10, no. 5 (May 1966), pp. 60–65.

Robert Pincus-Witten. Review of exhibition at Graham Gallery. *Artforum,* vol. 4, no. 9 (May 1966), p. 54.

Grace Glueck. "New York Gallery Notes: ABC to Erotic." *Art in America,* vol. 54, no. 5 (September–October 1966), pp. 105–8.

Hilton Kramer. "It's Art But Does It Matter?" *The New York Times,* September 25, 1966, sec. 2, pp. 27, 29.

David Antin. "Another Category: 'Eccentric Abstraction.' " *Artforum,* vol. 5, no. 3 (November 1966), pp. 56–57.

M[el] B[ochner]. Review of exhibition at Fischbach Gallery. *Arts Magazine,* vol. 41, no. 1 (November 1966), pp. 57–58.

Robert Smithson. "Quasi-Infinities and the Waning of Space." *Arts Magazine,* vol. 41, no. 1 (November 1966), pp. 28–31.

Lucy R. Lippard. "Eccentric Abstraction." *Art International,* vol. 10, no. 9 (November 20, 1966), pp. 28, 34–40.

Lucy R. Lippard. "Eros Presumptive." *The Hudson Review,* Spring 1967, pp. 91–99. (Revised and reprinted in Gregory Battcock, ed., *Minimal Art,* pp. 209–21. New York, E. P. Dutton, 1968.)

Mel Bochner. "Serial Art Systems: Solipsism." *Arts Magazine,* vol. 41, no. 8 (Summer 1967), pp. 39–43.

Sol LeWitt. "Paragraphs on Conceptual Art." *Artforum,* vol. 5, no. 10 (Summer 1967), pp. 79–83.

James Monte. " 'Making It' with Funk." *Artforum,* vol. 5, no. 10 (Summer 1967), pp. 56–59.

Mel Bochner. "The Serial Attitude." *Artforum,* vol. 6, no. 4 (December 1967), pp. 28–33.

David Lee. "Serial Rights." *ARTnews,* vol. 66, no. 8 (December 1967), pp. 42–45, 68.

Charlotte Willard. "Primary Forms." *New York Post,* December 9, 1967, p. 46.

John Perreault. "Repeating Absurdity." *The Village Voice,* December 14, 1967, p. 18.

Lucy R. Lippard and John Chandler. "The Dematerialization of Art." *Art International,* vol. 12, no. 2 (February 1968), pp. 31–32.

Robert Morris. "Anti-Form." *Artforum,* vol. 6, no. 8 (April 1968), pp. 33–35.

John Chandler. "Tony Smith and Sol LeWitt: Mutations and Permutations." *Art International,* vol. 12, no. 7 (September 1968), pp. 16–19.

"The New Season: Mostly Minimal" (photographic essay). *The Village Voice,* September 19, 1968, pp. 18–19.

"Eva Hesse." *Arts Magazine,* vol. 42, no. 3 (November 1968), p. 58.

M[artin] L[ast]. Review of "Chain Polymers" at Fischbach. *ARTnews,* vol. 67, no. 7 (November 1968), p. 14.

Letter protesting Mayor Richard Daley (Hesse one of several signatories). *ARTnews,* vol. 76, no. 7 (November 1968), p. 29.

Hilton Kramer. Review of "Chain Polymers" at Fischbach. *The New York Times,* November 23, 1968, p. 54.

John Perreault. "The Materiality of Matter." *The Village Voice,* November 28, 1968, p. 19.

Peter Frank. Review of "Chain Polymers" at Fischbach. *Columbia Owl,* December 4, 1968, p. 6.

John Perreault. "Art: A Test." *The Village Voice,* December 19, 1968, p. 19.

John Perreault. "Illusions of Reality." *The Village Voice,* December 26, 1968, pp. 22–23.

Germano Celant. *Arte povera,* pp. 56–60. Milan: Gabriele Mazzotta, 1969. Also published as *Art Povera: Earthworks—Impossible Art—Actual Art—Conceptual Art.* New York: Praeger, 1969.

James R. Mellow. "New York Letter." *Art International,* vol. 8, no. 1 (January 1969), pp. 53–54.

Emily Wasserman. Review of "Chain Polymers" at Fischbach. *Artforum,* vol. 7, no. 5 (January 1969), p. 60.

"Floating Wit." *Time,* January 3, 1969, p. 44.

Max Kozloff. "Nine in a Warehouse." *Artforum,* vol. 7, no. 6 (February 1969), pp. 38–42.

Gregoire Müller. "Robert Morris Presents Anti-Form." *Arts Magazine,* vol. 43, no. 4 (February 1969), pp. 29–30.

Larry Smith. "Flexible Constructions: Floppy and Wonderful." *The Village Voice,* February 6, 1969, pp. 13, 34, 38.

John Chandler. "Art in the Electric Age." *Art International,* vol. 13, no. 2 (February 20, 1969), p. 24.

Ralph Pomeroy. "Soft Objects: At the New Jersey State Museum." *Arts Magazine,* vol. 43, no. 5 (March 1969), pp. 46–48.

Jean-Christophe Ammann. "Schweizer Brief." *Art International,* vol. 13, no. 5 (May 1969), pp. 47–50.

Amy Goldin. "Sweet Mystery of Life." *ARTnews*, vol. 68, no. 3 (May 1969), pp. 46–51, 62.

Barbara Rose. "Problems of Criticism, VI: The Politics of Art, Part III." *Artforum*, vol. 7, no. 9 (May 1969), pp. 46–51.

Hilton Kramer. Review of "Anti-Illusion" at the Whitney Museum. *The New York Times*, May 24, 1969, p. 31.

John Perreault. "Art." *The Village Voice*, May 29, 1969, p. 16.

Herb Aach. "The Materials of Art Versus the Art of Materials." *Craft Horizons*, July–August 1969, pp. 37–38.

Charles Harrison. "Against Precedents." *Studio International*, vol. 178, no. 914 (September 1969), pp. 90–93.

Emily Wasserman. Review of "Anti-Illusion" at the Whitney Museum. *Artforum*, vol. 8, no. 1 (September 1969), pp. 56–57.

Bernard Denvir. Review of "When Attitudes Become Form" at the Kunsthalle, Bern. *Art International*, vol. 13, no. 8 (October 1969), p. 72.

Peter Plagens. "The Possibilities of Drawings." *Artforum*, vol. 8, no. 2 (October 1969), pp. 50–55.

Gregoire Müller. Review of "A Plastic Presence" at the Jewish Museum. *Arts Magazine*, vol. 44, no. 2 (November 1969), pp. 36–37.

Peter Plagens. "557,087." *Artforum*, vol. 8, no. 3 (November 1969), pp. 64–67.

John Gruen. "A Sticky Hodgepodge." *New York*, November 17, 1969, p. 58.

John Perreault. "Plastic, Very Present." *The Village Voice*, December 4, 1969, pp. 28, 63.

Grace Glueck. "Art Notes: Building the Plastic Image." *The New York Times*, December 7, 1969, p. D28.

Gregoire Müller. "Art in Process, IV." *Arts Magazine*, vol. 44, no. 3 (December 1969/January 1970), pp. 54–55.

Letter to Sol LeWitt from Hesse. In *Sol LeWitt*, p. 27. Exhibition catalogue, Haags Gemeentemuseum, The Hague, 1970.

Robert Pincus-Witten. Review of "A Plastic Presence" at the Jewish Museum. *Artforum*, vol. 8, no. 5 (January 1970), p. 69.

Harold Rosenberg. "The Art World: Deaestheticization." *The New Yorker*, January 24, 1970, pp. 62–67.

Philip Leider. "Art in Process, IV." *Artforum*, vol. 8, no. 6 (February 1970), p. 70.

"Fling, Dribble, and Drip" (includes statement by Hesse). *Life*, vol. 68, no. 7 (February 27, 1970), pp. 62–66.

Dore Ashton. "Exhibition at Finch College." *Studio International*, vol. 179 (March 1970), p. 119.

Hilton Kramer. Review of "New Drawings" at Fischbach. *The New York Times*, April 18, 1970.

Cindy Nemser. "An Interview with Eva Hesse." *Artforum*, vol. 8, no. 9 (May 1970), pp. 59–63.

"Eva Hesse Dies: Sculptor Was 34." *The New York Times*, May 30, 1970, p. 23.

H[arris] R[osenstein]. "Reviews and Previews: Exhibition at Fischbach Gallery." *ARTnews*, vol. 69, no. 4 (Summer 1970), p. 62.

James R. Mellow. "Three Sculptors in a Plastic Mode." *The New York Times*, July 5, 1970, p. B17.

Elizabeth C. Baker. "Sexual Art—Politics." *ARTnews*, vol. 69, no. 9 (January 1971), pp. 47–48, 60–62. (Revised and reprinted in Baker, *Art and Sexual Politics*. New York: Collier Books, 1973.)

Lucy R. Lippard. "Eva Hesse—The Circle." *Art in America*, vol. 59, no. 3 (May–June 1971), pp. 68–73. (Reprinted in Lippard, *From the Center*, pp. 155–66. New York: E. P. Dutton, 1976.)

John Perreault. "Art." *The Village Voice*, October 21, 1971, p. 35.

Robert Pincus-Witten. "Eva Hesse: Post-Minimalism into Sublime." *Artforum*, vol. 10, no. 3 (November 1971), pp. 32–44. (Reprinted in Pincus-Witten, *Postminimalism*, pp. 42–62. New York: Out of London Press, 1977.)

Douglas Davis. "The Invisible Woman Is Visible." *Newsweek*, November 15, 1971, pp. 130–31.

E[lizabeth] C. B[aker]. Review of exhibition at School of Visual Arts. *ARTnews*, vol. 70, no. 8 (December 1971), p. 16.

Achille Bonito Oliva. *Il territorio magico: Comportamenti alternativi dell'arte*, pp. 67, 111. Florence: Centro Di, 1972.

Leah Gordon. "Myth of Sensibility." *Time*, March 20, 1972, pp. 72–77.

John Canaday. "Win, Draw, or Lose at Chicago's All-American Show." *The New York Times*, June 25, 1972, p. 19.

Hilton Kramer. Review of "Documenta 5." *The New York Times*, July 1, 1972, p. 11.

Hilton Kramer. Review of "Documenta 5." *The New York Times*, July 9, 1972.

Robert Pincus-Witten. "Rosenquist and Samaras: The Obsessive Image and Post Minimalism." *Artforum*, vol. 11, no. 1 (September 1972), pp. 64–69.

Lizzie Borden. "Cosmologies." *Artforum*, vol. 11, no. 2 (October 1972), pp. 35–40.

Robert Pincus-Witten, ed. "Eva Hesse: Last Words." *Artforum*, vol. 11, no. 3 (November 1972), pp. 74–76.

Joyce Purnick. "A Portrait of the Artist, Tortured and Talented." *New York Post*, December 13, 1972.

Emily Genauer. "Art and the Artist." *New York Post*, December 16, 1972.

Hilton Kramer. "A Career Cut Short by Death." *The New York Times*, December 17, 1972.

Hilton Kramer. "Memorial for an Admired Art Talent." *The New York Times*, December 18, 1972, p. 31.

John Perreault. "Knotted and Split at the Seams." *The Village Voice*, December 21, 1972, pp. 31–32.

"Sculptures: Eva Hesse" (illustrations only). *Aphra*. vol. 3, no. 1 (Winter 1972–1973), pp. 42–45.

Lucy R. Lippard. *Six Years: The Dematerialization of the Art Object*. New York: Praeger, 1973.

Robert Hughes. "Vulnerable Ugliness." *Time,* January 1, 1973, p. 37.

Barbara Rose. "The Real Thing." *New York,* vol. 6, no. 1 (January 1, 1973), p. 60.

Tommaso Trini. "Tregua fra tendenze negli USA." *Corriere della sera* (Milan), January 7, 1973.

Judith Helfer. "Eva Hesse: Wirkungs- und gehaltvolle Retrospektive." *Aufbau,* January 12, 1973, p. 19.

Douglas Davis. "Cockroach or Queen." *Newsweek,* January 15, 1973, p. 73.

Judith Helfer. "Szene: Künstlerinnen." *Der Spiegel,* January 15, 1973.

Cindy Nemser. "All About Eva" (letter to the editor). *The Village Voice,* January 18, 1973.

Jill Johnston. "As Anybody Lay Dying." *The Village Voice,* January 25, 1973, pp. 23–26.

Lil Picard. "Aus dem Nachlass der Avantgarde." *Die Welt,* January 25, 1973.

Elizabeth C. Baker. "Sculpture: The Eva Hesse Memorial Exhibition." *Saturday Review,* February 1973, pp. 57–58.

Kim Levin. "Eva Hesse: Notes on New Beginnings." *ARTnews,* vol. 72, no. 10 (February 1973), pp. 71–73.

David Shapiro. "The Random Forms in Soft Materials and String by the Late Young Innovator Eva Hesse." *Craft Horizons,* vol. 33 (February 1973), pp. 40–45, 77.

Lee Sheridan. "Eva Hesse; Memorial Exhibition: Art Show of Astonishing Beauty." *Springfield Daily News* (Massachusetts), February 7, 1973.

Kenneth Baker. "Memorial Exhibition." *The Christian Science Monitor,* February 16, 1973.

Bruce Boice. "Eva Hesse: The Guggenheim Museum." *Artforum,* vol. 11, no. 7 (March 1973), pp. 89–91.

Douglas Crimp. "New York Letter." *Art International,* vol. 17, no. 3 (March 1973), pp. 40–42, 69.

Barbara Rose. "A Special Woman; Her Surprise Art." *Vogue,* March 1973, p. 50.

Kenneth Wahl. "A Great Talent Was Lost." *Birch Bark,* March 1973, p. 7.

Jean Reeves. "Eva Hesse Sculpture Exhibits Wide Range of Materials." *Buffalo Evening News,* March 6, 1973.

Nancy Tobin Willig. "Eva Hesse: Cries and Whispers Live in Sculpture." *Buffalo Courier-Express,* March 11, 1973, p. 5.

"Eva Hesse" (includes statement by Hesse). *Art Press* (Paris), no. 3 (March–April 1973), pp. 20–21.

Peter Schjeldahl. "Eva Hesse at the Guggenheim." *Art in America,* vol. 61 (March–April 1973), p. 99.

Lizzie Borden. "3D into 2D." *Artforum,* vol. 11, no. 8 (April 1973), p. 74.

Kasha Linville Gula. "Eva Hesse: No Explanation." *Ms.,* April 1973, pp. 39–42.

Ruth Berenson. "New Realists." *National Review,* May 11, 1973, p. 53.

"Conceptual Art—Arte Povera—Land Art—Body Art, 1966–1969." *Bolaffiarte* (Turin), vol. 4, no. 31 (June–July 1973), p. 74.

Fidel Danieli. "L.A. Art Sight Lines." *Los Angeles Weekly News,* September 28, 1973.

Lizzie Borden. "Art Economics and the Whitney Drawing Show." *Artforum,* vol. 12, no. 2 (October 1973), p. 87.

Melinda Terbell. "Eva Hesse Retrospective." *Artweek,* vol. 4, no. 33 (October 6, 1973), pp. 1, 16.

William Wilson. "Eva Hesse's Memorial to a Life of Pain." *Los Angeles Times,* October 7, 1973, p. 52.

Editha Flora Carpenter. "Eva Hesse: The Mystery of Art in Form." *Greensboro Daily News* (North Carolina), October 28, 1973, p. E16.

Barbara Smith. "Eva Hesse Retrospective." *Los Angeles Weekly News,* November 2, 1973, p. 24.

Thomas Albright. "A Moving Experience." *San Francisco Chronicle,* November 13, 1973.

Charles Shere. "U.C. Retrospective Explores the Work of Eva Hesse." *Oakland Tribune,* December 23, 1973.

Cindy Nemser. "Eva Hesse: Her Life." *Feminist Art Journal,* vol. 2, no. 1 (Winter 1973), pp. 13–14.

Cindy Nemser. "My Memories of Eva Hesse." *Feminist Art Journal,* vol. 2, no. 1 (Winter 1973), pp. 12–13.

"Announcement." *Artweek,* vol. 5, no. 2 (January 12, 1974), p. 1.

John Markell. "The Tragic Life and Forceful Sculpture of Eva Hesse." *U. C. Berkeley Daily California Arts Magazine,* January 18, 1974.

Cindy Nemser. *Art Talk: Conversations with Twelve Women Artists,* pp. 201–24, 229. New York: Scribner's, 1975.

Henry P. Raleigh. "The Aesthetic of Change." *Journal of Aesthetics and Art Criticism,* vol. 34, no. 2 (Winter 1975), pp. 177–82.

Lucy R. Lippard. *Eva Hesse.* New York: New York University Press, 1976.

Richard Lorber. "Eva Hesse." *Arts Magazine,* vol. 51, no. 4 (December 1976), p. 7.

Rosalind Krauss, *Passages in Modern Sculpture,* pp. 272, 275, fig. 204. Cambridge, Massachusetts: MIT Press, 1977.

Hilton Kramer. Review of Lippard, 1976. *The New York Times,* March 20, 1977, p. D27.

Jeff Perrone. Review of Lippard, 1976. *Artforum,* vol. 16, no. 1 (September 1977), pp. 54–55.

Naomi Spector. Review of Lippard, 1976. *Print Collector's Newsletter,* vol. 8, no. 4 (September–October 1977), pp. 117–18.

John Russell. "It Could Have Been a Disaster But . . .". *The New York Times,* November 2, 1977.

Roberta Smith. Review of Lippard, 1976. *Art in America,* vol. 66, no. 1 (January–February 1978), pp. 19–21.

Nancy Holt, ed. *The Writings of Robert Smithson,* p. 35, no. 25. New York: New York University Press, 1979.

"Zu kurze Schaffensjahre: Eva-Hesse-Retrospektive in zwei Londoner Galerien." *Du,* no. 7 (1979), p. 18.

Carolyn Carr. "Grids: Format and Image in 20th Century Art." *Dialogue*, no. 4 (March 1979).

Monica Petzal. Review of Whitechapel Art Gallery exhibition. *Art Monthly*, vol. 27 (June 1979), pp. 15–16.

E. Cooper. Review of Whitechapel Art Gallery exhibition. *Art & Artists*, vol. T14 (July 1979), pp. 8–10.

Andrea Hill. Review of Whitechapel Art Gallery exhibition. *Artscribe*, no. 18 (July 1979), pp. 41–43.

B. Marcelis. "Per la prima volta in Europa, una grande mostra . . .". *Domus*, no. 599 (October 1979), pp. 48–49.

Peter Winter. Review of Kestner-Gesellschaft exhibition. *Kunstwerk*, vol. 32, no. 5 (October 1979), pp. 55–56.

"Eva Hesse: Skulpturen und Zeichnungen in der Kestner-Gesellschaft/Hannover." *Flash Art*, October–November 1979, p. 50.

Antje von Graevenitz. Review of Rijksmuseum Kröller-Müller exhibition. *Pantheon*, vol. 37, no. 4 (October–December 1979), pp. 331–33.

"Whitechapel Art Gallery." *Print Collector's Newsletter*, vol. 10, no. 5 (November–December 1979), p. 166.

Carl Goldstein. "Teaching Modernism: What Albers Learned in the Bauhaus and Taught to Rauschenberg, Noland, and Hesse." *Arts Magazine*, vol. 54 (December 1979), pp. 109, 111, 114–15, 116.

Vivian Endicott Barnett. *Handbook: The Guggenheim Museum Collection*, 1900–1980, pp. 514–15, no. 247. New York: Solomon R. Guggenheim Museum, 1980.

N. MacGregor. "Some Recent Sculpture Acquisitions by British Public Collections." *The Burlington Magazine*, vol. 122 (January 1980), p. 84.

Rosy Parker and Griselda Pollock. *Old Mistresses: Women, Art, and Ideology*, pp. 153, 156, fig. 92. London: Oresko Books, 1981.

Clara Weyergraf. "The Holy Alliance: Populism and Feminism." *October*, no. 16 (Spring 1981), pp. 23–24.

S. Platt. "Testing the Studies" (review of University Art Museum, Berkeley, exhibition). *Artweek*, vol. 13 (October 2, 1982), p. 3.

Joyce Fernandes. Review of Allen Memorial Art Museum exhibition. *New Art Examiner*, vol. 10, no. 3 (December 1982), p. 25.

Grace Glueck. "How an American Sculptor Found Her True Métier." *The New York Times*, January 23, 1983.

Kay Larson. "The James Dean of Art." *New York*, January 31, 1983, p. 50.

Judith Russi Kirshner. "Eva Hesse: A Retrospective of the Drawings" (at the Renaissance Society, Chicago). *Artforum*, vol. 21, no. 6 (February 1983), p. 84.

Michael R. Klein. Review of Grey Art Gallery drawings exhibition. *ARTnews*, vol. 82, no. 4 (April 1983), pp. 151–52.

Ellen H. Johnson. "Order and Chaos: From the Diaries of Eva Hesse." *Art in America*, vol. 71 (Summer 1983), pp. 110–18.

William Rubin, ed. *"Primitivism" in 20th Century Art*, vol. 2, p. 673. New York: Museum of Modern Art, 1984.

Peter Schjeldahl. *Art of Our Time: The Saatchi Collection*, vol. 1, pp. 23–25. London: Lund Humphries, 1984.

"Rose Will Host Hesse Exhibit." *Waltham News-Tribune* (Massachusetts), October 24, 1985.

"Rose Presents First Area Show of Early Works by Artist Hesse." *Brandeis Reporter*, vol. 3, no. 6 (November 8, 1985).

Robert Taylor. "Hesse Show Demonstrates Creative Growth." *The Boston Globe*, November 17, 1985.

Nancy Stapen. "The Idiosyncratic Hesse." *Boston Herald*, November 21, 1985.

"Choices: Art." *The Boston Review*, December 1985.

"Eva Hesse: The Early Drawings and Selected Sculpture." *Brandeis Reporter*, vol. 3, no. 8 (December 13, 1985).

Claudia Betti and Teel Sale. *Drawing: A Contemporary Approach*. New York: CBS College Publishing, 1986.

William Zimmer. "At the Neuberger: Windows Allow Artists to Share a Theme." *The New York Times*, October 12, 1986.

Ray Faulkner, Edwin Ziegfeld, and Howard Smagula. *Art Today*, pp. 250, 251, fig. 249. New York: Holt, Rinehart & Winston, 1987.

Karen Lee Spaulding, ed. *Albright-Knox Art Gallery: The Painting and Sculpture Collection: Acquisitions Since 1972*, pp. 166–67, ill. New York: Hudson Hills Press, 1987.

Roberta Hershenson. "The Fine, Painstaking Art of Arranging a Major Exhibition." *The New York Times*, November 9, 1987.

UNPUBLISHED SOURCES

Taped review of "Chain Polymers." New York, WNCN, December 3, 1968.

Taped lecture by Hesse. Boston, Boston Museum School, January 26, 1969.

Taped interview with Cindy Nemser. New York, artist's studio, January 13, 21, 27, 1970.

Marytha Smith-Allen. "The Art of Eva Hesse, Mel Bochner, and Vito Acconci as Indicative of Shifts in Mainstream Art Between 1966 and 1973." Ph.D. dissertation, New York University, 1983.

Exhibitions

ONE-PERSON EXHIBITIONS

Allan Stone Gallery, New York. "Eva Hesse: Recent Drawings." Opened March 12, 1963.

Kunstverein für die Rheinlande und Westfalen, Kunsthalle, Düsseldorf. "Eva Hesse: Materialbilder und Zeichnungen." August 6–October 17, 1965. Catalogue.

Allen Memorial Art Museum, Oberlin, Ohio. "Recent Drawings by Eva Hesse." Opened January 17, 1968.

Fischbach Gallery, New York. "Eva Hesse: Chain Polymers." November 16–December 5, 1968.

Fischbach Gallery, New York. "Eva Hesse: New Drawings." April 3–23, 1970.

Visual Arts Gallery, School of Visual Arts, New York. "Eva Hesse." October 4–November 1, 1971. Organized by Linda Shearer.

Detroit Institute of Arts. "Eva Hesse." September 27–November 5, 1972. Organized by Frank Kolbert. Brochure.

Solomon R. Guggenheim Museum, New York. "Eva Hesse: A Memorial Exhibition." December 8, 1972–February 11, 1973. Traveled to Albright-Knox Art Gallery, Buffalo, March 6–April 22, 1973; Museum of Contemporary Art, Chicago, May 19–July 1, 1973; Pasadena Art Museum, September 18–November 11, 1973; University Art Museum, University of California, Berkeley, December 12, 1973–February 3, 1974. Organized by Linda Shearer. Catalogue.

Mayor Gallery, London. "Eva Hesse, 1936–1970: An Exhibition of Sculpture and Drawings." September 25–October 31, 1974. Catalogue with an essay by Linda Shearer.

Droll/Kolbert Gallery, New York. "Eva Hesse." June 9–July 15, 1977.

Mayor Gallery, London. "Eva Hesse, 1936–1970: A Retrospective of Works on Paper." May 4–June 9, 1979. Catalogue with an essay by David Brown. Traveled to Otterlo and Hannover with the Whitechapel sculpture exhibition; Kestner-Gesellschaft combined and published both English catalogues in one German edition.

Whitechapel Art Gallery, London. "Eva Hesse: Sculpture." May 4–June 17, 1979. Traveled to Rijksmuseum Kröller-Müller, Otterlo, June 30–August 5, 1979; Kestner-Gesellschaft, Hannover, August 17–September 23, 1979. Catalogue.

Allen Memorial Art Museum, Oberlin, Ohio. "Eva Hesse: A Retrospective of the Drawings." April 20–May 30, 1982. Traveled to Renaissance Society, University of Chicago, September 28–November 7, 1982; Contemporary Arts Museum, Houston, November 20, 1982–January 2, 1983; Grey Art Gallery and Study Center, New York, January 18–February 27, 1983; Baltimore Museum of Art, March 15–April 24, 1983. Catalogue by Ellen H. Johnson.

Metro Pictures, New York. "Eva Hesse: Paintings and Reliefs." January 8–29, 1983.

Rose Art Museum, Brandeis University, Waltham, Massachusetts. "Eva Hesse: The Early Drawings and Selected Sculpture." November 10–December 19, 1985. Catalogue.

Pat Hearn Gallery, New York. "Eva Hesse." November 20–December 31, 1987.

SELECTED GROUP EXHIBITIONS

Wadsworth Atheneum, Hartford, Connecticut. "Drawings." Dates unknown. Organized by Samuel Wagstaff.

Brooklyn Museum. "21st International Watercolor Biennial." April 10–May 28, 1961. Catalogue with an essay by Hertha Wegener.

John Heller Gallery, New York. "Drawings: 3 Young Americans." April 11–May 2, 1961. Illustrated brochure.

Amel Gallery, New York. "First Showing of Gallery Group." December 19, 1963–January 6, 1964.

Park Place Gallery, New York. "Invitational Show." Opened March 16, 1964.

Kunstverein für die Rheinlande und Westfalen, Kunsthalle, Düsseldorf. "Winterausstellung." Opened November 29, 1964.

Isabel and F. Arnhard Scheidt Residence, Kettwig-am-Ruhr, West Germany. "Tom Doyle and Eva Hesse." May 15, 1965.

Graham Gallery, New York. "Abstract Inflationism and Stuffed Expressionism." March 1–26, 1966. Organized by Joan Washburn. Brochure.

Fischbach Gallery, New York. "Eccentric Abstraction." September 20–October 8, 1966. Organized by Lucy R. Lippard. Brochure.

Riverside Museum, New York. "30th Annual Exhibition: 'Yesterday and Today,' 1936–1966." September 25–November 27, 1966.

Visual Arts Gallery, School of Visual Arts, New York. "Working Drawings and Other Visible Things on Paper Not Necessarily Meant to Be Viewed as Art." December 2–23, 1966. Organized by Mel Bochner.

Ithaca College Museum of Art, Ithaca, New York. "Drawings 1967." January 17–February 25, 1967. Catalogue.

New York State Fair, Syracuse. "Art Today, 1967." August 29–September 4, 1967. Organized in cooperation with the New York State Council on the Arts.

Weatherspoon Gallery, University of North Carolina, Greensboro. "Art on Paper Invitational, 1967." October 15–November 22, 1967. Organized by Gilbert H. Carpenter. Catalogue.

Lannis Museum of Normal Art, New York. "Normal Art." Opened November 12, 1967. Organized by Joseph Kosuth.

Finch College Museum of Art, New York. "Art in Series." November 22, 1967–January 6, 1968. Organized by Elayne H. Varian and Mel Bochner.

Moore College of Art, Philadelphia. "American Drawings, 1968." January 13–February 16, 1968. Organized by Richard Anuskiewicz, Brian O'Doherty, and Stephen Prokopoff.

Galerie Ricke, Cologne, West Germany. "Programm 1." May 29–September 15, 1968.

Milwaukee Art Center. "Directions 1: Options, 1968." June 22–August 18, 1968. Traveled to Museum of Contemporary Art, Chicago, September 14–October 20, 1968. Catalogue with an essay by Lawrence Alloway.

John Gibson Gallery, New York. "Anti-Form." October 5–November 7, 1968.

American Federation of Arts. "Soft and Apparently Soft Sculpture." October 6, 1968–October 12, 1969. Traveling exhibition organized by Lucy R. Lippard. Catalogue.

Kunsthalle, Cologne, West Germany. "Kunstmarkt 1968." October 15–20, 1968.

Flint Institute of Arts, Flint, Michigan. "Made of Plastic." October 18–December 1, 1968. Catalogue.

Leo Castelli Warehouse, New York. "Nine at Leo Castelli." December 4–28, 1968. Organized by Robert Morris.

Whitney Museum of American Art, New York. "Annual Exhibition." December 17, 1968–February 9, 1969. Organized by Robert Doty and John Gordon. Catalogue.

Institute of Contemporary Art, University of Pennsylvania, Philadelphia. "Plastics and New Art." January 15–February 25, 1969. Traveled to Marion Koogler McNay Art Institute, San Antonio, Texas, March 16–April 13, 1969. Catalogue with an essay by Stephen Prokopoff.

Wilcox Gallery, Swarthmore College, Swarthmore, Pennsylvania. "Hard, Soft, and Plastic." February 7–March 3, 1969.

Finch College Museum of Art, New York. "Drawings: Some Recent Trends." March 1969. Catalogue.

New Jersey State Museum, Trenton. "Soft Art." March 1–April 27, 1969. Organized by and catalogue by Ralph Pomeroy.

New York Shakespeare Festival, Public Theater, New York. "Art/Peace Event." March 5–May 4, 1969.

Museum of Modern Art, New York. "New Media, New Methods." Traveling exhibition organized by Kynaston McShine, March 16, 1969–August 16, 1970.

University Gallery, University of Minnesota, Minneapolis. "The Artist and the Factory." March 19–April 16, 1969. Catalogue with an essay by Charles Savage.

Galerie Heiner Friedrich, Munich. "Drawings." March 20–April 4, 1969.

Kunsthalle, Bern. "When Attitudes Become Form/Works — Concepts — Processes — Situations — Information." March 22–April 27, 1969. Traveled to Museum Haus Lange, Krefeld, West Germany, May 10–June 15, 1969; Institute of Contemporary Arts, London, September 28–October 27, 1969. Organized by Harold Szeemann. Catalogue with essays by Scott Burton, Gregoire Müller, and Tommaso Trini; English catalogue by Charles Harrison.

Whitney Museum of American Art, New York. "Anti-Illusion: Procedures/Materials." May 19–July 6, 1969. Organized by and catalogue by Marcia Tucker and James Monte.

New Gallery, Cleveland, Ohio. "Seven Objects." May 24–June 30, 1969. Traveled to Galerie Ricke, Cologne, West Germany, Summer 1969.

Westmoreland County Museum of Art, Greensburg, Pennsylvania. "Recent Trends in American Art." May 25–July 6, 1969.

Aldrich Museum of Contemporary Art, Ridgefield, Connecticut. "Highlights of the 1968–1969 Art Season." June 22–September 14, 1969. Organized by Dorothy Mayhall. Catalogue.

Seattle Art Museum, "557,087." September 5–October 5, 1969. Traveled to Vancouver Art Gallery, British Columbia, as "955,000," January 13–February 8, 1970; Centro de Arte y Comunicación, Buenos Aires, as "3,549,000." Organized by Lucy R. Lippard. Catalogue on loose index cards.

Fort Worth Art Museum. "American Drawings." October 28–December 6, 1969. Organized by Peter Plagens and Henry Hopkins. Catalogue.

Jewish Museum, New York. "A Plastic Presence." November 19, 1969–January 4, 1970. Traveled to Milwaukee Art Center, January 20–March 8, 1970; San Francisco Museum of Art, April 24–May 24, 1970. Organized by Susan Tumarkin Goodman. Catalogue.

Galerie Ricke, Cologne, West Germany. "Profile." December 3, 1969–January 5, 1970.

Finch College Museum of Art, New York. "Art in Process, IV." December 11, 1969–January 26, 1970. Organized by Elayne H. Varian. Catalogue.

Heckscher Museum, Huntington, New York. "The Expressive Line." December 21, 1969–January 25, 1970. Catalogue.

Trinity College Art Gallery, Hartford, Connecticut. "Works in Plastic, 1970." 1970. Organized by Mitchell Pappas.

Hawthorne Gallery, Skidmore College, Saratoga Springs, New York. "Group." January 6–30, 1970.

Sidney Janis Gallery, New York. "String and Rope." January 7–31, 1970. Catalogue.

Reese Palley Gallery, San Francisco. "Multiples and Graphics." January 13–31, 1970.

Vancouver Art Gallery, British Columbia. "955,000" January 13–February 8, 1970. Originated at the Seattle Art Museum as "557,087."

Emily Lowe Gallery, Hofstra University, Hempstead, New York. "Hanging/Leaning." February 2–27, 1970. Organized by Robert Littman. Catalogue.

Cooper-Hewitt Museum of Decorative Arts and Design, Smithsonian Institution, New York. "The Drawing Society of New York Regional Exhibition, 1970." March 9–May 9, 1970. Circulated nationally by the American Federation of Arts, Fall 1970–Fall 1971. Catalogue.

Art Museum, Princeton University. "American Art Since 1960." May 5–27, 1970.

Owens-Corning Fiberglas Center, New York. "Tony Delap/Frank Gallo/Eva Hesse: Trio." May 14–September 5, 1970. Traveled to Owens-Corning Fiberglas Center, Detroit, as "Art in Automobile," October 1970.

Galerie Ricke, Cologne, West Germany. "Zeichnungen Amerikanischer Künstler." May 15–June 25, 1970. Catalogue.

Whitney Museum of American Art, New York. "Recent Acquisitions." June–July 1970.

Fondation Maeght, St. Paul-de-Vence, France. "L'Art Vivant aux États-Unis." July 16–September 30, 1970. Organized by and catalogue essay by Dore Ashton.

Museum of Modern Art, New York. "Recent Acquisitions." July 31–October 18, 1970.

Galerie Yvon Lambert, Paris. "American Drawings." September 1970.

Institute of Contemporary Art, Boston. "Works Mostly on Paper." October 20–November 14, 1970.

Institute of Contemporary Art, University of Pennsylvania, Philadelphia. "Against Order: Chance and Art." November 14–December 22, 1970. Catalogue with an essay by Robert Pincus-Witten.

Museum of Modern Art, Art Lending Service, New York. "Paperworks." November 24, 1970–January 10, 1971. Organized by Pierre Apraxine.

Janie C. Lee Gallery, Dallas. "Drawings." December 1970–January 1971.

University of Maryland Art Gallery, College Park. "Editions in Plastic." December 3, 1970–January 23, 1971. Catalogue.

Whitney Museum of American Art, New York. "The Permanent Collection—Women Artists." December 16, 1970–January 19, 1971. Organized by Elke Solomon.

Paula Cooper Gallery, New York. "Drawings." December 19, 1970–January 13, 1971.

International Council of the Museum of Modern Art, New York. "1971 Triennale of India." New Delhi, January 31–March 31, 1971. Organized by Waldo Rasmussen. Brochure.

Finch College Museum of Art, New York. "Projected Art: Artists at Work." March 13–May 2, 1971. Organized by Elayne H. Varian. Brochure.

Katonah Gallery, Katonah, New York. "Materials and Methods: A New View." March 21–May 2, 1971. Catalogue with an essay by Robert Pincus-Witten.

Corcoran Gallery of Art, Washington, D.C. "Depth and Presence." May 3–30, 1971. Catalogue with an introduction by Stephen Prokopoff.

Museum of Modern Art, Art Lending Service, New York. "Summer Show." July 8–September 30, 1971.

M. Knoedler & Co., New York. "Selections of Work by Gallery Artists." September 14–October 15, 1971.

Aldrich Museum of Contemporary Art, Ridgefield, Connecticut. "Sculpture and Shapes of the Last Decade." October 3–December 12, 1971.

Museum of Contemporary Art, Chicago. "Six Sculptors: Extended Structures." October 30–December 12, 1971. Catalogue with an introduction by Stephen Prokopoff.

Bykert Gallery, New York. "Drawings and Prints." Nfovember 6–December 2, 1971.

School of the Museum of Fine Arts, Boston. "Changing Terms." December 3, 1971–January 14, 1972.

Institute of Contemporary Art, University of Pennsylvania, Philadelphia. "Grids." January 26–March 1, 1972. Organized by Suzanne Delehanty. Catalogue by Lucy R. Lippard.

Salem Fine Arts Center, Winston-Salem, North Carolina. "Women: A Historical Survey of Works by Women Artists." February 27–March 19, 1972. Organized in conjunction with the North Carolina Museum of Art, Raleigh, March 25–April 20, 1972. Catalogue.

Kunsthaus, Hamburg. "American Women Artists Show." April 14–May 14, 1972. Catalogue by Lil Picard and Sibylle Niester.

High Museum of Art, Atlanta. "The Modern Image." April 15–June 11, 1972. Catalogue.

Philadelphia Museum of Art. "Friends' Purchase Party." Opened April 20, 1972. Organized by Anne d'Harnoncourt.

Art Institute of Chicago. "Seventieth American Exhibition." June 24–August 21, 1972.

Museum Fridericianum and Neue Galerie, Kassel, West Germany. "Documenta 5." June 30–October 8, 1972. Catalogue with an essay by Lucy R. Lippard.

Copenhagen. "Young American Artists: Drawings and Graphics." 1973.

Storm King Art Center, Mountainville, New York. "The Emerging Real." 1973.

New York Cultural Center. "3D into 2D: Drawing for Sculpture." January 18–March 10, 1973. Organized by and catalogue introduction by Susan Ginsburg.

Whitney Museum of American Art, New York. "American Drawings, 1963–1973." May 25–July 22, 1973. Organized by and catalogue introduction by Elke Solomon.

Seattle Art Museum Pavilion. "American Art: Third Quarter Century." August 22–October 14, 1973. Organized by Jan van der Marck. Catalogue.

International Program of the Museum of Modern Art, New York. "Some Recent American Art." Traveled to National Gallery of Victoria, Melbourne, February 12–March 10, 1974; Art Gallery of New South Wales, Sydney, April 5–May 5, 1974; Art Gallery of South Australia, Adelaide, May 31–June 30, 1974; Western Australian Art Gallery, Perth, July 26–August 21, 1974; City of Auckland Art Gallery, October 14–November 17, 1974. Curated by and catalogue by Jennifer Licht.

William Zierler, Inc., New York. "American Works on Paper, 1944–1974." November 2–30, 1974.

Städtisches Museum, Leverkusen, West Germany. 1975.

Wadsworth Atheneum, Hartford, Connecticut. "Matrix 5." March–April 1975. Catalogue by Andrea Miller-Keller.

Whitney Museum of American Art, New York. "Sculpture of the Sixties: Selections from the Permanent Collection." March–April 1975.

Museum of Modern Art, New York. "Drawing Now." January 21–March 19, 1976. Traveling exhibition. Catalogue.

Whitney Museum of American Art, New York. "Two Hundred Years of American Sculpture." March 16–September 26, 1976. Catalogue.

New Orleans Museum of Art. "Sculpture: American Directions, 1945–1975." April 1–May 16, 1976. Catalogue.

Seibu Museum of Art, Tokyo. "Three Decades of American Art." June–July 1976.

Pratt Institute Gallery, Brooklyn. "Alumni Fine Arts Show." 1977.

Rosa Esman Gallery, New York. "Photonotations." 1977.

Renaissance Society, University of Chicago. "Ideas in Sculpture, 1965–1977." May 1–June 11, 1977.

Fitzwilliam Museum, Cambridge, England. "Jubilation: American Art During the Reign of Elizabeth II." May 10–June 18, 1977.

Museum Fridericianum, Orangerie, and Neue Galerie, Kassel, West Germany. "Documenta 6: Handzeichnungen, Utopisches Design, Bücher." June 24–October 2, 1977.

Whitney Museum of American Art, New York. "20th Century American Art from Friends' Collections." July 27–September 27, 1977.

Museum of Contemporary Art, Chicago. "A View of a Decade, 1967–1977." September 10–November 10, 1977. Catalogue.

Solomon R. Guggenheim Museum, New York. "Recent Gifts and Purchases." September 16–October 16, 1977.

Brooklyn Museum Art School. "Contemporary Women: Consciousness and Content." October 1–November 27, 1977.

New York State Museum, Albany. "New York, the State of Art." October 8–November 27, 1977.

Vancouver Art Gallery, British Columbia. "Strata: Nancy Graves, Eva Hesse, Michelle Stuart, Jackie Winsor." October 9–November 6, 1977. Organized by and catalogue essay by Lucy R. Lippard.

Leo Castelli, New York. "Numerals, 1924–1977." January 7–28, 1978. Organized by Independent Curators, Inc., New York. Traveled until 1979. Catalogue by Rainer F. Crone.

Whitney Museum of American Art, New York. "Collection: American Sculpture." January 24–April 16, 1978.

Storm King Art Center, Mountainville, New York. "Sculpture: A Study in Materials." May 17–October 30, 1978.

Stedelijk Museum, Amsterdam. "Door Beeldhouwers Gemaakt; Made by Sculptors." September 14–November 4, 1978.

Pace Gallery, New York. "Grids: Format and Image in Twentieth Century Art." December 16, 1978–January 20, 1979. Traveled to Akron Art Institute, Akron, Ohio, March 24–May 6, 1979.

Roosevelt Public Library, Art Workshop, Roosevelt, New York. "Lines, Points, Plains." 1979.

Touchstone Gallery, New York. "Drawings by Sculptors." 1979.

Museum of Modern Art, New York. "Contemporary Sculpture: Selections from the Collection of the Museum of Modern Art." May 18–August 7, 1979.

David Winton Bell Gallery, List Art Center, Brown University, Providence, Rhode Island. "Invitational." February 2–24, 1980.

Allen Memorial Art Museum, Oberlin, Ohio. "From Reinhardt to Christo." Opened February 20, 1980. Catalogue.

Neuberger Museum, State University of New York, Purchase. "Hidden Desires." March 9–June 15, 1980.

Kunsthaus, Zurich. "Weich und Plastisch—Soft-Art." November 16, 1979–February 4, 1980. Catalogue by Erika Billeter.

Yale University Art Gallery, New Haven, Connecticut. "Twenty Artists: Yale School of Art, 1950–1970." January 29–March 29, 1981. Catalogue with an essay by Irving Sandler.

Museen der Stadt Köln, Cologne, West Germany. "Westkunst: Zeitgenössische Kunst seit 1939." May 30–August 16, 1981.

Wesleyan University Art Gallery and Davison Art Center, Middletown, Connecticut. "No Title: The Collection of Sol LeWitt." October 21–December 20, 1981. In association with the Wadsworth Atheneum, Hartford, Connecticut.

Centre d'Arts Plastiques Contemporains, Bordeaux, France. ". . . Sculptures, 1966–1969." March 13–April 30, 1982. Catalogue by Germano Celant.

University Art Museum, University of California, Berkeley. "Matrix." July 1982.

Whitney Museum of American Art, New York. "Sculpture from the Permanent Collection." July–September 1982.

Whitney Museum of American Art, New York. "From Minimalism to Expressionism: Painting and Sculpture Since 1965." June–December 1983.

Museum of Contemporary Art, Los Angeles. "The First Show: Painting and Sculpture from Eight Collections, 1940–1980." November 1983–February 1984. Catalogue.

Grand Rapids Art Museum, Grand Rapids, Michigan. "Women in Art." 1984.

Merian-Park, Basel. "Skulptur im 20. Jahrhundert." 1984. Catalogue.

Sidney Janis Gallery, New York. "American Women Artists, Part 1: Twentieth Century Pioneers." January–February 1984. Catalogue.

Moderna Museet, Stockholm. "Flyktpunkter/Vanishing Points." April 14–May 27, 1984. Catalogue.

Museum of Modern Art, New York. " 'Primitivism' in 20th Century Art." September 19, 1984–January 15, 1985. Traveled to Detroit Institute of Arts, February–May 19, 1985; Dallas Museum of Art, June 23–September 1, 1985. Catalogue edited by William Rubin.

Columbus Museum of Art, Columbus, Ohio. "Partners in Purchase." 1985.

Hudson River Museum, Yonkers, New York. "A New Beginning: 1968–1978." 1985.

Whitney Museum of American Art at Philip Morris, New York. "The Box Transformed." February 15–April 25, 1985. Brochure.

Edith C. Blum Art Institute, Bard College Center, Annandale-on-Hudson, New York. "The Maximum Implication of the Minimal Line." March 24–April 28, 1985. Catalogue.

Whitney Museum of American Art, Stamford, Connecticut. "Affiliations: Recent Sculpture and Its Antecedents." June 27–August 24, 1985. Catalogue.

Weatherspoon Art Gallery, University of North Carolina, Greensboro. "Summer Sculpture Exhibition." Summer 1985.

Grey Art Gallery and Study Center, New York. "From the Collection of Sol LeWitt." July 9–August 26, 1985. Organized by Independent Curators, Inc., New York. Traveled to University Art Museum, California State University, Long Beach, October 16–November 11, 1984; Ackland Art Museum, University of North Carolina, Chapel Hill, January 26–March 3, 1985; Everhart Museum, Scranton, Pennsylvania, April 27–June 8, 1985; Meadow Brook Art Gallery, Oakland University, Rochester, Michigan, October 6–November 17, 1985; Museum of Art, Fort Lauderdale, Florida, March 5–April 16, 1986. Catalogue.

Blum/Helman, New York. "American Eccentric Abstraction." November 16–December 14, 1985.

Solomon R. Guggenheim Museum, New York. "Transformations in Sculpture: Four Decades of American and European Art." November 22, 1985–February 16, 1986.

Museum of Art, Fort Lauderdale, Florida. "An American Renaissance: Painting and Sculpture Since 1940." January 12–March 30, 1986. Catalogue.

Palacio de Velázquez, Madrid. "Between Geometry and Gesture: American Sculpture, 1965–1975." May–July 1986.

List Visual Arts Center, Massachusetts Institute of Technology, Cambridge, Massachusetts. "Natural Forms and Forces: Abstract Images in American Sculpture." May 9–June 29, 1986. Catalogue.

Centre Georges Pompidou, Musée National d'Art Moderne, Paris. "Qu'est Que C'est la Sculpture Moderne?" July 3–October 13, 1986.

Neuberger Museum, State University of New York, Purchase. "The Window in Twentieth Century Art." September 20, 1986–January 18, 1987. Traveled to Houston Contemporary Arts Museum, April 18–June 19, 1987. Catalogue.

Museum of Contemporary Art, Los Angeles. "Individuals: A Selected History of Contemporary Art, 1945–1986." December 10, 1986–January 10, 1988.

Xavier Fourcade, Inc., New York. "Drawings." January 9–February 7, 1987.

Wadsworth Atheneum, Hartford, Connecticut. "From the LeWitt Collection." March 12–May 4, 1987.

Institute of Contemporary Art, University of Pennsylvania, Philadelphia. "1967: At the Crossroads." March 13–April 26, 1987. Catalogue.

David Winton Bell Gallery, List Art Center, Brown University, Providence, Rhode Island. "Alternative Supports: Contemporary Sculpture on the Wall." April 25–May 25, 1987.

Kent Fine Art, Inc., New York. "Assemblage." May 12–July 2, 1987. Catalogue.

Kunstmuseum, Düsseldorf. "Brennpunkt Düsseldorf . . . 1962–1987." Summer 1987. Catalogue.

Städtische Kunsthalle, Düsseldorf. "Similia/Dissimilia: Modes of Abstraction in Painting, Sculpture, and Photography Today." August–September 1987. Traveled November–December 1987 to Wallach Art Gallery, Columbia University, New York; Leo Castelli Gallery, New York; and Sonnabend Gallery, New York. Catalogue.

Pat Hearn Gallery, New York. "Group Show." September 25–October 18, 1987.

Solomon R. Guggenheim Museum, New York. "Fifty Years of Collecting: An Anniversary Selection." November 13, 1987–March 13, 1988.

Whitney Museum of American Art, New York. "Vital Signs: Organic Abstraction." April 28–July 17, 1988.

Index of Sculptures *(Keyed to entry numbers)*

Photograph Credits *(keyed to page numbers)*

Albright-Knox Art Gallery 231

Courtesy Australian National Gallery 227

Bill Barrette back flap, 48, 90, 98, 102, 116, 137 bottom, 138, 140, 146, 148 bottom, 149, 180, 230

Ben Blackwell 171, 195, 244, 245

Michael Bleichfeld 221

Detroit Institute of Art 141

Richard Eells 223

Lynton Gardiner cover, 23, 25, 26, 27, 33, 35, 37, 39, 41, 43, 45, 47, 53, 63, 67, 73, 77, 79, 83, 89, 93, 95, 97, 99, 103, 107, 109, 111, 115, 119, 122, 125, 127, 129, 133, 135, 137 top, 143, 151, 153, 155, 167, 169, 177, 179, 181, 185, 191, 197, 199, 201, 203, 209, 211, 213, 217, 219, 224, 225, 233, 235, 236, 237

Courtesy Stephen Giannakos 228, 229

N. and C. Heinrich 75

Robert Hensleigh 21, 91

Courtesy Eva Hesse Estate back cover, 22, 26, 29, 44, 51, 55, 60, 61, 63, 69, 71, 86, 87, 101, 145 top, 147, 161, 163, 173, 189, 193, 204, 205, 207, 242, 243

Israel Museum 139

H. Landshoff 2, 56, 58, 82, 104, 105, 164

Museum Ludwig 175

Daniel Martinez 131

Museum of Modern Art 148 top

Courtesy Ohio State University 187

Edward Owen 121

Philadelphia Museum of Art 113, 157

Eric Pollitzer 239

Rijksmuseum Kroller-Muller 183

Courtesy Robert Miller Gallery 20, 52

Courtesy Saatchi Collection 159

John Seyfried 85

Courtesy Sotheby's Inc. 117

Courtesy Naomi Spector 145 bottom

Manfred Tischer 18

Whitney Museum of American Art 214, 215

Gareth Winters 31, 57, 59, 81